Sewing

FOR

Twentieth Century Dolls

Sewing

Twentieth Century Dolls

Revised Edition

Johana Gast Anderton

Published by

Wallace-Homestead
authoritative books on antiques & collectibles

Wallace-Homestead Book Co.
1912 Grand Avenue
Des Moines, Iowa 50309

WHAT THE COPYRIGHT MEANS

These patterns and the contents of this book are protected by United States and International copyright laws. The patterns are intended for use by hobbyists and doll dressmakers and may be traced for use by such persons in the creation of doll clothes for their own or customers' dolls.

At no time may the patterns herein be traced or otherwise reproduced by any method for purposes of selling the patterns or for giving the patterns as a gift. Neither may the patterns be reproduced in a magazine, newspaper or other publication without the written consent of the copyright owner herein named.

When patterns are traced for purposes of sewing doll clothes, the following notation should be made on each pattern piece:

"From Anderton's 'SEWING FOR TWENTIETH CENTURY DOLLS', p. no."

Any misuse of the material contained in this book will be prosecuted under above mentioned copyright laws.

ISBN 0-87069-276-3
LIBRARY OF CONGRESS CATALOG
CARD NUMBER 72-77829

Typography by Craftsman Composition, North Kansas City, Missouri
Dustjacket and Book Design by the Author.

Published by

Wallace-Homestead Book Co.
1912 Grand Avenue
Des Moines, Iowa 50309

To my sisters, Shirley and Carol
for the many happy hours we spent together
playing dolls and sewing for our doll families
– to the three little girls we used to be.

CONTENTS

Frontpiece 2

What The Copyright Means 4

Dedication 5

Acknowledgments 7

Introduction 8

Tips on Sewing for Dolls 9

Making Patterns from This Book 13

Fitting Patterns to Your Doll 14

Hats and Other Accessories 16

Bodies . . . . : 18

Stockings and Shoes 25

The 1900's 29

The 1910's 48

The 1920's 77

The 1930's 127

The 1940's 155

The 1950's 173

The 1960's 206

Entering the 1970's 260

Sources 261

Index 262

Backplate 264

ACKNOWLEDGEMENTS

My sincere thanks to the many collectors, friends and members of my own family who allowed their dolls' costumes to be examined and sketched.

Thanks also to my proof-reading friends and to my Mother who stitched up checking samples of the patterns whenever there was any doubt of fit or draftsmanship.

Special appreciation is extended to The H. D. Lee Company which so generously shared the original patterns for the Buddy Lee doll uniforms and Lee Riders.

And finally, thanks to all of you, the readers without whom this book would not have been possible.

INTRODUCTION

As work progressed in preparation of an earlier book, the seeds of this book began to germinate. Many of the dolls then being photographed for *"TWENTIETH CENTURY DOLLS, From Bisque to Vinyl"* were still wearing their original clothes, or were arrayed in home-sewn fashions made from original patterns. As I admired and mentally catalogued these old doll things, the thought recurred that other collectors might enjoy being able to reproduce authentic costumes for their dolls.

A companion to the *"TWENTIETH CENTURY DOLLS"* book was clearly the answer. As work on this earlier book neared completion, my new file was growing larger each day. This file was crammed with fashion notes from old catalogs, sketches, and actual drafts of patterns taken from the doll clothes found on the dolls as they were photographed.

Since many of the dolls appearing in the doll book *lived* in other cities, it was necessary to travel again to those places to examine the clothes and draft patterns. These were the dolls discovered early in the work on the doll book, prior to the *great idea* for this book. Revisiting the collectors and their dolls proved a delightful and rewarding experience, for in several cases *new* old dolls had been added to collections and more pictures were taken.

As the file grew, several things became clear. First, it seemed wise to divide the patterns chronologically wherever possible; therefore they have been arranged by decade. There will be, of course, some overlap since fashions do not automatically change as the pages of a calendar are turned. What was considered the latest thing in 1919 would still hold some merit in 1920 or perhaps 1921.

Moreover, gentle mutations may be seen in fashions, so that a detail introduced as revolutionary in one year becomes softened and refined in later seasons. Then, too, there are the classic fashions which change little. The cardigan, the blazer, the nautical costume, the shirtwaist dress, these are all examples of classics which are subjected to subtle changes in order that they may conform to the profile of current fashion.

Second, it seemed wise to give full-size patterns wherever possible, and for this reason we have used large-size pages. With a little manipulation of pattern parts, it has been possible to draw patterns full-size, even for the 28-inch **K (STAR) R** doll. In a few cases it has been necessary to break the lines and rearrange the pattern on a page, but careful study of the chapter, "MAKING PAPER PATTERNS", will provide answers to most questions.

Last, it seemed probable that the whole project would benefit from a discussion of fabrics, accessories, and fashions of each period (decade). While there is a danger of taking oneself too seriously in such an undertaking, it seems worthwhile to provide a certain background or framework in which to set the dolls. One would not wish, for example, to costume a Bye-Lo of the 1920s in nylon or dacron which was not available until the 1950s.

Since spare heads are sometimes available, it seemed a good idea to give a few body patterns. These have been provided in variety and should meet most needs. Old bodies may be ripped apart and additional patterns made. Notes are also included on making your own patterns, on making patterns fit your dolls, and on making shoes and stockings. The latter seemed of imminent importance since these bits of doll apparel are usually the first to be lost.

No one realizes more than this writer the shortcomings of this book, yet a real attempt has been made to be of assistance to doll collectors and costumers. Many of the patterns appearing here have not been previously attempted. Yet it seems good to record the vagaries of even this latest decade.

We live in a swiftly moving civilization. Paper dresses and disposable fashions are a reality. Tomorrow may see us walking through a dressing room each morning where a film of dressing material is automatically wrapped about us. At night we may return to a refreshing shower which distintegrates the costume of the day and gently wraps us in a sleeping garment. Stranger things we have known in these past seventy years and two.

Though we certainly cannot know what the future will bring us of fashion, we can enjoy what has passed and we can see that each of our dolls is adequately prepared to represent us in that future. To this end this book is submitted for your use and enjoyment.

Johana Gast Anderton
Gladstone, Missouri
February 15, 1972

TIPS ON SEWING FOR DOLLS

Since most collectors or doll costumers have at least a speaking knowledge of sewing techniques, we will not begin with a basic sewing course. Rather, having assumed each of us to be acquainted with the ways of needle and thread, a discussion of the peculiarities of sewing for dolls is in order.

One of the first and most common mistakes made in sewing for dolls is not allowing sufficient width of trouser legs or sleeves. All too often, when the garment is completed and ready to be placed on the doll, the seamstress discovers the dress or shirt will not pass over the doll's extremeties. The rule must be "CHECK THE FIT, RE-CHECK IT, AND CHECK IT AGAIN".

As work progresses on a garment, keep the doll at hand and fit as you stitch. Since dolls, for the most part, do not move, it is usually not necessary to allow for movement and *give* in fitting doll fashions. If the doll is a walking doll or a performing doll, by all means switch it on and check the fit while the doll is in action.

Another oft-repeated mistake in making doll clothes is in the selection of fabrics. How saddening to see a beautiful doll, dressed in a fine outfit which has obviously cost the dressmaker many hours, but made of such stiff, heavy fabric as to be completely out of proportion to the size of the doll.

Fine fabrics drape more easily and becomingly than heavy ones. Tiny prints are more in proportion to small garments and doll measurements. Stripes should be narrow, checks minute, and plaids softly defined. Laces should be of proportionate widths, ruffles not so tightly gathered as to appear ludicrous on a small doll. Buttons and other fasteners ought to be doll-sized.

Bear in mind that we are not talking here about the forty-four inch ball-jointed bisque doll or a thirty-two inch vinyl Pollyana. These, of course, will require larger, even normal sized fasteners and patterns. The small and average sized doll, however, requires fine thread and delicate buttonholes, the narrowest of bias tape and ribbon, and carefully trimmed seams to avoid bulkiness.

Just as we consider our own features, coloring of hair, skin, and eyes, when selecting colors and fabrics for our own wardrobe, so ought we to choose for our dolls. A red-haired bisque with high coloring could look well in a cooling green or blue. Or a pink chosen for its precise shade may be just the right color to highlight the red hair. If time is valuable and much running to and fro with samples is not possible, then pack up the doll in question and carry it with you to the fabric shop. A possible combination may occur which otherwise would not have been considered had the doll been left at home.

When an old doll is found in an original or very old dress which is tattered and quite soiled. It is often a temptation to throw everything out and begin anew. What a tragic mistake to destroy such valuable evidence. Many collectors tell stories of their zeal as beginning collectors in making every doll spotless and perfect.

There are times, of course, when it is wise to renew or replace an old dress. Often the underwear is in good condition and only the dress needs redoing. In such cases, the old dress may be copied carefully, cleaned as carefully and safely as possible, then filed away with a full description of the doll to which it belongs. Some collectors even pin these old garments to the underclothes of the doll.

In keeping with the wish for authenticity, consideration should be given to the age of each individual doll. As fashion changes, so too the *face* of fashion undergoes sometimes striking transformations. Eyebrows are considered important one year, and are dusted to diminish their effect the next. Lashes are blackened, curled, and even lengthened with new products designed to perform such magic. This season the eyes may be slanted at the corners with a bit of pencil; next year they may be required to appear quite round.

In each decade there is a *face,* representative of the aspirations of every young lady or gentlemen who wishes to appear *au courant.* Dolls usually reflect this image even in the facial contours. In an age when obviously well-fed children were considered the most attractive, dolls were plump, well-stuffed dumplings. Slender, active, outdoor children have their counterparts in the long-legged, slim, almost boyish girl dolls of another decade.

It is often with results bordering on the ridiculous that dolls are dressed in fashions not of their period. Equally ludicrous is the child doll dressed in the velvet, brocades, and laces of a matronly lady. A study should be made of the child fashions of each period as well as the adult designs. Consideration of the doll's proportions will give the final clue as to the age-type the doll represents.

Hair styles are another point at which mistakes may be made in the finishing of a doll's *couture*. Do not create, for a girl doll, the piled-up pompadour of a lady of fashion. Pigtails, ponytails, bangs, bobs, long curls, and loose, flowing tresses are all suitable for the girl doll of several decades. All these may be tied up with bows and ribbons, or tucked under a flop hat or beanie, depending upon the period.

Human hair has been considered one of the finest materials ever used in the making of dolls' wigs. The next most satisfactory material and one most often used is mohair, a fine woolen material which lends itself to careful combing and to realistic styling. Mohair has a soft, low sheen especially flattering to the composition dolls.

Newer, man-made materials have been introduced which have much durability and may be shampooed easily and combed, brushed and curled. These fibres, dynel, Saran, nylon, and various blends, are of various qualities and features. Saran is rather coarse, has high lustre, and is a good quality material. Chatty Cathy and other early dolls from Mattel featured Saran wigs rooted in the vinyl heads. Saran does not seem to break off easily as do some of the other synthetic fibres.

Dynel is a finer, softer fibre with a duller sheen than Saran, and is more suitable for smaller dolls. Nylon has a sheen somewhat higher than Dynel and is a tough fibre, although both these and some of the blends do have the tendency to break off rather badly. These fibres also tend to frizz when exposed to heat.

A general rule for replacing wigs is to replace with a wig of similar material to that with which the doll was first produced: Human hair or mohair, sometimes fur, wigs for bisque, china, and composition dolls; Saran, dynel, nylon, and synthetic blends for hard plastic, vinyl and soft vinyl dolls. Hard plastic dolls were sometimes issued with mohair wigs; the choice for these is a matter of taste. Styling of the wig may be matched to the old wig as nearly as possible.

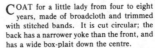
COAT for a little lady from four to eight years, made of broadcloth and trimmed with stitched bands. It is cut circular; the back has a narrower yoke than the front, and has a wide box-plait down the centre.

Simple Embroidery Stitches

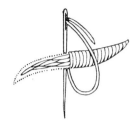

Satin Stitch may be padded or not. It consists of regular smooth stitches taken close together side by side across a space, either straight across or on a slant. This is the most important stitch in French Embroidery.

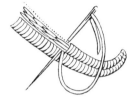

Voided Satin Stitch is made in exactly the same manner, working two sections side by side. Often a space is voided only a part of the way, then the two portions converge into one. This stitch is especially useful in working broad spaces which seem too wide for a single stitch.

Bullion Stitch. Bring the thread up at the base of the petal, insert the needle at the apex and bring the point out at the base again; wrap the thread a number of times around the needle and draw through, then carry down at the apex.

Buttonholing may be padded or not and is worked from left to right. Holding the thread down with the left thumb, a stitch is taken across the space to be covered, and the loop formed when the thread is drawn up makes a purling on the edge of the space.

Running Outline is made by running a row of short stitches along the line of stamping and then going back, putting the needle under every stitch and always putting in under from the same side.

Simple Outline is made from left to right, putting the needle forward a short distance along the line of stamping and bringing it up at the end of the last stitch. Always keep the thread on the same side of the line.

Long Eyelet. Run a thread around the stamped line, slit the space, roll back the edges on the wrong side and whip over and over with short, close stitches.

A Shaded Eyelet, one which is heavier on one side, is padded between the double lines, and otherwise worked in the ordinary way.

Round Eyelet. Run stamped line with fine stitches, punch with stiletto, clip material if it does not separate easily, hold edges under and work in over-and-over stitch from right to left with thread below needle as in illustration.

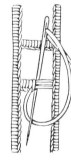

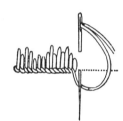

Italian Cut Work consists of long, narrow spaces buttonholed on the sides, with buttonhole bars across and the material cut away beneath. The bars are put in before the edges are buttonholed.

Long and Short Buttonholing is made like simple buttonholing except that the stitches are of unequal length. This stitch is used when an irregular effect is desired.

Snail Trail is made from right to left along a single line of stamping. The thread is held on the line while a short buttonhole stitch is made over it.

Woven Bar, used in Italian cut work. Carry two threads across the space, fasten securely in edge of material, and weave over and under the threads. Buttonhole or satin-stitch the edges before cutting away linen beneath the bars.

Fagoting, usually employed for joining two edges, consists of buttonhole-stitches taken on first one edge and then the other, letting the work progress towards one. When two bands are fagoted together, they are first basted on stiff paper and then the stitches added.

Chain Stitch is a form of outlining which is also used for filling large spaces. It is really a succession of buttonhole stitches made along a single line, putting the needle back into the last stitch each time and working towards one.

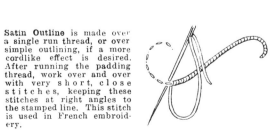

Satin Outline is made over a single run thread, or over simple outlining, if a more cordlike effect is desired. After running the padding thread, work over and over with very short, close stitches, keeping these stitches at right angles to the stamped line. This stitch is used in French embroidery.

French Knots. Bring the thread out on the right side, then, holding it with the left hand, wrap once, twice, or several times around the needle; insert the needle near where it was brought up and hold the thread taut while the needle is carried through.

German Knot is made from left to right. Take a short tight stitch at right angles to the stamped line, put a loose simple stitch and a loose buttonhole stitch into the first stitch. Repeat at intervals.

Couching consists of sewing down a cord or several strands of thread by taking short stitches across at regular intervals.

Lazy Daisy or Bird's-Eye Stitch is another form of buttonholing. Long loop stitches, beginning and ending at the same place, are caught down with a short stitch in the end of the loop.

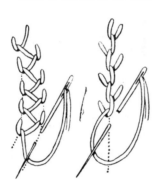

Briar Stitch and Feather Stitch are both forms of buttonholing made toward the worker. The first is made along two lines by taking a short buttonhole-stitch first on one line and then on the other. Feather-stitch is made with short, slanting buttonhole-stitches taken alternately on the left and right of a single line.

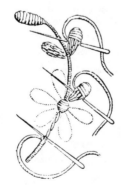

Padding for Satin Stitch is one of the most important factors in producing beautiful work. Pad by rows of close stemstitching or outlining, running lengthwise the design, taking up as little material as possible on the wrong side. Make padding compact, but do not draw stitches so tightly as to pull the linen. Pad sufficiently to give good relief.

Cross Stitch consists of two short stitches crossing at right angles. The top threads should all run in the same direction.

Spaced Buttonholing or Blanket Stitch is made in same manner as simple buttonholing, except that a short space is left between stitches.

Darning consists of parallel rows of short, regular stitches; the stitches of each row alternate with those of the last. It is used for filling large spaces or backgrounds.

Honeycomb Stitch, which is used for filling irregular spaces or backgrounds, is a simple loose buttonhole stitch worked into the preceding row and the fabric beneath. The illustration shows the method of working very plainly.

Seed Stitch consists of one, two, or more short stitches taken over and over at regular intervals to fill a space. The work progresses from right to left with needle pointed towards the left.

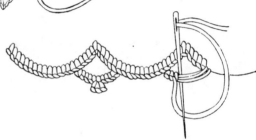

Buttonholed Scallops with Picot Bars: buttonhole one complete scallop and to the bar on the next; carry thread across to first scallop and back three times, then buttonhole back over the threads and continue second scallop. Make three buttonhole stitches in the top of one stitch in the centre to form the picot.

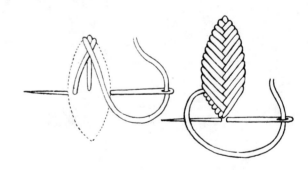

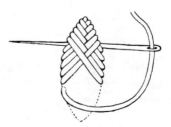

Self-Padding Stitch. Bring needle through at upper point of leaf, take a long stitch across centre from right to left, carry thread again to the point and take a short stitch just below it from side to side, then another long stitch at centre just below previous long stitch and repeat until leaf is filled.

MAKING PAPER PATTERNS FROM THE BOOK

Every effort has been made to keep the patterns as clear and easy to follow as possible. Patterns are all full-size and ready to be traced. Only occasionally has it been necessary, because of size, to break the lines of a pattern. In such instances, the end of each line is keyed to match the end of the line where the pattern continues. With one exception, (the Buddy Lee overalls), the broken lines are continued on the same page, placed at a different angle.

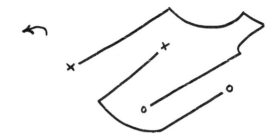

To trace patterns, never use a ball-point pen. The rolling ball-point will press through the tracing paper and have a tendency to cut into the book pages. When the book pattern is traced more than once, there will be gradual damage to the printed page. The ideal method of tracing patterns is to use a lead pencil or a soft-tipped fibre pen, good quality artists' tracing paper, available at art supply shops padded in several sizes, and a clear, acetate shield to protect the book page. This acetate shield may be slipped under the edge of the dustjacket in the back of the book where it will be available for future use.

To trace patterns with broken lines, place paper and shield over the page and trace one section, carefully following the lines and ending exactly where the printed line ends. Lift the paper and move it about to determine where the corresponding lines take up. Replace the paper, aligning the marks and complete the pattern tracing.

Seam and hem allowances are not drawn on the pages because of space which would have to be allowed on each page. After the pattern is traced and before cutting it out, draw seam allowances on the paper. Cut out paper pattern with hem and seam allowances, mark all instructions on your pattern, including matching instructions and fold indications. Also mark each pattern piece with the size, type, and any other pertinent information. While this may seem time-consuming, a few minutes at this point may save hours later. Mark each piece: "From Anderton's Sewing for Twentieth Century Dolls, p. (no.)," fold pattern pieces together neatly, and place in individual envelope with description on the outside. Keep all such pattern envelopes in a special box and you will be ready at all times for a session of doll clothes sewing without the fuss of finding patterns and instructions.

Further use may be made of the individual pattern envelopes as you sew. Any alterations for a particular doll, any special effects, or other items of importance may be duly noted on the reverse of the envelope and will be available to anyone using the pattern in future.

FITTING PATTERNS TO YOUR DOLL

The patterns in this book are as accurate in size and fit as it is possible to make them. It is possible, however, that a given pattern will not fit the doll of your choice even though the doll is the "same" or nearly the same as the doll from which the pattern was made.

Wide variations are often found in body styling. This is particularly true in the case of the old ball-jointed bodies. One doll may have a fat "tummy" and a protuberant *derriere* while another doll of the same height will be quite *willowy* or perhaps *bosomy*.

Measure your doll by taking the front measurements, underarm across the front to opposite underarm, and back measurements, underarm across the back to opposite underarm. Do not measure simply by placing the measuring tape around the body. This will be misleading since front and back measurements are usually not the same.

Now check the measurements of the pattern you have selected, both with a tape measure and by placing the pattern pieces against the doll. When you are satisfied the pattern actually fits, you are ready to cut the fabric.

There are several methods of enlarging and decreasing patterns. One of the simplest methods, when a minimal alteration is required, is bisecting the pattern laterally and vertically, and cutting it apart on those lines. This gives four pattern pieces from one. These four pieces may either be moved apart to enlarge the pattern piece or slightly overlapped to decrease. A bit of transparent tape will hold them together at the new measurement.

As previously stated, this method works only if the adjustment is a minor one. For alterations requiring major size changes, the most efficient method is one which takes a little practice, but which is actually quite easy to accomplish. Without cutting out the paper pattern you have traced from the book, divide it carefully into one inch squares.

Now for some computation: Let us suppose your doll is eighteen inches tall whereas the pattern is for a twelve inch doll. Your doll is one and one-half times as tall as the doll of the pattern. Mark off another, larger piece of paper in one and one-half inch squares and transfer the pattern line-for-line, using the squares as guide-lines. This same method, in reverse, may be used to decrease a pattern.

Widening or narrowing of shoulders may be necessary since some dolls, especially some of the ball-jointed ones, have rather wide shoulders owing to the large ball joints, while others may have quite sloping shoulders. Do check carefully to be sure the pattern gives adequate length of skirt for your particular doll. Generally, alterations of doll clothes are the same as for full-size fashions.

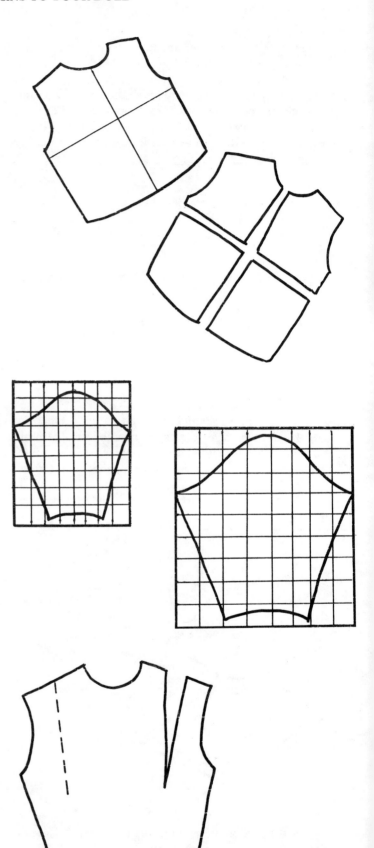

The Smartest of the Autumn Hats

They may flare or dip, they may be large or small, but all are feather-trimmed

Selected by GRACE MARGARET GOULD

Illustrated by AUGUSTA REIMER

VELVET, Fur, Feathers—these three proclaim the fashions in millinery for fall and winter. There is scarcely a hat for the autumn that does not show the introduction of velvet, if it is not entirely made of that material; and as for the trimming, it is bound to be of feathers, one kind or another, and often fur, too, is introduced.

LARGE and small, high and low, these are the new hats for the autumn. No one definite shape is a necessity, but rather to suit the individuality of the wearer is the mission of the hat this season. Well down on the head it must be placed, with a slight dip to the right side, to be correct. It is worn again this year without even the suggestion of a bandeau.

15

HATS AND OTHER ACCESSORIES

Whether your interest in this book stems from a desire to costume a collection or to dress play dolls, consideration should be given to accessories. Although usually the first things lost in a doll's wardrobe, accessories are a great deal of fun. Ingenuity and imagination must be called upon to invent many of the tiny personal oddments which every well-dressed doll counts among her possessions.

Hats are perhaps the obvious place to begin and, indeed, an entire book might be devoted to the construction of really elaborate headgear of every imaginable style. Patterns for hats and bonnets are given throughout the book wherever the original matching *chapeau* was available. If a hat pattern is not given with the style of your choice, simply borrow suitable headgear from another pattern.

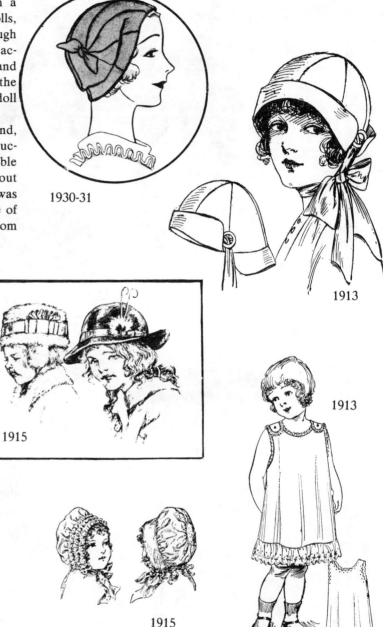

1930-31

1913

1915

1913

1915

1913

Underthings are adequately described in each section along with patterns for dresses and other garments. Stockings and shoes have a separate section to which you may refer and are also occasionally included along with certain patterns.

Castoffs are often the source of material for doll clothes; the lone stocking or glove offers many possibilities, for example. From the toe or the top of an ankle sock come skating caps, ear huggers, neck scarves, and beanies. A leather helmet for a boy doll may be made from a discarded glove. Make fur-lined hoods and other accessories from a fur-lined driving glove.

Bits of leather also provide materials for shoes, boots, purses, and vests. The fingers of white kid gloves become upper arms for bisque dolls with kid bodies. Long white dress gloves for teen fashion dolls are made from the fingers of ladies' nylon gloves. The fingers of leather gloves are also excellent as boots for small dolls. The leather may be dampened and shaped to the foot and when dry will retain the boot shape.

Discarded underwear often has areas of little wear which provide adequate material for dolls' underthings. Some stockings make excellent seamless undersuits for small dolls.

Old, worn, much-laundered sheets and white shirts give the softness required for slips, petticoats, and underpants.

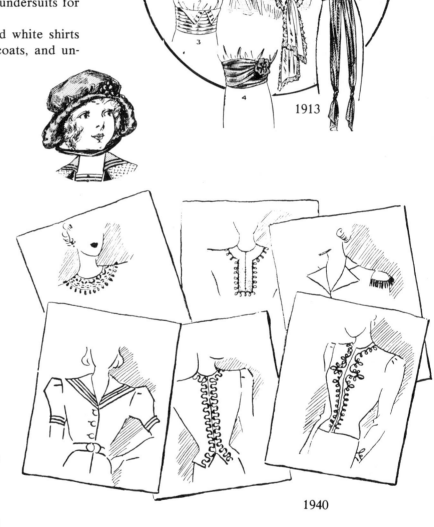

1913

1930-31

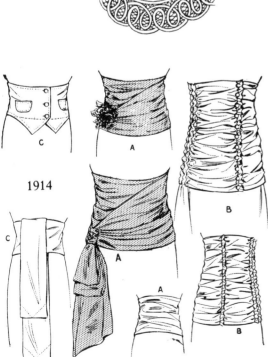

1914

1940

The crowns of old straw or felt hats may be cleaned, steamed, and shaped over fruit jars or other forms and emerge as the best of dolls' hats.

In most homes, a buttonbox or special drawer houses a collection of beads, buttons, spools, pins and other oddities which lend themselves to the creation of doll jewelry. A fancy button, for example, may be just right as a brooch at the throat of a special doll's dress. The remaining pearls of a broken strand may be adequate for a doll necklace; an old ring could become a doll bracelet; map pins or even some hat pins may be changed into perfect dolls' earrings.

The secret is imagination — yours.

17

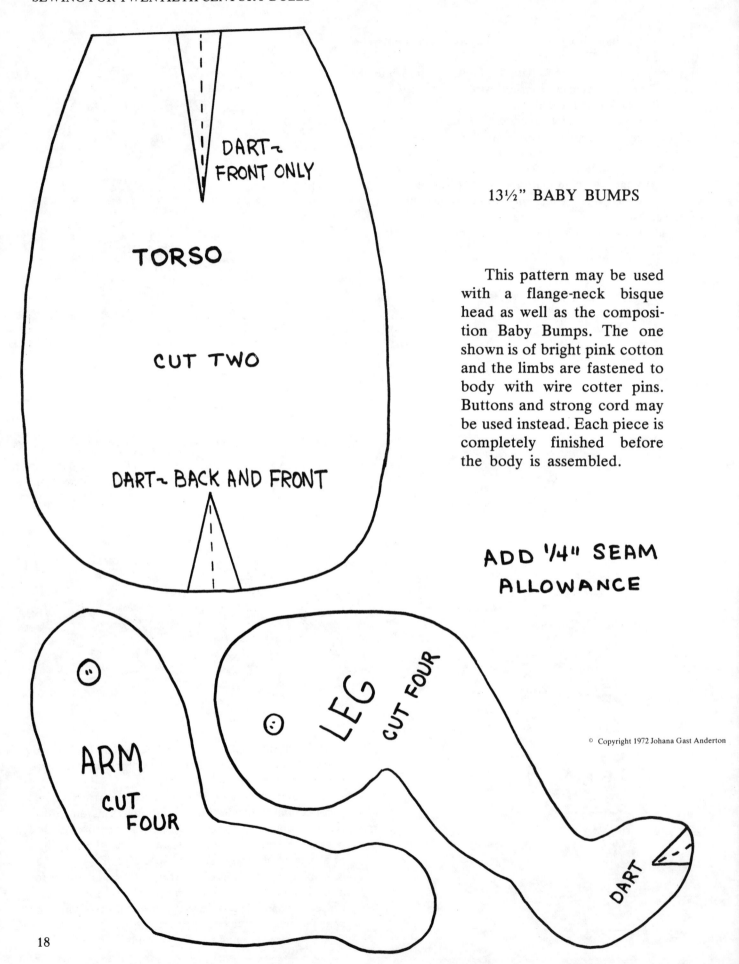

DART ~
FRONT ONLY

TORSO

CUT TWO

DART ~ BACK AND FRONT

13½" BABY BUMPS

This pattern may be used with a flange-neck bisque head as well as the composition Baby Bumps. The one shown is of bright pink cotton and the limbs are fastened to body with wire cotter pins. Buttons and strong cord may be used instead. Each piece is completely finished before the body is assembled.

ADD ¼" SEAM ALLOWANCE

ARM
CUT FOUR

LEG
CUT FOUR

DART

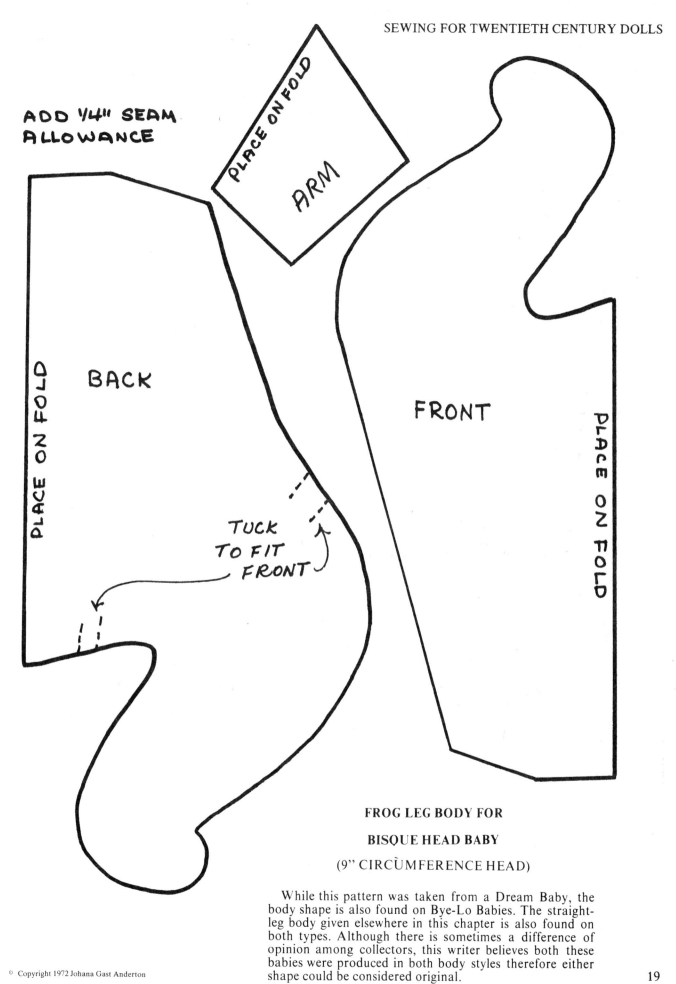

ADD ¼" SEAM ALLOWANCE

PLACE ON FOLD

ARM

PLACE ON FOLD

BACK

FRONT

PLACE ON FOLD

TUCK TO FIT FRONT

FROG LEG BODY FOR

BISQUE HEAD BABY

(9" CIRCUMFERENCE HEAD)

While this pattern was taken from a Dream Baby, the body shape is also found on Bye-Lo Babies. The straight-leg body given elsewhere in this chapter is also found on both types. Although there is sometimes a difference of opinion among collectors, this writer believes both these babies were produced in both body styles therefore either shape could be considered original.

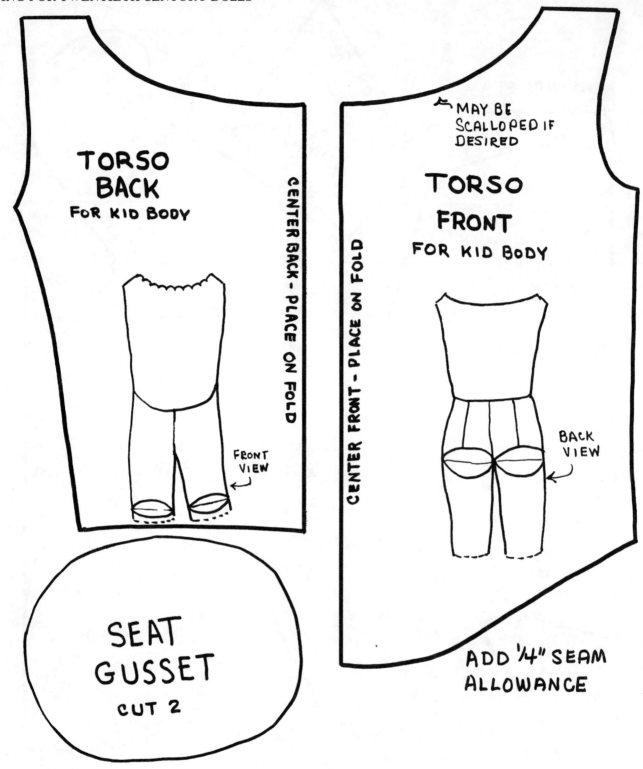

TORSO BACK
FOR KID BODY

CENTER BACK - PLACE ON FOLD

FRONT VIEW

MAY BE SCALLOPED IF DESIRED

TORSO FRONT
FOR KID BODY

CENTER FRONT - PLACE ON FOLD

BACK VIEW

ADD ¼" SEAM ALLOWANCE

SEAT GUSSET
CUT 2

This body may also be made of heavy unbleached muslin or pink sateen. The pattern makes a body approximately 12" from shoulder to mid-calf. Length of leg below knee may require adjustment depending on type of lower limb to be used. A cloth lower leg and foot may be added in place of bisque, composition, or celluloid.

1. Insert knee gussets in leg sections.
2. Seam each leg section together, matching double and triple dots.
3. Insert seat gusset in each leg section.
4. Seam leg sections together along crotch seam.
5. Sew side seams of torso.
6. Seam leg assembly to torso.

20

© Copyright 1972 Johana Gast Anderton

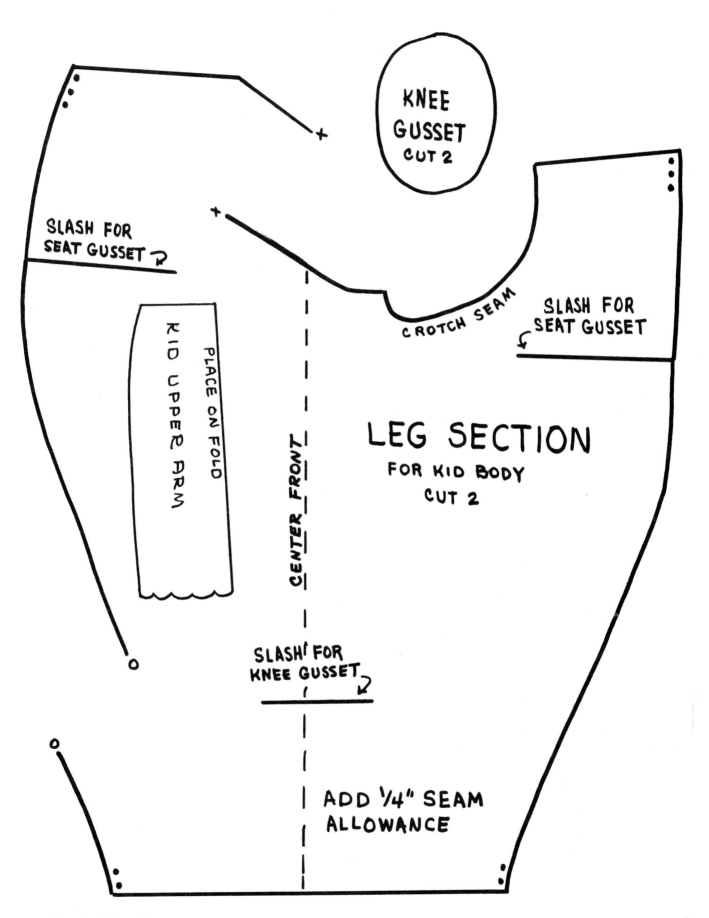

KNEE
GUSSET
CUT 2

SLASH FOR
SEAT GUSSET

SLASH FOR
SEAT GUSSET

CROTCH SEAM

KID UPPER ARM

PLACE ON FOLD

CENTER FRONT

LEG SECTION
FOR KID BODY
CUT 2

SLASH FOR
KNEE GUSSET

ADD ¼" SEAM
ALLOWANCE

BODY FOR 11½" DREAM BABY
(WITH 8" CIRC. HEAD)

Use unbleached muslin or other sturdy cotton. If celluloid, bisque or composition hands are not available, cut fabric to include hands with arm. Stuff finger area lightly, stitch to define fingers, then stuff hands fatter.

1. Seam, turn and stuff legs.

2. Baste tops of legs closed, matching back seam to front seam.

3. Sew side seams of body, taking tucks in back to fit back to front.

4. With body wrong side out insert stuffed legs with feet toward neck opening. Match seams to O's on pattern front. Check to be sure front of legs and body are together. Baste across lower body, turn and check position of legs in relationship to body. If correct, turn and stitch across lower body twice for added strength.

5. Turn, stuff body, attach head, wrapping several times with heavy thread or cord.

6. Attach arms.

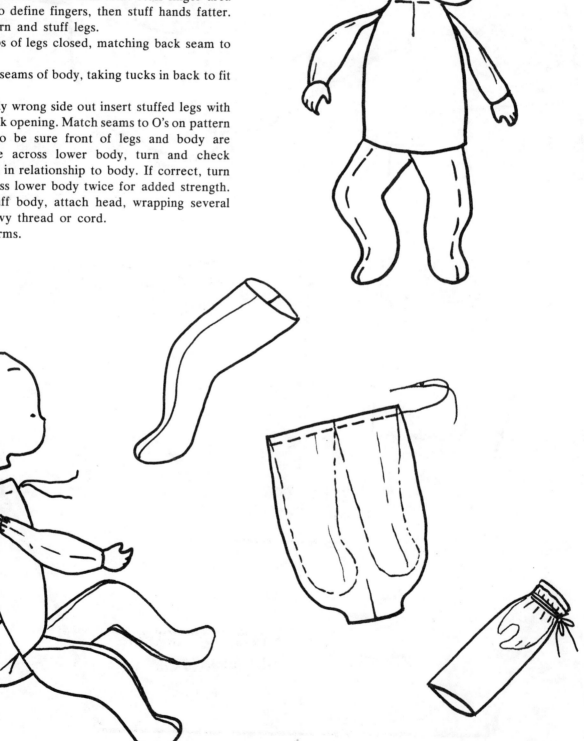

22

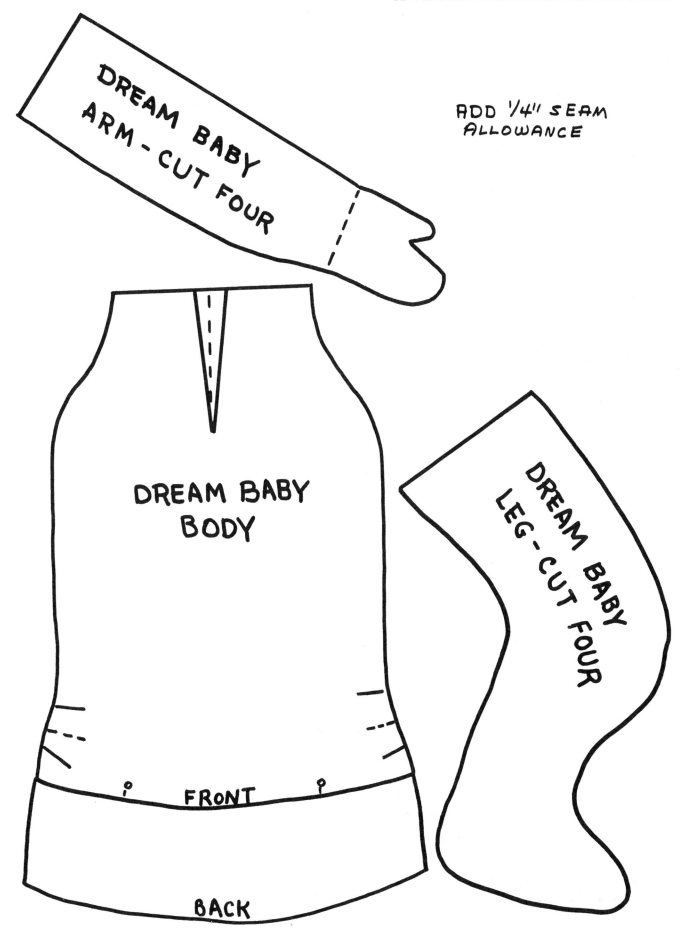

DREAM BABY
ARM - CUT FOUR

ADD ¼" SEAM
ALLOWANCE

DREAM BABY
BODY

FRONT

BACK

DREAM BABY
LEG - CUT FOUR

FLAPPER BED DOLL

If composition arms and feet are not available, use patterns to cut them from fabric. For legs, cut two pieces fabric 4"x11" of same material as body or use dress material. Fold lengthwise and stitch.

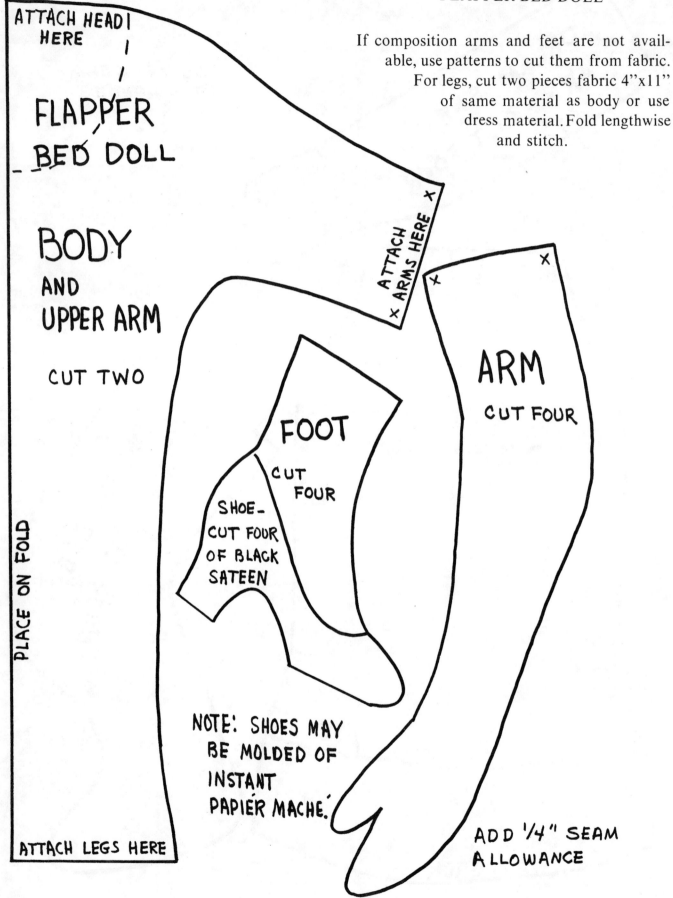

ATTACH HEAD HERE

FLAPPER BED DOLL

BODY AND UPPER ARM

CUT TWO

PLACE ON FOLD

ATTACH LEGS HERE

ATTACH ARMS HERE

ARM CUT FOUR

FOOT CUT FOUR

SHOE- CUT FOUR OF BLACK SATEEN

NOTE: SHOES MAY BE MOLDED OF INSTANT PAPIER MACHE.

ADD 1/4" SEAM ALLOWANCE

STOCKINGS AND SHOES

Shoes are not difficult to make if taken step by step. Complete each step on both shoes before proceeding to the next step. In this way, the shoes will be a matching pair, and will also be easier to finish.

Stockings, too, are quite simple since they may often be made of old discarded hosiery which has a finished top waiting to be utilized. The *Chatty Cathy* socks may be cut of any knit such as an old undershirt. Fold over the top along dash line, then stitch the side seam, turn to right side and you have a finished sock.

Several patterns for stockings and shoes are shown elsewhere in this volume. Consult the index to learn their location.

TO MAKE SHOES

1. Cut all pieces and lay out in sets for each shoe. Cut side piece, one innersole and one outer sole, and any other sections.

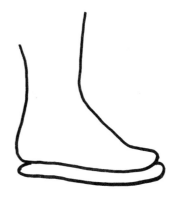

2. Attach innersole to bottom of doll's foot with bit of floral clay, sew any seams required for side of shoe and place on doll's foot. Put dots of glue all around and glue side to innersole.

3. Fold over seam allowance, snip to ease all around, dot glue all around outer sole and folded-over section, allow to set, then glue together. Additional reinforcement may be made by stitching back and forth across bottom of foot before glueing on outer sole. Add heel if desired.

SANDALS

SANDAL SOLE

DOLL SOCKS FROM DISCARDED HOSIERY

GIGGLES AND OTHER 'MOD' DOLLS WEAR THIS SANDAL. CUT SOLE OF FELT, PLASTIC OR LEATHER; MAKE STRAPS OF VARIOUS WIDTHS AND COLORS, ELASTIC OR CLOTH.

TIE SLIPPER USE SOLE BELOW

MCGUFFEY ANA, ALICE IN WONDERLAND AND OTHERS WORE THIS TYPE SHOE.

INCREASE TO THREE SNAPS FOR LARGER SHOES.

SOLE

HEEL

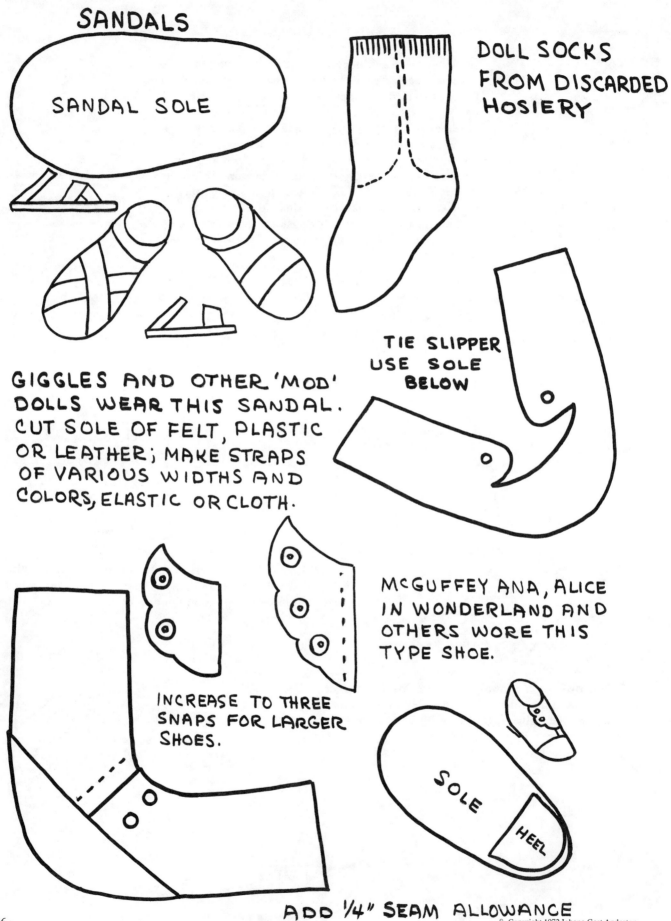

ADD ¼" SEAM ALLOWANCE

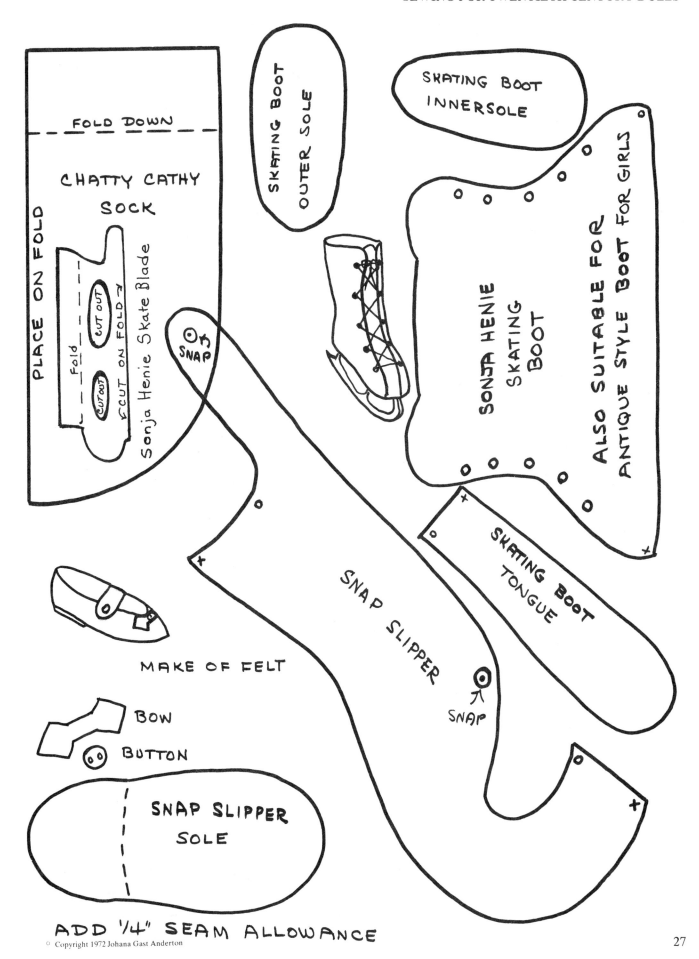

FOLD DOWN

CHATTY CATHY
SOCK

PLACE ON FOLD

Fold

CUT OUT

CUT ON FOLD

CUT OUT

CUT ON FOLD

Sonja Henie Skate Blade

SKATING BOOT
OUTER SOLE

SKATING BOOT
INNERSOLE

SONJA HENIE
SKATING BOOT

ALSO SUITABLE FOR
ANTIQUE STYLE BOOT FOR GIRLS

SNAP

SNAP SLIPPER

SKATING BOOT
TONGUE

SNAP

MAKE OF FELT

BOW

BUTTON

SNAP SLIPPER
SOLE

ADD 1/4" SEAM ALLOWANCE

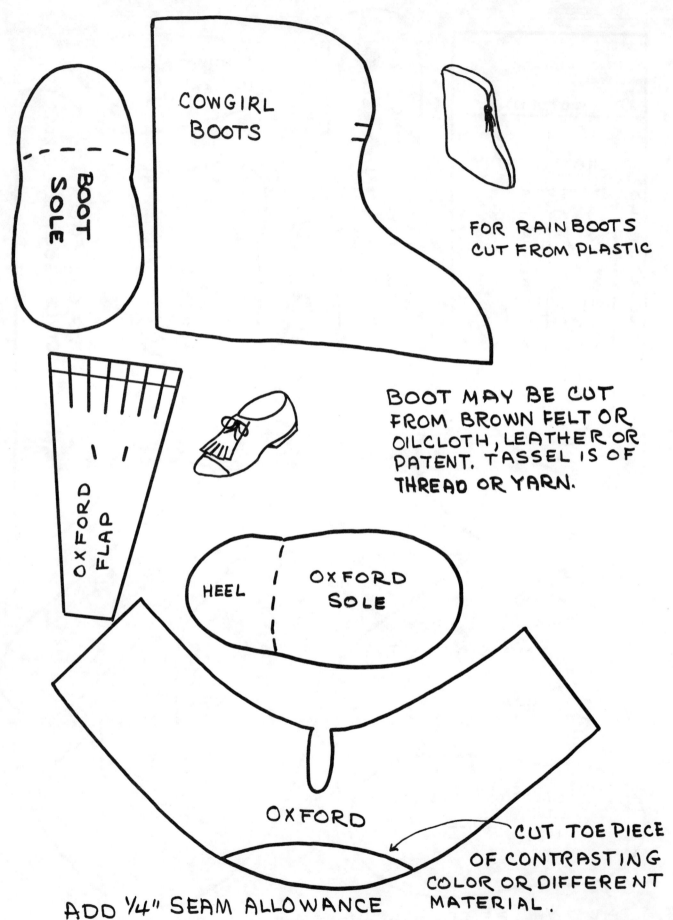

COWGIRL BOOTS

BOOT SOLE

FOR RAIN BOOTS CUT FROM PLASTIC

BOOT MAY BE CUT FROM BROWN FELT OR OILCLOTH, LEATHER OR PATENT. TASSEL IS OF THREAD OR YARN.

OXFORD FLAP

HEEL

OXFORD SOLE

OXFORD

ADD ¼" SEAM ALLOWANCE

CUT TOE PIECE OF CONTRASTING COLOR OR DIFFERENT MATERIAL.

Dressy, with Little Trimming

THE 1900s

The turn of the Century, although the dawn of a *new era*, nevertheless saw many 1890s styles holding their own. Sailor collars, always a classic, were still popular for little girls and boys. Sweeping skirts, large sleeves, bustles, and bosom padding continued in style, although changing in shape and size from year to year.

Where climate or school buildings permitted, school clothes were of wash fabrics such as pique, challis, lawn, batiste, and lace. Heavier fabrics in use were navy blue serge, fine striped worsted, cashmere, dark challis, lawn, batiste, and lace. Heavier fabrics in use were navy blue serge, fine striped worsted, cashmere, dark challis and wool batiste. Navy blue was brightened with white or red braid, piping, or gilt buttons. Black and white shepherd's check worsted was highlighted with piping of cardinal, emerald green, cerise, or other light colors, set off with fancy buttons and a colored patent leather belt. Blue dotted French flannel with solid blue bands and a white sailor collar was trimmed with braid and a patent leather belt.

Boys' coats were double breasted, boxy, and of diagonal storm serge, chinchilla cloth or polo cloth. Suits were of serge, woven checks, or worsted. Early in the decade the Eton collar with soft tie, worn with a suit having a straight jacket and bloused short trousers was proper dress for a young man. This suit was worn with long, dark hose, and a vest.

Lace, tucks, cording, piping, and smocking were used as trims on ladies' dresses of challis, lawn, linen, broadcloth, or India mull. Velvet ribbon trims were much in evidence.

1904

A Street Suit with Gored Jacket

A Smart Suit for Street Wear

Silk Girdle Strewn with Sequins

Black Silk with Gold Buckle

A Model in Challis

29

3071

3428

3208

3265

2791

3371

3196

3045

3144

3735

3449

3727

3668

3585

3618

2686

PICTORIAL REVIEW

3288

3345

3166

3634

3219

3262

2512

3522

3710

3145

Pictorial Review for December 1910

25" GERMAN BISQUE CHILD
(MARKED DEP 11)

ATTACH SHOULDER RUFFLE HERE

BACK VIEW

This bisque-head doll has a ball-jointed, composition and wood body. Here is an excellent example of differences in proportion among similar types of dolls. This child, though definitely not a toddler type, is proportionately narrow across the back with protuberant chest and stomach. The patterns reflect this proportioning. Her measurements are:

Height	25"
Waist	13½"
Hips	16"
Chest	14½"
Neck to Wrist	9"
Front, neck to crotch	12"
Back, neck to crotch	11"

UNDERWEAR

As always, fit and complete the underwear first. Although this child wears only a slip with a double ruffle and a pair of drawers, it would be simplicity itself to construct a vest of the same fine cotton, using the slip bodice pattern lengthened by one and one-half inches.

Diagrams for the drawers are self-explanatory. To finish legs of the drawers, cut two pieces of same cotton fabric ten inches long and three inches wide. Sew five very narrow tucks along the length of each piece. Hem and trim with lace one long side on each piece, following sketch of finished drawers. Seam two short sides together, gather remaining long sides to fit lower edges of leg openings. Cover this seam with insertion lace.

For slip, fit and complete slip bodice and set aside.

For skirt of slip, cut a piece of fabric ten inches by twenty-eight inches long. Attach one inch lace to one long side. Seam short sides together to a point six inches from bottom edge of lace. Add flounce — sew along a line marked four inches from bottom of lace.

To make flounce, cut a piece of fabric two inches by fourty inches long. Stitch two narrow tucks full length of piece. Attach two and one-half inches wide lace to long side of piece. Gather remaining long side and attach to skirt of slip as above. Attach skirt to bodice.

DRESS

This original dress, in a turn-of-the-Century style, offers a construction challenge yet is quite simply made. Alternating panels of fragile pink silk and ecru lace combine to achieve an artistic, stylish appearance. While the back is straight, the front is slightly bloused, although not as decidedly as the white dress shown for our 28" K (STAR) R.

A step-by-step approach is basic to the construction of this dress; therefore, do not skip ahead and become confused.

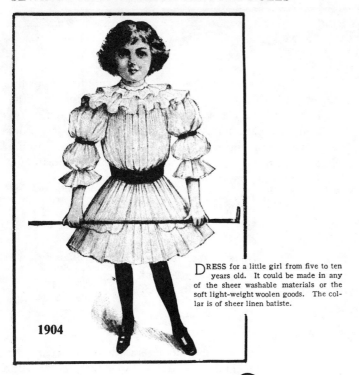

DRESS for a little girl from five to ten years old. It could be made in any of the sheer washable materials or the soft light-weight woolen goods. The collar is of sheer linen batiste.

1904

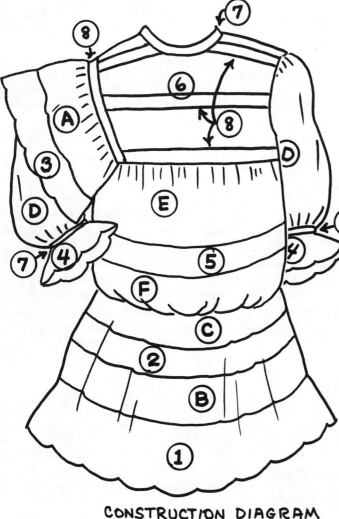

CONSTRUCTION DIAGRAM

34

DRESS REQUIREMENTS

Make the following paper patterns to be cut from dress material and mark each one as it is cut out:

- A. Shoulder Ruffle A — 2 pieces   2¼" x 17".
- B. Skirt Flounce B — 1 piece   2½" x 60".
- C. Skirt Flounce C — 1 piece   1¾" x 26".
- D. Sleeve D — 2 pieces   Pattern Piece D.
- E. Bodice Panel E — 1 piece   4" x 13".
- F. Bodice Panel F — 1 piece   3" x 13".
- G. Bodice Back — 4 pieces   Pattern Piece G.
- H. Bodice Front — 1 piece   Pattern Piece H.

Pin, cut and set aside above pattern pieces.

Measure and lay out the following pieces of lace; pin an identification slip of notepaper to each:

1. Skirt Ruffle — 1 piece 2" lace, 88" long.
2. Skirt Section — 1 piece 1½" lace, 36" long.
3. Shoulder Ruffle — 2 pieces 2" lace, 36" long.
4. Sleeve Ruffle — 2 pieces 2" lace, 15" long.
5. Bodice Front — 1 piece 1½" lace, 13" long.
6. Sufficient lengths of lace to construct the Lace Bodice section (see Pattern Piece 6).
7. Narrow Lace for neck edge finish and sleeve band.
8. Sufficient ½" Lace trim for Lace Bodice and for attaching shoulder ruffle.

DRESS CONSTRUCTION

Bodice is lined with fine cotton; dress is fine silk alternating with fine lace. Do not use cotton lace or eyelet for these are too heavy and will not hang properly.

1. Sew tucks in pieces B, E, F, and G. Refer to diagrams and sketches.
2. Using Pattern Piece 6, construct Lace Bodice section.
3. Open out Bodice Front H lining.
4. Construct bloused over-section following dress diagram and using Pieces E, F, and Lace 5.
5. Gather upper edge of construction (in 4 above) to fit lower edge of Lace Bodice section 6 and seam together.
6. Pin this construction unit to Bodice Front Lining H.
7. Pin one back lining section to each back dress section and assemble bodice and lining front to backs as one.
8. Gather sleeves along dotted lines, fitting upper edge to armhole and lower edge to narrow flat lace cut to fit over doll's hand.
9. Gather Lace Piece 4 to fit Sleeve Band 7 and attach.
10. Construct shoulder ruffle by gathering upper edge of Lace Piece 3 to long edge of dress material section A. Gather remaining long edge of A to fit line marked on pattern with XXXs. Cover this seam with narrow Lace 8.
11. Finish back opening, crochet three button loops and attach three buttons.

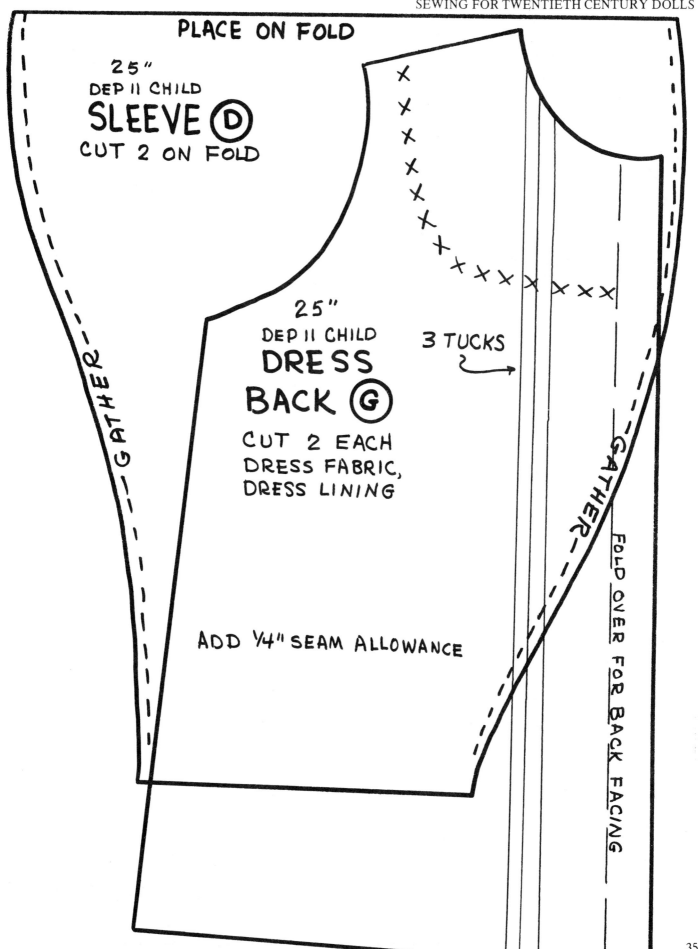

PLACE ON FOLD

25"
DEP II CHILD
SLEEVE Ⓓ
CUT 2 ON FOLD

25"
DEP II CHILD
DRESS
BACK Ⓖ
CUT 2 EACH
DRESS FABRIC,
DRESS LINING

3 TUCKS

GATHER

GATHER

FOLD OVER FOR BACK FACING

ADD ¼" SEAM ALLOWANCE

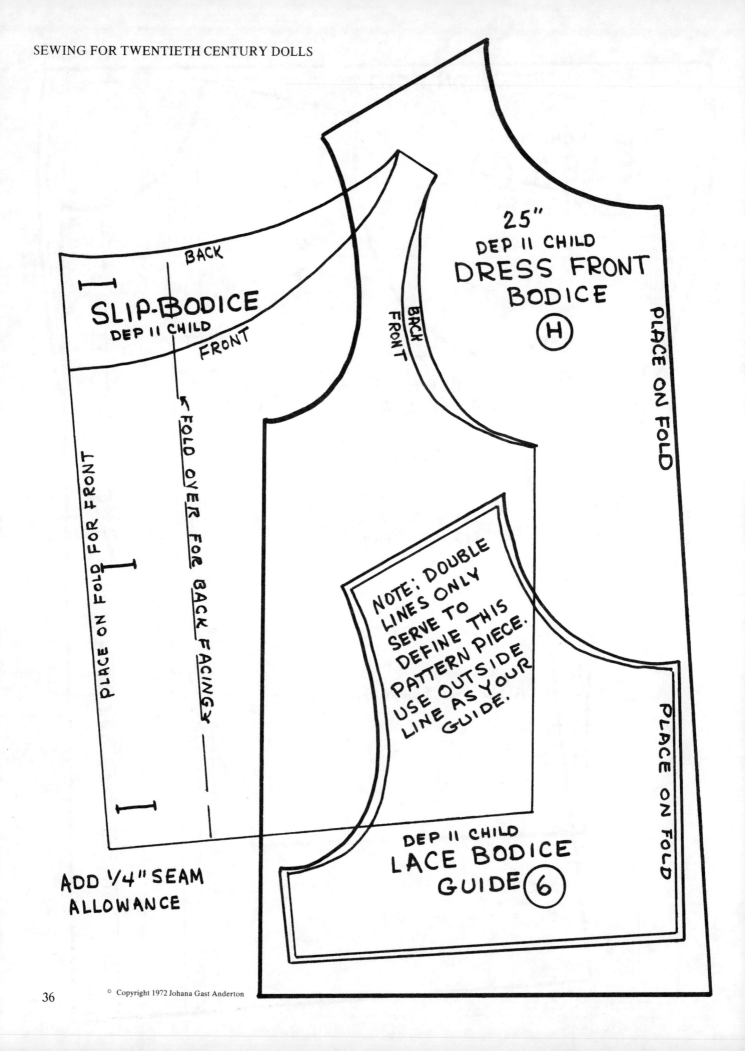

BACK

SLIP-BODICE
DEP II CHILD

FRONT

FOLD OVER FOR BACK FACING

PLACE ON FOLD FOR FRONT

ADD ¼" SEAM
ALLOWANCE

BACK

FRONT

25"
DEP II CHILD
DRESS FRONT
BODICE
Ⓗ

PLACE ON FOLD

NOTE: DOUBLE
LINES ONLY
SERVE TO
DEFINE THIS
PATTERN PIECE.
USE OUTSIDE
LINE AS YOUR
GUIDE.

DEP II CHILD
LACE BODICE
GUIDE ⑥

PLACE ON FOLD

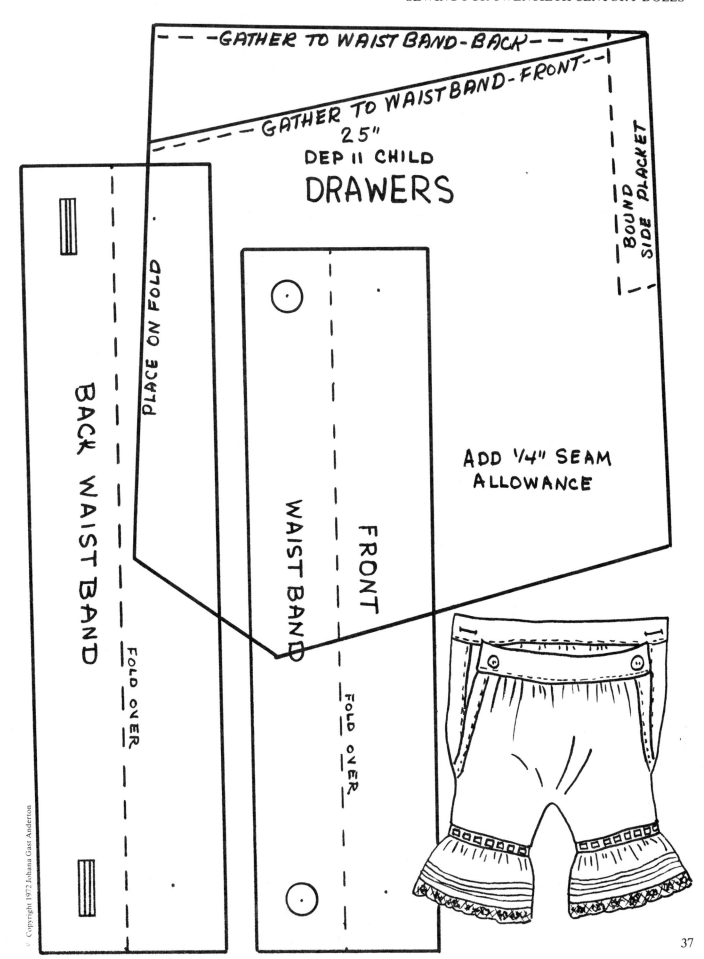

GATHER TO WAIST BAND - BACK

GATHER TO WAISTBAND - FRONT

2 5"
DEP II CHILD
DRAWERS

BOUND SIDE PLACKET

PLACE ON FOLD

BACK WAIST BAND

FOLD OVER

WAIST BAND

FRONT

FOLD OVER

ADD ¼" SEAM ALLOWANCE

"SLIDELL" — A 21" GERMAN BISQUE
(HANDWERCK 10911)

"Slidell" is named for a little town in Louisiana across Lake Ponchartrain from New Orleans. In a flea market one vacation time we found her lying in a box in all her original finery, waiting for us. Rebekka and I knew she must come home with us. We also knew that someday we would share her so that others could enjoy being able to duplicate her costume.

Bright rose-pink cotton made up the dress, with an overdress of some more fragile material, probably silk, which now hangs almost completely in shreds. The narrow black velvet ribbon trim, the underthings, the pink stockings and the shoes are all in good condition. The shoes are of fine white leather with tiny eyelets and flat heels, pink shoe laces and a numeral 6 on the sole of each.

UNDERCLOTHES

Begin with the underthings. Cut them from fine cotton such as lawn or batiste and trim with antique lace or good quality new eyelet or lace. Cotton trim may be salvaged from discarded garments if in good condition. The flounce for the slip is made from a piece of cotton 4 inches by 30 inches. Sew the two tucks, add 1 and ½ inch wide lace along one long side, then gather to fit body of slip. Cover this seam with insertion lace, topstitched.

THE STOCKINGS

This stocking pattern may seem to make no sense whatever but is actually quite easy to assemble once the cut-out material is in hand.

Cut two on fold from discarded hosiery or fine knit underwear. If positioned properly on old stockings, the top will have a ready-made finished edge.

THE SHOES

See chapter STOCKINGS AND SHOES for general directions on constructing these shoes.

THE DRESS

Work the dress and overdress as one, sewing sleeve seams together, etc.

Cut the dress along solid lines of pattern. Cut the back of overdress same as dress. Cut the front of overdress extending along the dotted lines as shown. Gather overdress front at neck opening and bottom edge to fit dress.

For dress flounce, cut piece of fabric 4 inches by 36 inches plus hem allowance. Hem one long side; add ¾" lace along hemmed side. Repeat for overdress flounce, apply narrow ribbon trim (see sketch). (Note: Overdress should be of much lighter, finer material than dress.) Gather remaining long sides of dress flounce and overdress flounce as one to fit lower edge of body of dress. Cover this seam with same ribbon.

DRESS for a little girl from six to ten years of age. It would be very pretty if made of a light figured or plain challis and trimmed with narrow black velvet ribbon.

1904

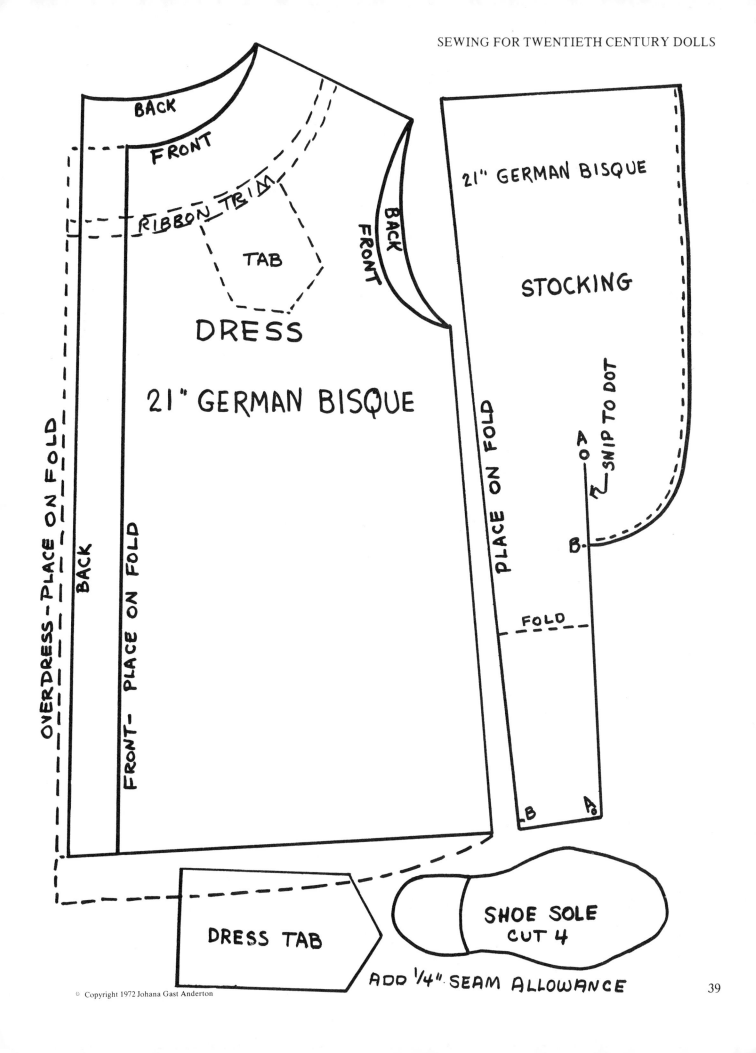

BACK

FRONT

RIBBON TRIM

TAB

BACK
FRONT

21" GERMAN BISQUE

STOCKING

DRESS

21" GERMAN BISQUE

A
SNIP TO DOT

B

OVERDRESS - PLACE ON FOLD

BACK

FRONT - PLACE ON FOLD

PLACE ON FOLD

FOLD

B   A

DRESS TAB

SHOE SOLE
CUT 4

ADD ¼" SEAM ALLOWANCE

GATHER

21" GERMAN BISQUE
OUTER
SLEEVE
DRESS

PLACE ON FOLD

PLACE ON FOLD

21" GERMAN BISQUE
SLEEVE LINING
DRESS

VELVET RIBBON

VELVET RIBBON

GATHER

SHOE
CUT TWO

ADD ¼" SEAM ALLOWANCE

21" GERMAN BISQUE

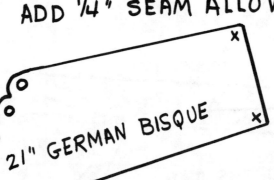

1904

A PRETTY party dress for a little lady from four to six years old. It is made of soft India mull, and trimmed with a yoke of all-over embroidery. The edge of the yoke is laid in a cluster of cordings.

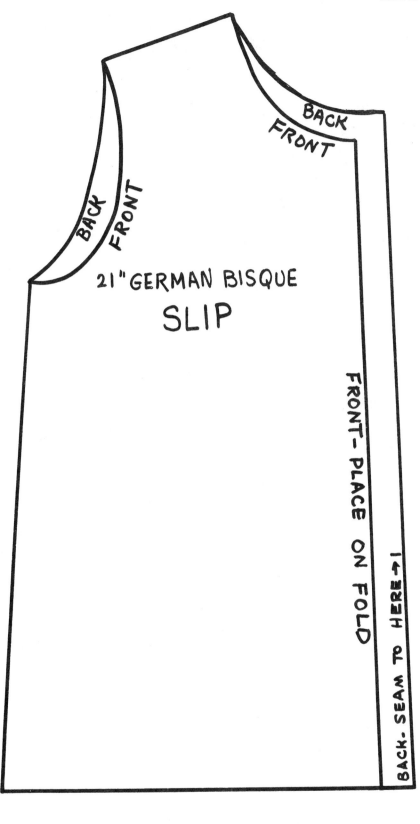

21" GERMAN BISQUE
SLIP

BACK
FRONT

BACK
FRONT

FRONT - PLACE ON FOLD

BACK - SEAM TO HERE →|

1904

SUIT for a little boy from five to seven years. Could be made of white duck or linen. It has full bloomer trousers, and the blouse has a pointed stitched yoke and fastens at the right side.

THIS DOLL
LACKED UNDER-
PANTS WHEN
FOUND. USE
SUITABLE
PATTERN FROM
ELSEWHERE IN
THIS BOOK.

STAND-UP COLLAR - DRESS FOLD OVER
CUT ONE

ADD ¼" SEAM ALLOWANCE

28" K (STAR) R — ORIGINAL COSTUME

Always fit and make the underwear first, fitting the clothes one layer over the last.

UNDERWEAR

The undersuit and slip diagrams are largely self-explanatory. Fig. A shows method of attaching underwear buttons with tape.

DRESS

A dropped-waist style is typical of the 1900 period; this one is of white cotton trimmed with tucks and lace.

Complete the bodice before adding the skirt. Evenly space seven buttons and buttonholes down the back, which is open to the insertion lace. To achieve the stylish, *bloused* effect, sew tapes inside the bodice, attached at neckline and lower edge of bodice, and underarm and lower edge of bodice. Underarm tapes are 7 and ¾ inches long; back tapes are 10 and ½ inches long. There is no tape at the front.

The dress flounce or skirt is a piece of dress fabric 4 and ¾ inches (plus hem allowance) by 56 inches long. The piece of insertion lace which joins the bodice and flounce is 19 inches long. Sleeves are also gathered to insertion lace cut 4 inches long. Do measure the arms of your doll to be sure finished sleeve band will pass over the doll's hand.

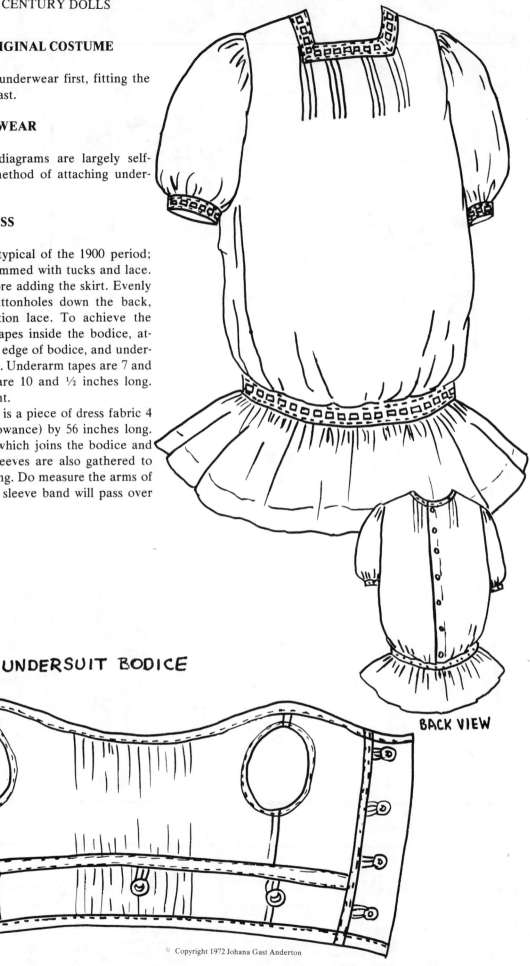

BACK VIEW

UNDERSUIT BODICE

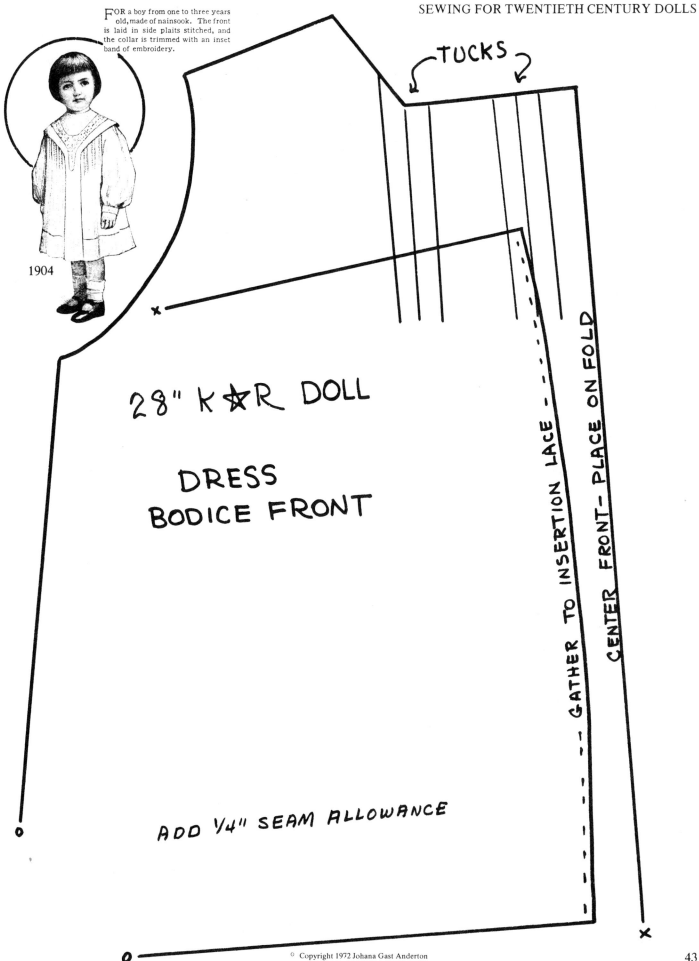

FOR a boy from one to three years old, made of nainsook. The front is laid in side plaits stitched, and the collar is trimmed with an inset band of embroidery.

1904

TUCKS

28" K☆R DOLL

DRESS
BODICE FRONT

GATHER TO INSERTION LACE

CENTER FRONT – PLACE ON FOLD

ADD 1/4" SEAM ALLOWANCE

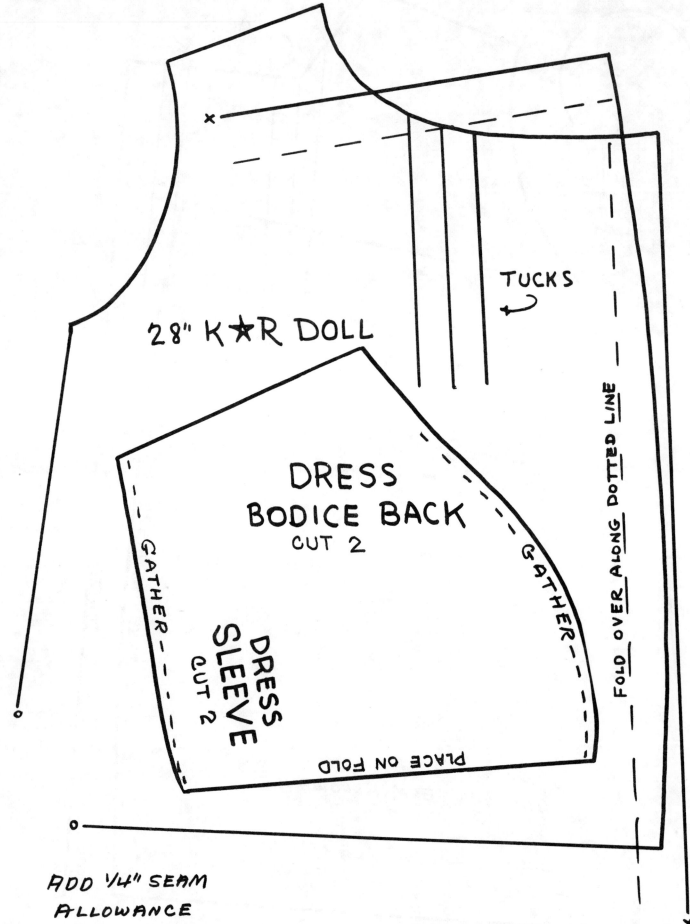

TUCKS

28" K★R DOLL

FOLD OVER ALONG DOTTED LINE

DRESS
BODICE BACK
CUT 2

GATHER

GATHER

DRESS
SLEEVE
CUT 2

PLACE ON FOLD

ADD ¼" SEAM
ALLOWANCE

1904

Dress for a little lady from two to five years old, made in the straight Mother Hubbard fashion and trimmed with a scalloped yoke embroidered in French knots.

SLIP
CUT 2

28" K★R DOLL

PLACE ON FOLD

ADD 2" TUCKED RUFFLE EDGED WITH 3/8" LACE

45

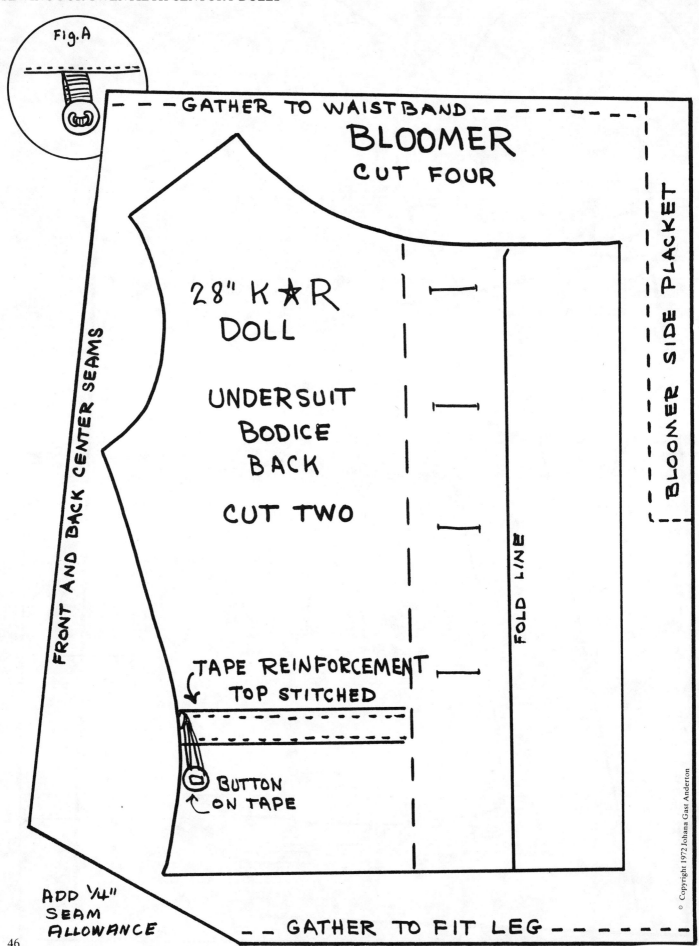

Fig. A

GATHER TO WAISTBAND

BLOOMER
CUT FOUR

BLOOMER SIDE PLACKET

FRONT AND BACK CENTER SEAMS

28" K★R
DOLL

UNDERSUIT
BODICE
BACK

CUT TWO

FOLD LINE

TAPE REINFORCEMENT
TOP STITCHED

BUTTON
ON TAPE

ADD ¼"
SEAM
ALLOWANCE

GATHER TO FIT LEG

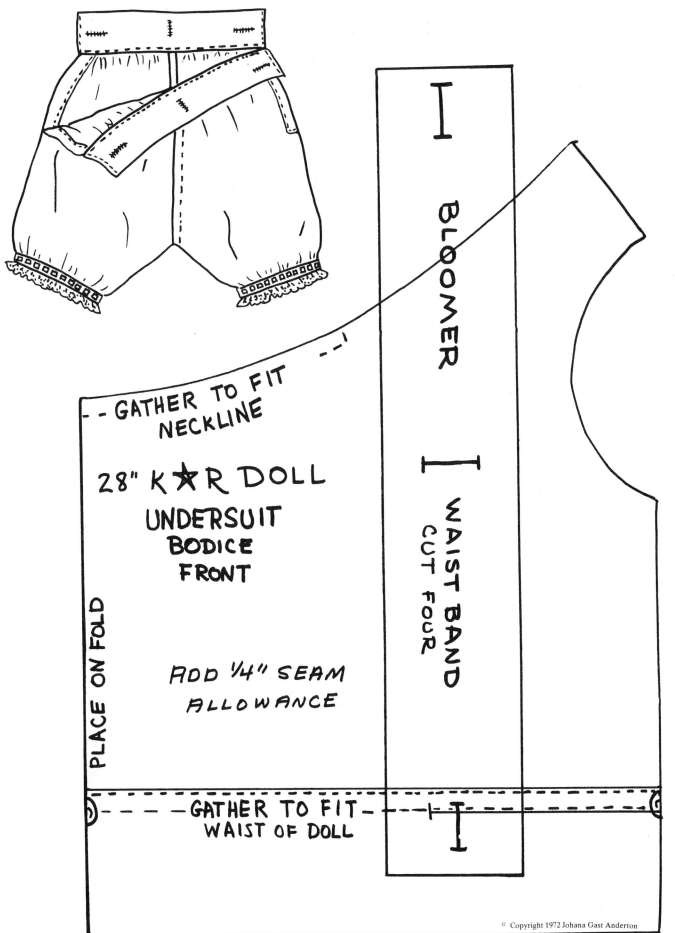

BLOOMER

WAIST BAND
CUT FOUR

GATHER TO FIT
NECKLINE

28" K★R DOLL
UNDERSUIT
BODICE
FRONT

PLACE ON FOLD

ADD ¼" SEAM
ALLOWANCE

GATHER TO FIT
WAIST OF DOLL

47

THE 1910s

In 1911, little boys dressed in blouse suits of *Galatea,* linen, rep or chambray in light or dark blue, tan or brown tones, trimmed with braid, binding, contrasting stitching or dickeys of striped material. Muslin, pongee, silk, and flannel were the vogue for night shirts.

In 1913, noting the latest trends, *Pictorial Review* stated:

"It is not alone woman's outer garments that are affected by style changes, but her underclothing as well. For, whenever a radical change is made in dress like the introduction of the present fashion in clinging garments, it becomes necessary that the underwear be made to conform with the new lines."

The article goes on to describe the latest in corset covers *"designed to preserve the slender lines of the figure."* Nainsook, long cloth, and *crepe de Chine* were popular fabrics for lingerie.

In 1914 this same magazine describes the latest in small boys' apparel as being of *"deepest pink and rose tints from his tiny sister's rainbow of colors".* Another innovation is the belt for his suits in the fabric of the suit rather than a leather belt as in former years. Older boys were dressing like father in mannish tweeds and polos.

Boys' clothes reflected the influences of war in the years 1917 through 1919; many soldier's uniforms for boys were shown. The military note was present in girls' clothes as well as in their mother's, although generally women's clothes were soft and feminine.

In 1919, little girls wore their hair in long curls with large hairbows perched at the crown. Sweaters were long; dresses slightly high-waisted, belted, made of cotton serge, chambray, closely woven cotton *Galatea* cloth, poplin, plaid ginghams and lawn. Silk chiffon was for party dresses. Children wore three-piece knit suits for outdoor play consisting of long sweater, below the hips, leggings and hat.

Romper, creepers, and bloomers were of flannelette, cotton knit, and duckling-fleeced cotton, seersucker, chambray and percale. Underwear was muslin, nainsook, cotton cambric, flannel, or knit flannelette, and undershirts had diaper tabs. Dresses for toddlers were "walking length" with machine embroidery, gathered from the neck, front and back.

Coats were of cream color cotton bedford cord, cream white belted chinchilla cloth, white on Liberty Blue velour-finished corduroy, double breasted, black or burgundy velour, walking length, belted with false flap pockets. A cream white cashmere long cloak for Baby had yoke cape in silk embroidery, with matching embroidery on the cloak skirt.

Baby dresses were of nainsook and lawn predominantly. Fresh air was highly thought of and a must was an outdoor sleeping bag of heavy blanket fleece. Undershirts were "vests". Boys and little fellows wore corduroy suits, belted long jackets and caps to match, long stockings, and high-lace shoes. Small boys were resplendent in Buster Brown suits, sailor suits and Lord Fauntleroy suits of dark blue velveteen.

The Little Boy's Blouse Suit

The Ladies' Home Journal for March 1, 1911

Designs by Selina Yorke

1913

5261   4980

5297   5331   5320

5331

5320

5261   4980   5317

5315   4499   4152

5315   4499   4152   5297   5317

49

Paris says—

Puffs, frills, pantalettes, laced sleeves,
Sleeveless bodices and high, high collars

Drawings by
EDWARD POUCHER

PLAITED tulle opens fan-like above a white satin choker. Colored velvet ribbon spans the back, held in front with tiny flowers.

JUST enough of 1860 and 1915 mingled! A dress from Martial et Armand shows a tight-fitting bodice and a bouffant skirt. Like most evening dresses, front and back are flat, the sides distended.

"BUSTLES now!" says Premet. Sometimes he compromises on a huge wired sash bow, one loop black, one red, the ends reversed for oddity.

CAN this narrow velvet ribbon be a belt? Jenny says so, and lets the ends fly loosely under the upstanding loops.

FUR from top to toe—and out to finger tips! Black kid and white fur deck these gloves.

UNDENIABLY they are pantalettes, Paris-sponsored, dark for daytime, with fur and lace for dancing.

MME. ROBERTS lights up a somber waist with brocaded silk, and uses jet buttons for a note of contrast. The inside of the collar, revers and chemisette are starched white organdie, and a cord marks the waist line.

This one-piece princess dress will make a charming wedding dress for the doll, and if made without the train it will serve for less formal wear. It takes little material to make it, and the softest fabrics are the best for the shirred style.

1915

NOW gloves and sleeves lace, *on dit*,—the one below right up to the elbow.

LANVIN trims a skirt with heavy braid, fluted braid in a V-shaped design over it. An upstanding frill at the hem is Paquin's device. Jenny, to continue the success of her transparent hem, yet to give novelty, introduces knotted silk fringe. Weeks's petticoat, with net yoke and wired ruffles, has seams strengthened by ribbon.

BEER devises a wristband of plaited silk with a loose turn-over white linen cuff.

HERE'S French inconsistency! This cuff turns back to shorten the sleeve—then two lace ruffles give it length.

A MARTIAL et Armand sleeve shows a roll shirred over solid stuffing, while an inch tuck forms a close cuff. 51

Reefer 9735

Dress 9180

Suit 9525

Jumper 9733

1918

CLOTHES OF TO-DAY FOR MEN OF TO-MORROW

MAN'S work is never done—and for the saving of clothes, which is no small matter these days, there is a comfortable jumper (design 9733) that can be slipped right on over the suit. It is a splendid protection to a man's clothes. It is very simple in construction and inexpensive to make The pockets are very convenient. Use denim, duck, khaki or flannel.

A 36 breast measure requires 3⅞ yards denim 27 inches wide.

Design 9733, 10 sizes, 30 to 48 inches breast measure.

Suit 9588

Suit 9383

Suit 8930

Dress
1188

Suit 9588

Suit 9998

Military suit
1403

Suit 1429

FEBRUARY, 1919

1915

Here is an outfit for a doll, consisting of a dress, petticoat, and combination chemise and envelope drawers.

1913

WARDROBE FOR A 16"-18" DOLL OF ABOUT 1910

This doll had a trunk-full of beautiful clothes; so many in fact it was difficult to decide which garments to show in our limited space. At every opportunity I have drawn multi-purpose patterns to take full advantage of a page.

One of the most important articles of apparel in a doll's wardrobe was a raincape, judging from the fact that one appeared in nearly every large grouping of doll clothes examined by this writer. The pattern given may be varied with a fur collar and heavy lining for a winter cape.

A cream flannel petticoat was a must in the days of unreliable heating and long, cold winters. In addition there must be a fine tucked lawn petticoat, often edged with lace. Other petticoats were sometimes worn with dress-up clothes, or for added warmth.

This doll had a full array of hats and several are given here. She also had a muff and a neckpiece called a "tippet" which was worn over the coat collar. This was not only warm but also decorative. Remnants of fur "tails" hung from the end of this accessory. Any fur item may be duplicated with ease since the advent of the "fake furs" made of synthetic fibres.

Underwear included drawers with ruffles and bloomers. There was also a romper; however, these are all covered sufficiently elsewhere in the book.

Although the doll for which these clothes were made had a bisque head, the styles and size are correct for Schoenhut dolls.

1913

16"-18" BISQUE HEAD
OR SCHOENHUT DOLL

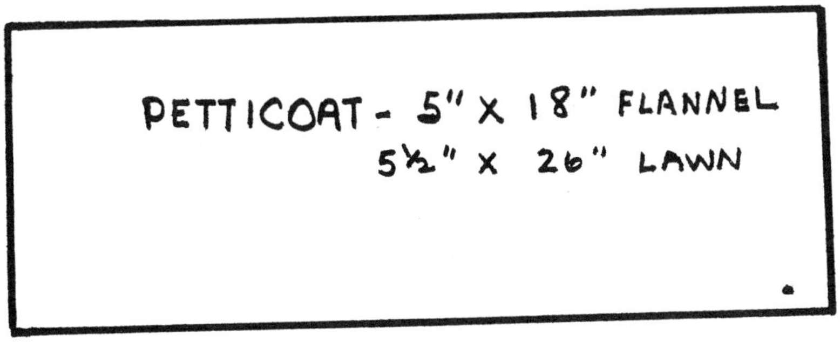

PETTICOAT- 5" X 18" FLANNEL
5½" X 26" LAWN

FLANNEL PETTICOAT HAS FEATHER-
STITCH TRIM, LAWN ONE HAS TUCKS.

ADD ¼" SEAM ALLOWANCE
FOR 18" DOLL. SEAMS ALLOWED
FOR 16" DOLL.

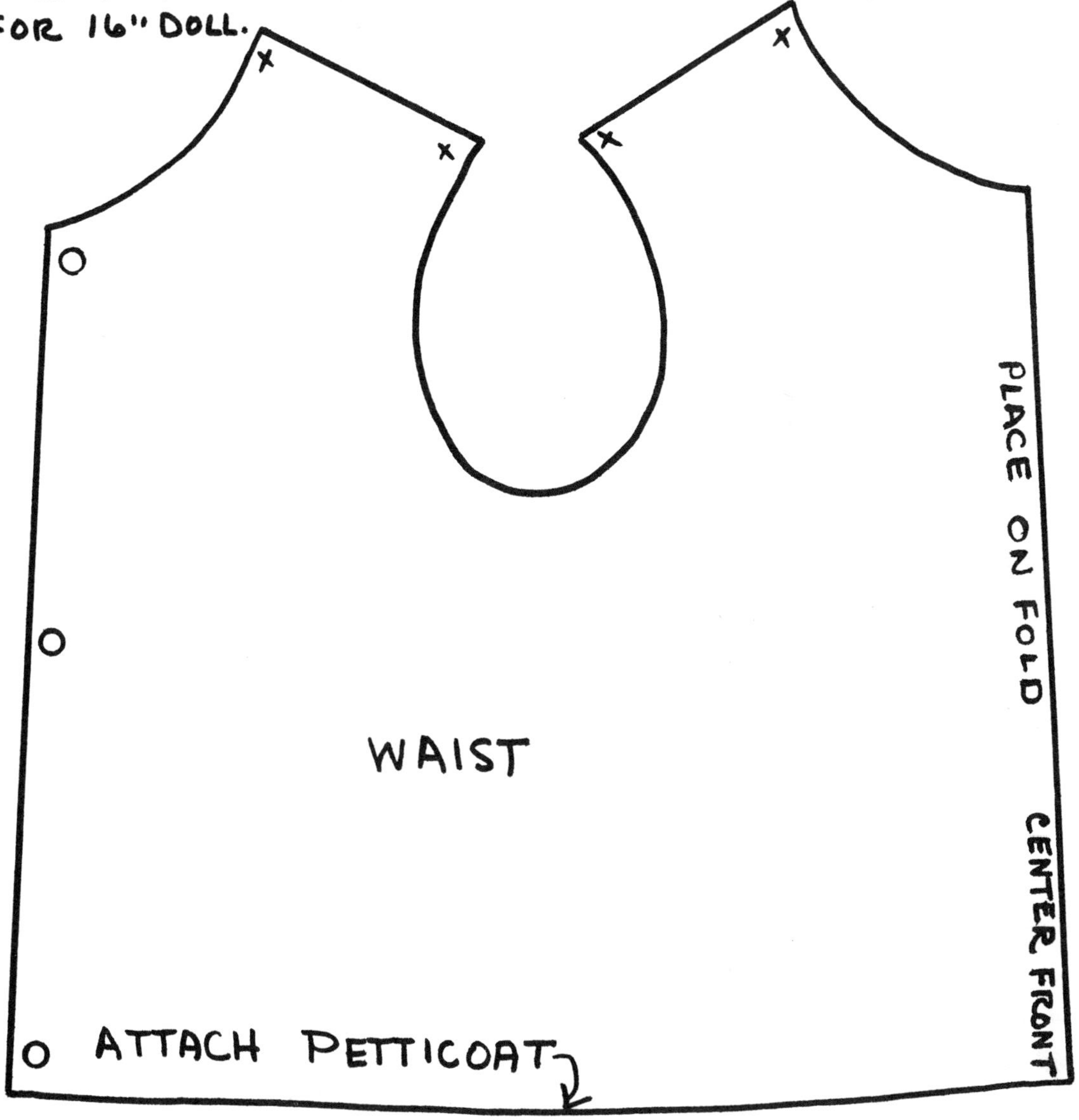

WAIST

PLACE ON FOLD

CENTER FRONT

o ATTACH PETTICOAT

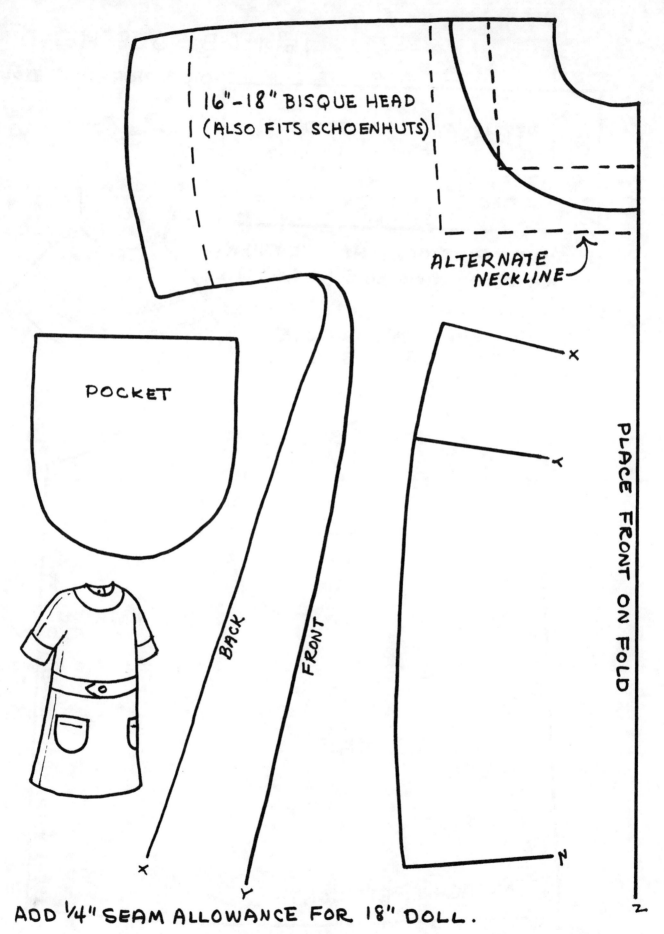

16"-18" BISQUE HEAD
(ALSO FITS SCHOENHUTS)

ALTERNATE
NECKLINE

POCKET

BACK

FRONT

PLACE FRONT ON FOLD

ADD ¼" SEAM ALLOWANCE FOR 18" DOLL.

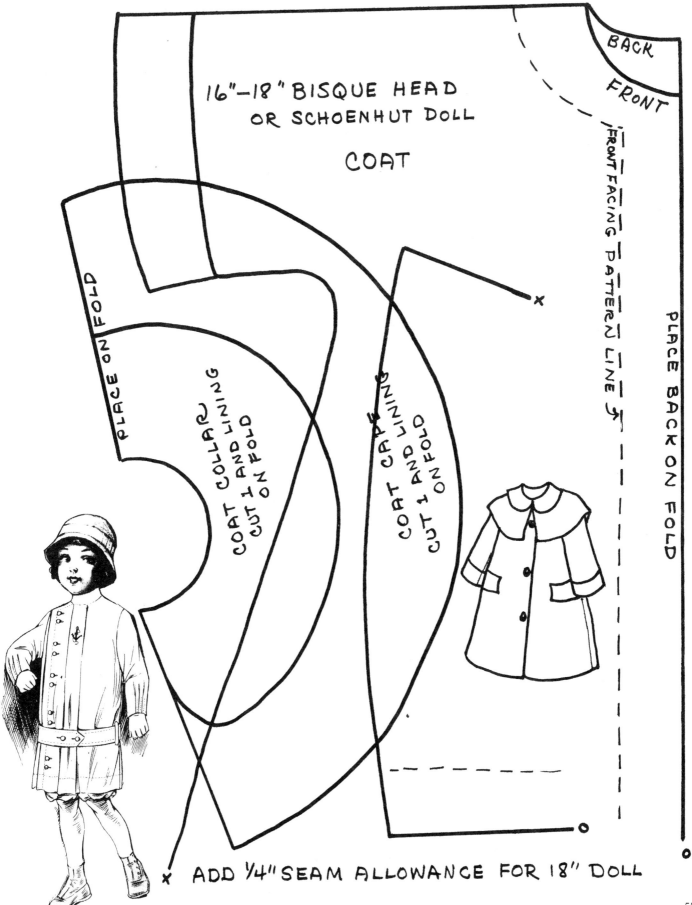

16"–18" BISQUE HEAD
OR SCHOENHUT DOLL

COAT

BACK

FRONT

FRONT FACING PATTERN LINE

PLACE BACK ON FOLD

PLACE ON FOLD

COAT COLLAR
CUT 1 AND LINING
ON FOLD

COAT CAPE LINING
CUT 1 AND LINING
ON FOLD

ADD ¼" SEAM ALLOWANCE FOR 18" DOLL

57

16"–18" BISQUE HEAD
RAIN CAPE

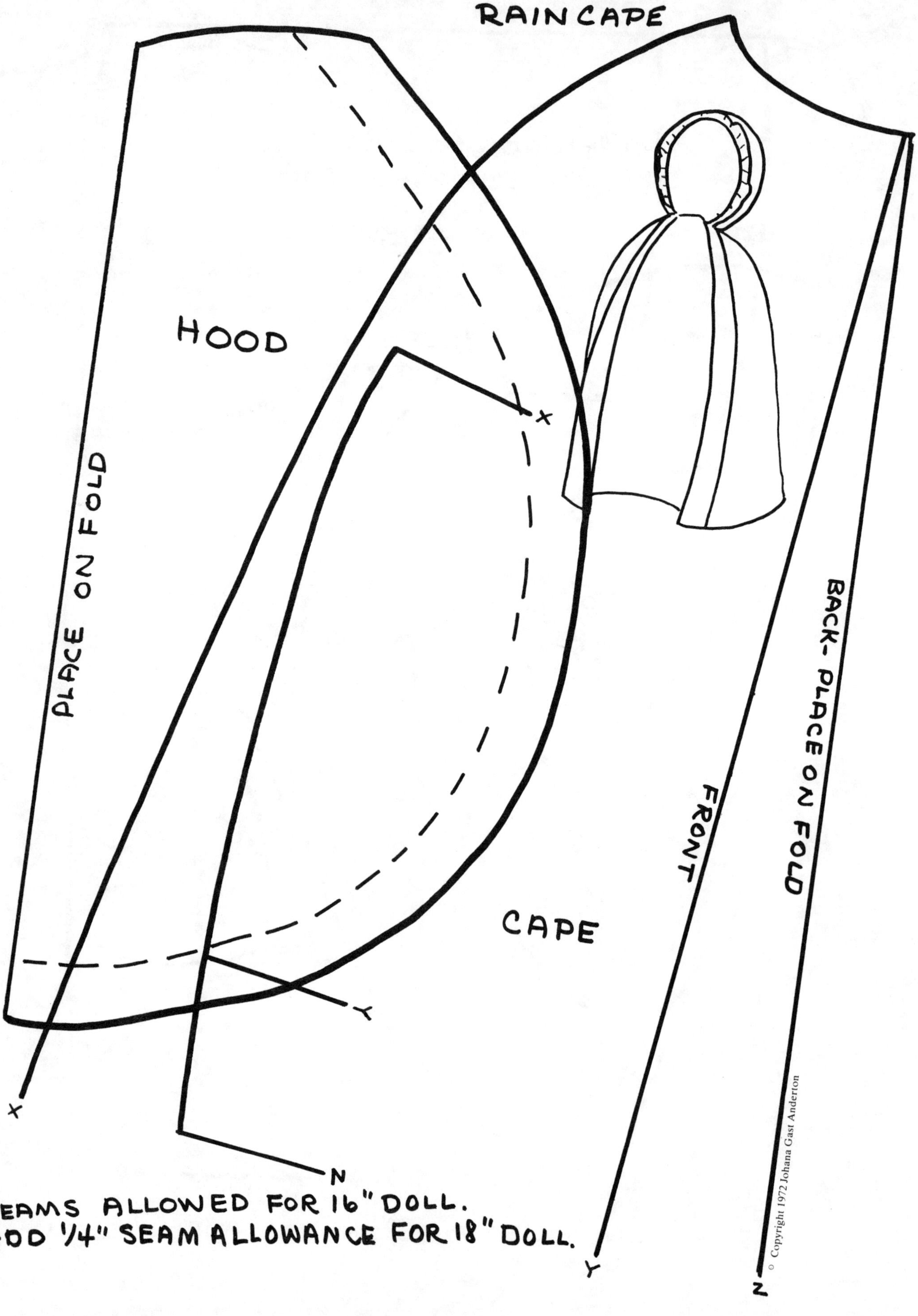

HOOD

PLACE ON FOLD

X

CAPE

FRONT

BACK- PLACE ON FOLD

X

Y

N

SEAMS ALLOWED FOR 16" DOLL.
ADD ¼" SEAM ALLOWANCE FOR 18" DOLL.

Y

Z

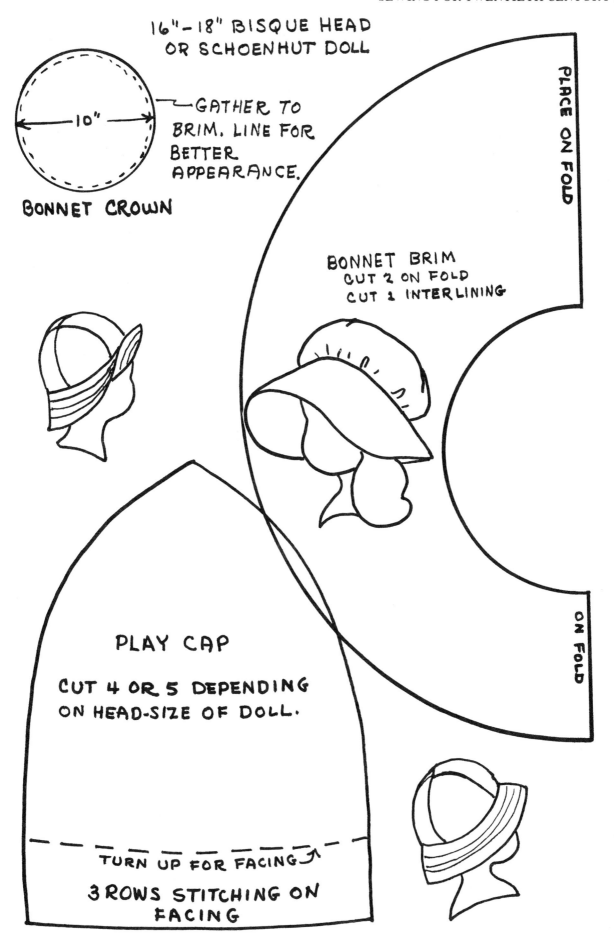

16"–18" BISQUE HEAD
OR SCHOENHUT DOLL

BONNET CROWN

—GATHER TO BRIM. LINE FOR BETTER APPEARANCE.

10"

PLACE ON FOLD

BONNET BRIM
CUT 2 ON FOLD
CUT 1 INTERLINING

ON FOLD

PLAY CAP

CUT 4 OR 5 DEPENDING ON HEAD-SIZE OF DOLL.

TURN UP FOR FACING

3 ROWS STITCHING ON FACING

16"–18" BISQUE HEAD OR SCHOENHUT DOLL

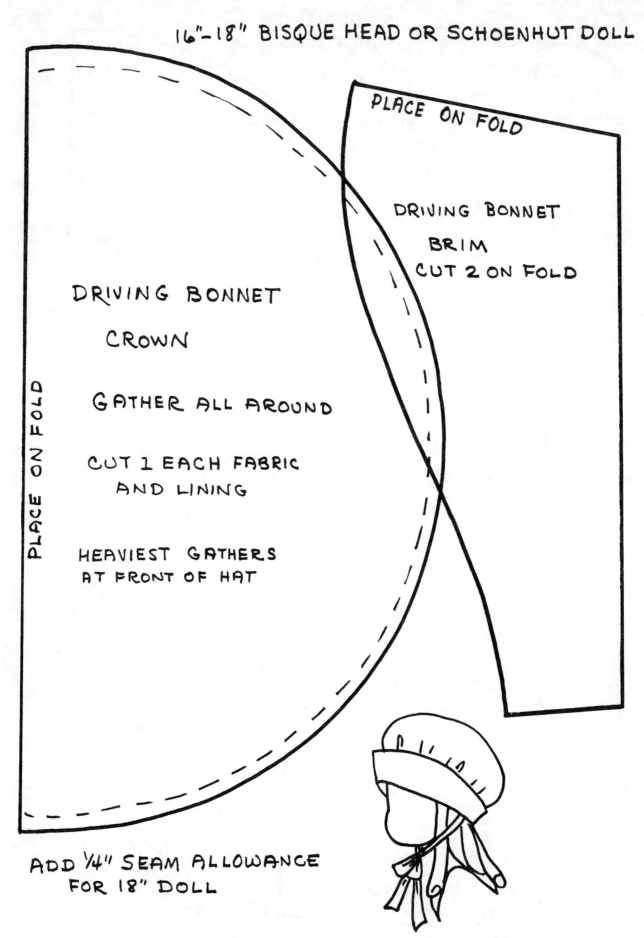

PLACE ON FOLD

DRIVING BONNET

BRIM

CUT 2 ON FOLD

DRIVING BONNET

CROWN

GATHER ALL AROUND

CUT 1 EACH FABRIC
AND LINING

HEAVIEST GATHERS
AT FRONT OF HAT

PLACE ON FOLD

ADD ¼" SEAM ALLOWANCE
FOR 18" DOLL

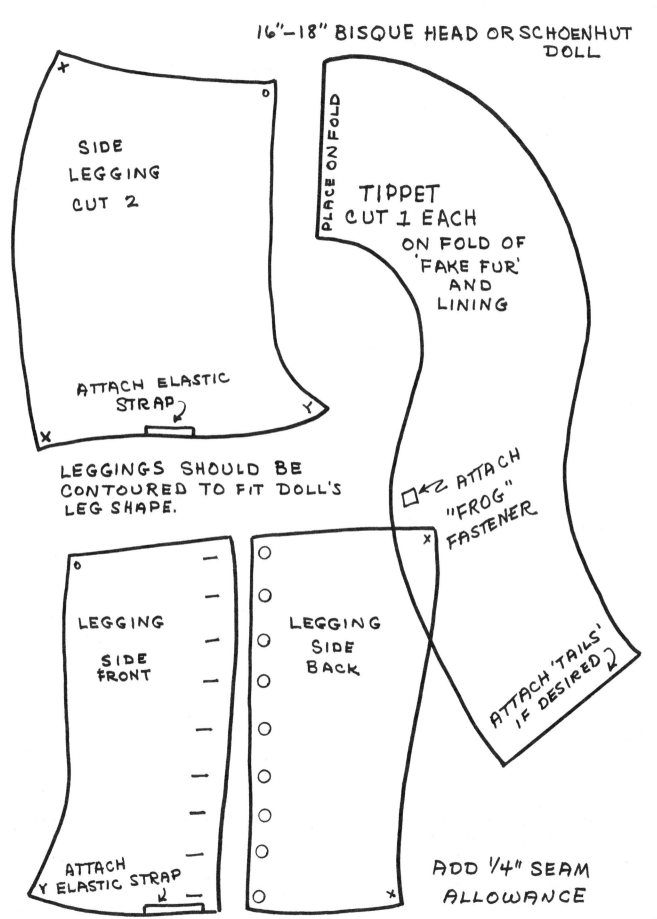

16"–18" BISQUE HEAD OR SCHOENHUT DOLL

SIDE LEGGING CUT 2

PLACE ON FOLD

TIPPET CUT 1 EACH ON FOLD OF 'FAKE FUR' AND LINING

ATTACH ELASTIC STRAP

LEGGINGS SHOULD BE CONTOURED TO FIT DOLL'S LEG SHAPE.

ATTACH "FROG" FASTENER

LEGGING SIDE FRONT

LEGGING SIDE BACK

ATTACH 'TAILS' IF DESIRED

ATTACH Y ELASTIC STRAP

ADD ¼" SEAM ALLOWANCE

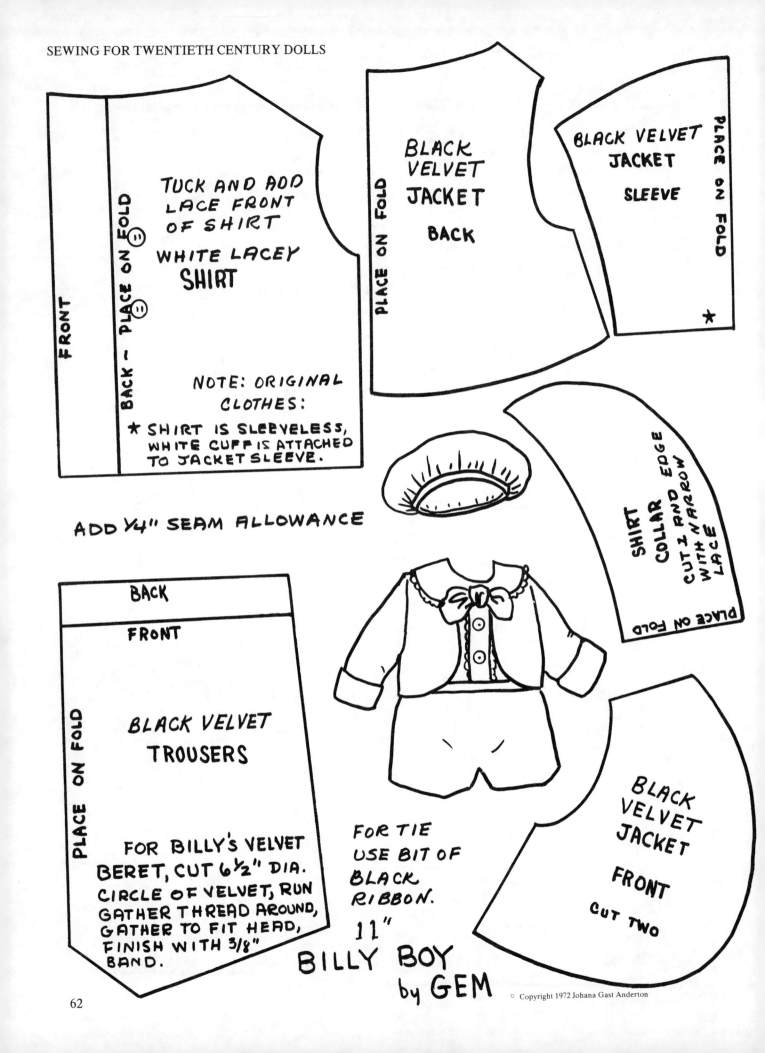

TUCK AND ADD
LACE FRONT
OF SHIRT

WHITE LACEY
SHIRT

FRONT

BACK – PLACE ON FOLD

NOTE: ORIGINAL
CLOTHES:

★ SHIRT IS SLEEVELESS,
WHITE CUFF IS ATTACHED
TO JACKET SLEEVE.

PLACE ON FOLD

BLACK
VELVET
JACKET

BACK

PLACE ON FOLD

BLACK VELVET
JACKET

SLEEVE

★

SHIRT
COLLAR
CUT 1 AND NARROW
WITH NARROW LACE

PLACE ON FOLD

ADD ¼" SEAM ALLOWANCE

BACK

FRONT

PLACE ON FOLD

BLACK VELVET
TROUSERS

FOR BILLY'S VELVET
BERET, CUT 6½" DIA.
CIRCLE OF VELVET, RUN
GATHER THREAD AROUND,
GATHER TO FIT HEAD,
FINISH WITH 3/8"
BAND.

FOR TIE
USE BIT OF
BLACK
RIBBON.

11"
BILLY BOY
by GEM

BLACK
VELVET
JACKET

FRONT

CUT TWO

© Copyright 1972 Johana Gast Anderton

62

X   O

PLACE ON FOLD

20" RAGGEDY ANDY'S HAT

CUT 1 ON FOLD

(WHITE FABRIC)

X   O

20" RAGGEDY ANDY'S HAT CROWN

CUT 1

(PLAIN FABRIC)

20" RAGGEDY ANDY'S SHIRT

(PRINT FABRIC)

PLACE FRONT ON FOLD

ADD ¼" SEAM ALLOWANCE

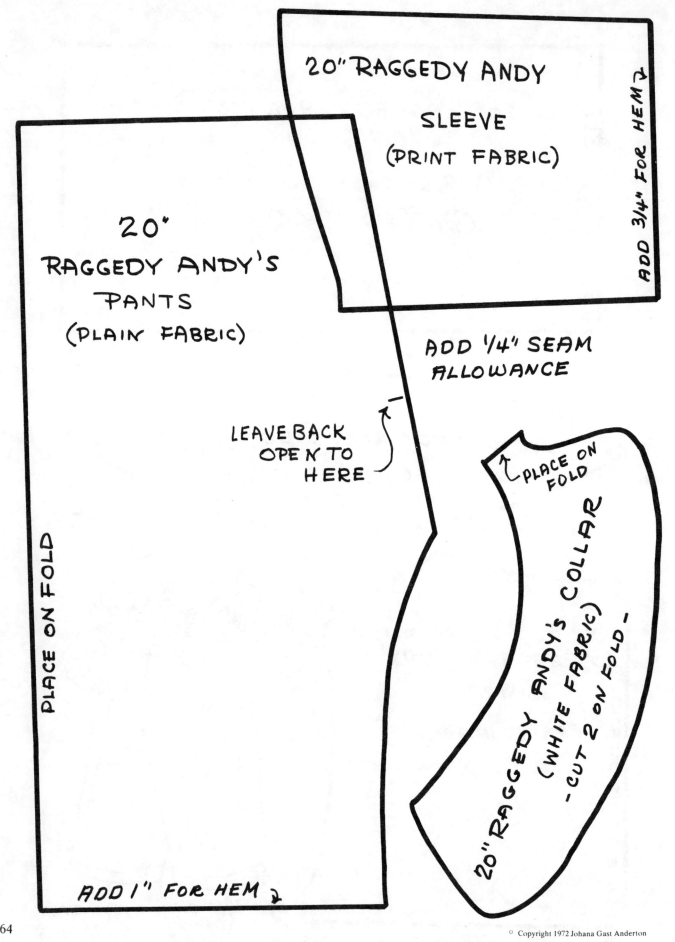

20" RAGGEDY ANDY
SLEEVE
(PRINT FABRIC)

ADD 3/4" FOR HEM ⤵

20"
RAGGEDY ANDY'S
PANTS
(PLAIN FABRIC)

ADD 1/4" SEAM
ALLOWANCE

LEAVE BACK
OPEN TO
HERE

PLACE ON
FOLD

PLACE ON FOLD

20" RAGGEDY ANDY'S COLLAR
(WHITE FABRIC)
- CUT 2 ON FOLD -

ADD 1" FOR HEM ⤵

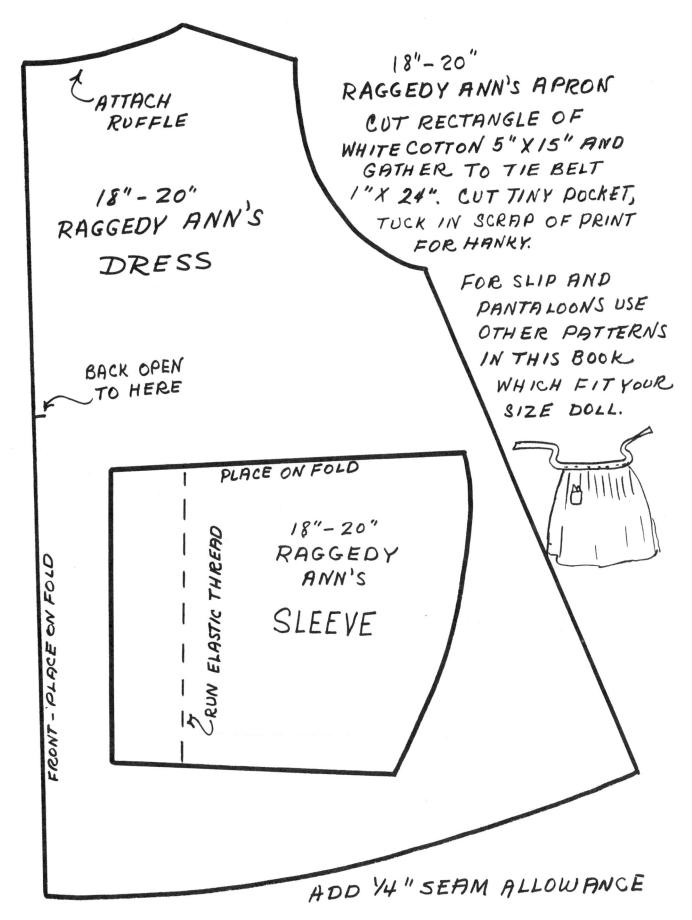

ATTACH RUFFLE

18"-20"
RAGGEDY ANN'S
DRESS

BACK OPEN
TO HERE

FRONT - PLACE ON FOLD

18"-20"
RAGGEDY ANN'S APRON
CUT RECTANGLE OF
WHITE COTTON 5"X15" AND
GATHER TO TIE BELT
1"X 24". CUT TINY POCKET,
TUCK IN SCRAP OF PRINT
FOR HANKY.

FOR SLIP AND
PANTALOONS USE
OTHER PATTERNS
IN THIS BOOK
WHICH FIT YOUR
SIZE DOLL.

PLACE ON FOLD

RUN ELASTIC THREAD

18"-20"
RAGGEDY
ANN'S
SLEEVE

ADD ¼" SEAM ALLOWANCE

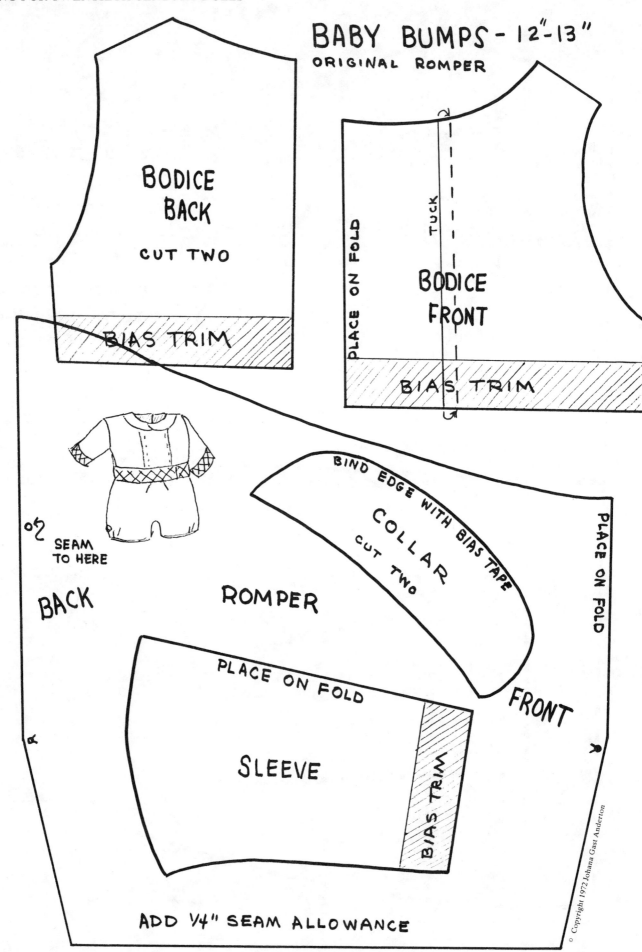

BABY BUMPS - 12"-13"
ORIGINAL ROMPER

BODICE BACK

CUT TWO

BIAS TRIM

PLACE ON FOLD

TUCK

BODICE FRONT

BIAS TRIM

BIND EDGE WITH BIAS TAPE

COLLAR

CUT TWO

PLACE ON FOLD

SEAM TO HERE

BACK

ROMPER

FRONT

PLACE ON FOLD

SLEEVE

BIAS TRIM

ADD ¼" SEAM ALLOWANCE

THE SCHOENHUT DOLLS

Here is a virtual panorama of original clothes for Schoenhut boy and girl dolls. The patterns I have drafted are all-purpose ones which may be used selectively to create many different dresses and suits. Each pattern piece is numbered, the costumes are numbered, and a list of required pattern pieces for each outfit is given along with a description of original fabrics and colors. The doll figures are taken from an old Schoenhut catalog. Patterns are drafted for a 16-17 inch doll, by adding seam allowances. They will fit a 14 inch doll as drawn.

Baby dresses and rompers are covered adequately elsewhere in this book, as are drawers, petticoats, stockings, shoes, and other wardrobe items. Pattern is given for the Schoenhut underwear since it is almost a trademark of these dolls. Made of fine knit, the girls' undersuit is plain. Both have three buttons in back.

Space has not been used to give patterns for skirts of dresses when pattern is merely a rectangle of proper size, such as in dress numbers 561 and 562. Some of these skirts are gathered to the bodice or to a belt, and some are pinch-pleated while others are box-pleated.

Note different belt treatments: number 569 is a separate belt with rounded ends, 570 is a ribbon tie, 530 is narrow, loose, and buttoned, 561, 562, 563 and others have sewn-in belts, topstitched, and 569 has a loose belt with buttonholes on both ends which is buttoned first to dress, then the dress is buttoned, and finally right end of belt goes over same button.

None of the views shows sailor bellbottom trousers, but many collectors like to dress their Schoenhut boys in this style and I have given the pattern along with three other trouser effects.

———

560 — Pink or blue chambray, white linene trim. Collar 2, dress pattern page 56, sleeve 1, belt 2 or 5, cuff 1.

561 — Pink or blue percale, colored chambray trim. Collar 3, bodice 3, 2, sleeve 1, cuff 1, belt 1.

562 — Pink or blue chambray, white linene trim, snap buttons. Collar 1, bodice 4, 6, sleeve 1, belt 4, cuff 1.

563 — Pink and blue gingham, embroidery and fancy braid trim. Collar 5, bodice 8, 7, sleeve 1, dickey 1.

564 — Fancy striped, or blue plaid gingham, colored piping, white tucked guimpe. Blouse (guimpe) bodice 4, 6, sleeve 1, dress 1, belt 2.

565 — Pink and blue gingham, pink or blue chambray trim. Collar 3, bodice 1, 2, belt 6, cuff 1.

566 — Pink or blue chambray, braid and button trim fancy white waist. Blouse, bodice 11, 12, collar 2, vest bodice 9, 7.

567 — Pink plaid or pink striped zephyr gingham, plain pink or white lawn trim. Dress, page 56, collar 3, overdress, bodice 7, 8, belt 1.

568 — Pink or fancy striped zephyr gingham, braid and embroidery trim. Dress, page 56, collar 4, vest, bodice 11, 12.

569 — Pink and blue striped zephyr gingham, braid trim, fancy guimpe. Dress, page 56, collar 4, overdress bodice 10, 13, belt 1.

570 — Blue and pink or yellow and pink flowered lawn, lace trim and fancy guimpe. Bodice 8, 13, blouse, bodice 5, 7, collar 4.

530 — White and blue linene, blue trim, red stars and tie. Dress, page 56, with front neck opening 9, collar 5, belt 4, sleeve 1.

580 — White, embroidery insertion, lace and ribbon trim. Bodice 1, 2, sleeve 2 with lace ruffle.

532 — White, embroidery insertion, tucking beading, ribbon trim. Adapt dress, page 42.

581 — Fancy white dress, skirt, yoke of embroidery lace, ribbon trim. Bodice 4, 6, sleeve 2 with ruffle.

582 — Fancy white dress, skirt and waist of embroidery, embroidery and ribbon trim. Dress, page 56 collar 4, sleeve 2.

583 — Fancy white dress, fine lawn, fine lace insertion, lace edge, ribbon trim. Bodice 1, 2, sleeve 2 with ruffle, lace ruffle over shoulders.

584 — Same as 583 with trim varied.

820 — Assorted Oliver Twist suits of blue or brown pants with blue and white or plain white waists. Bodice 11, 12, collar 1, sleeve 1, trousers 1.

821 — Same description as 820. Same as 820 except collar 2, trousers 2.

819 — Assorted Buster Brown Suits of blue and white or red and white striped seersucker, white trim and tie. Jacket 1, 2, sleeve 1, collar 1, trouser 3, elastic at hem.

812 — Assorted Russian Suits of white linene with pink or blue collars, shield, belt, and tie. Jacket 3, 2, sleeve 1, belt 4, dickey 1, collar 6.

813 — Assorted Russian Suits of blue and white stripe Galetea, white shield and tie. Same as 812.

818 — Fancy Suit of white linen pants, white shirt, red cloth coat, silk tie. Jacket 4, 2, collar 7, sleeve 1, trousers 3.

560   561   562   563

564   565   566   567

569 568 570 530

580 532 581 582

583

584

820

821

819

812

813

818

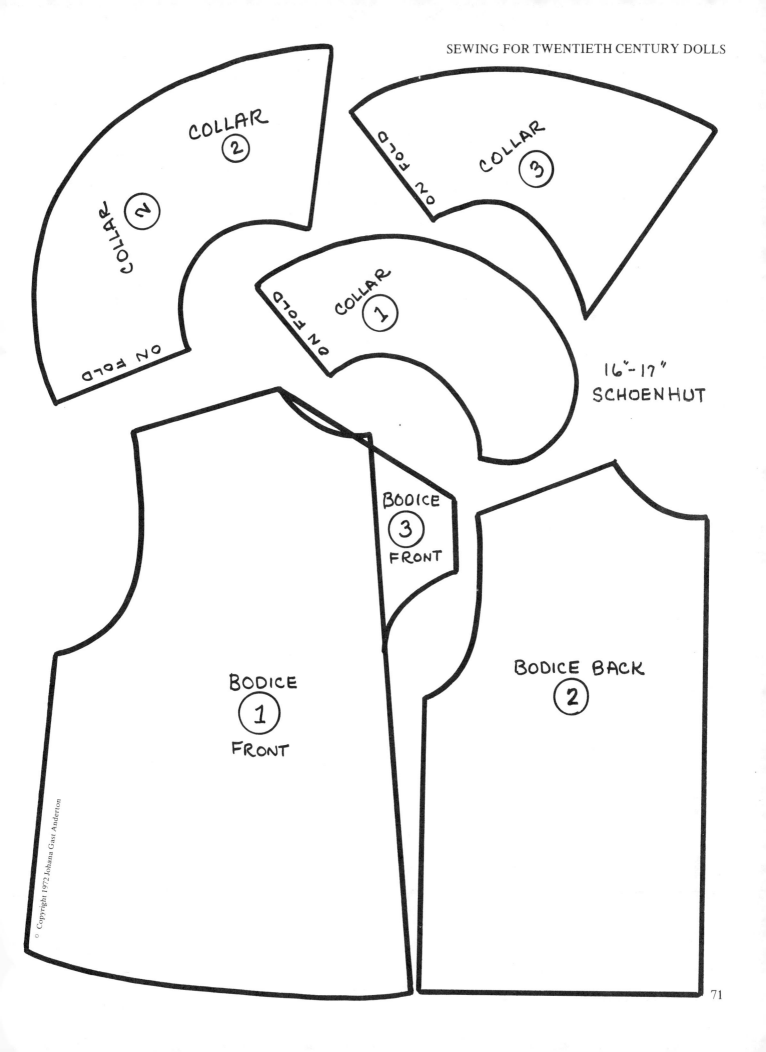

COLLAR
②

COLLAR
②

COLLAR
③

ON FOLD

ON FOLD

ON FOLD

COLLAR
①

ON FOLD

16"–17"
SCHOENHUT

BODICE
③
FRONT

BODICE
①
FRONT

BODICE BACK
②

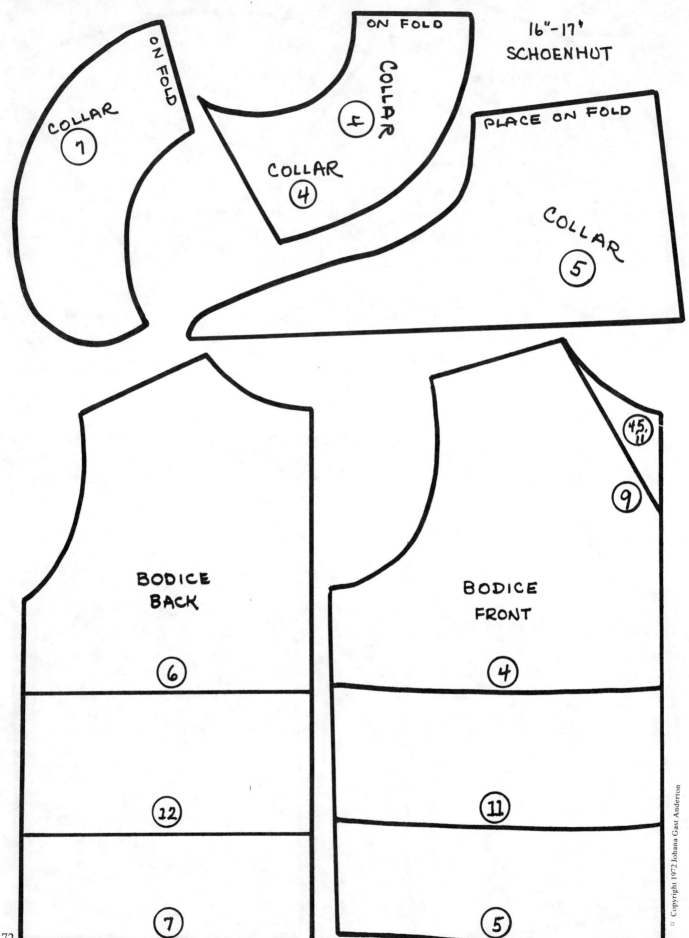

16"-17"
SCHOENHUT

COLLAR 7

ON FOLD

COLLAR 4

ON FOLD

COLLAR 4

PLACE ON FOLD

COLLAR 5

BODICE BACK 6

BODICE FRONT 4

45, 11

9

12

11

7

5

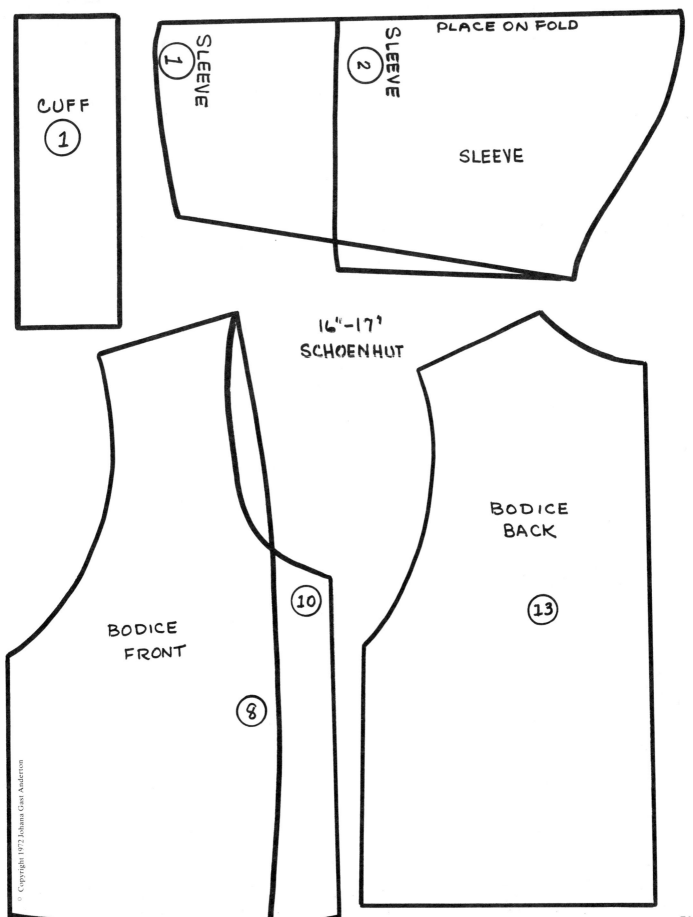

CUFF
①

SLEEVE
①

SLEEVE
②

PLACE ON FOLD

SLEEVE

16" – 17"
SCHOENHUT

BODICE
FRONT

⑩

⑧

BODICE
BACK

⑬

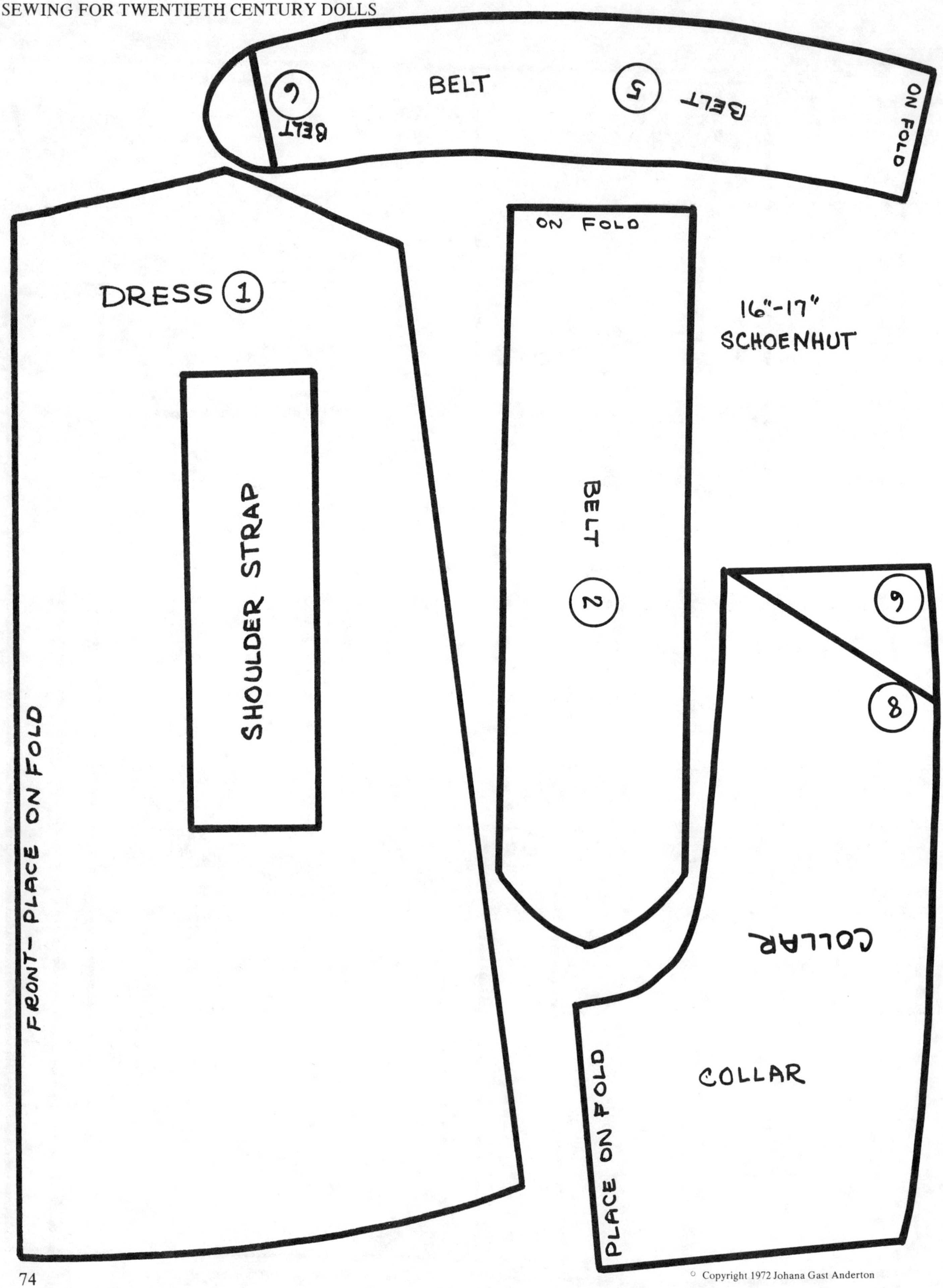

BELT ⑦

BELT

⑤ BELT

ON FOLD

DRESS ①

ON FOLD

16"-17"
SCHOENHUT

SHOULDER STRAP

BELT
②

⑨

⑧

FRONT— PLACE ON FOLD

COLLAR

COLLAR

PLACE ON FOLD

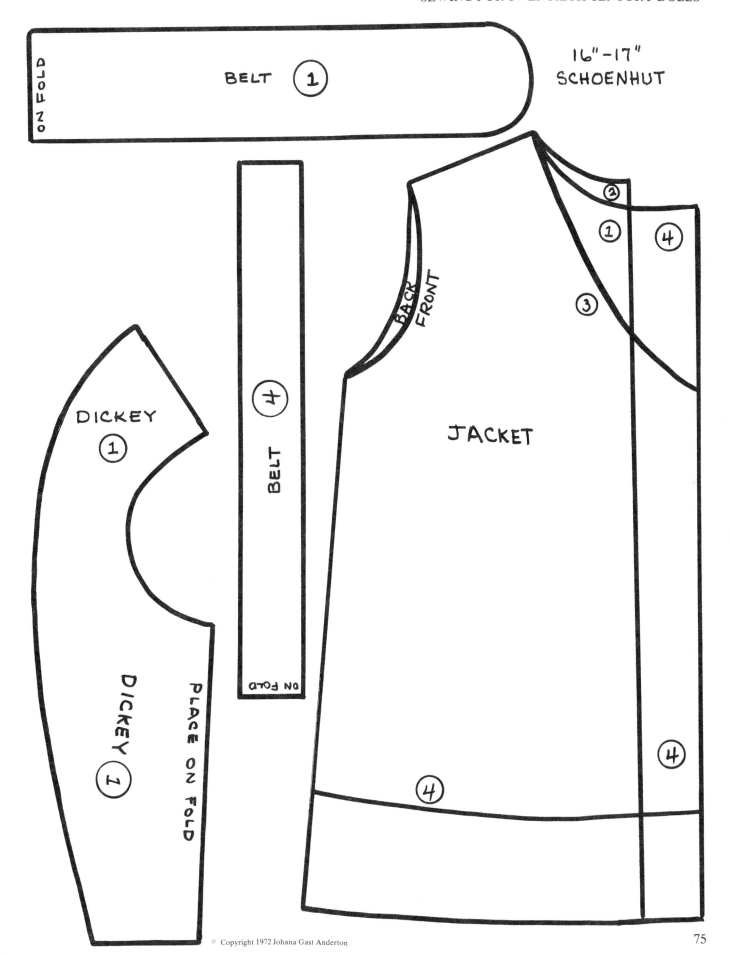

ON FOLD

BELT ①

16"-17"
SCHOENHUT

②

① ④

③

BACK
FRONT

DICKEY ①

BELT ④

JACKET

DICKEY ①

PLACE ON FOLD

ON FOLD

④

④

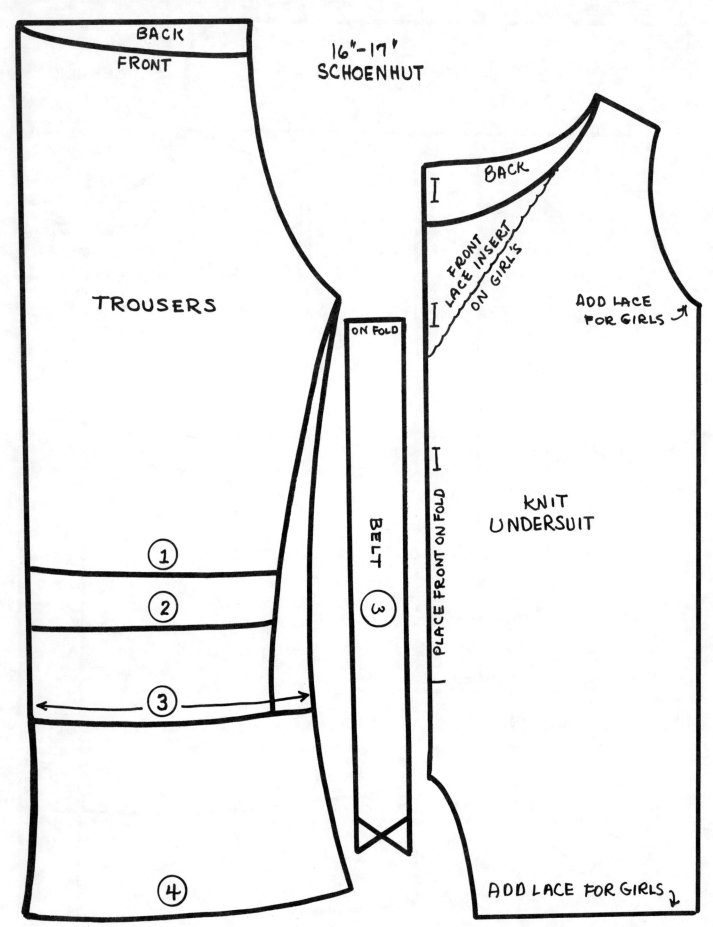

BACK

FRONT

16"-17'
SCHOENHUT

TROUSERS

BACK

FRONT LACE INSERT ON GIRL'S

ADD LACE FOR GIRLS ↗

ON FOLD

BELT

PLACE FRONT ON FOLD

KNIT UNDERSUIT

① ② ③ ④

ADD LACE FOR GIRLS ↘

THE 1920s

Dolls reflect, more than ever, the styles of their human counterparts. One 20" doll wears a "mushroom style" straw hat with tailored white cotton linene suit in 1921. Some have lawn dresses with matching hats trimmed with roses and ribbons. Dolls were being made with deep shoulder plates by 1923 to allow for the low neckline styles.

Shorter skirts for children were shown in 1926 with toddlers wearing balloon-shaped romper suits with belts or half-belts. Three-piece knitted suits were for cool days. Women's dresses were also shorter and trousers were shown for women. Sailor suits and two-piece Norfolk suits were popular for little boys. Also shown for the small male were cowboy, baseball, Indian, and Forest Ranger suits.

Styles were becoming very straight and narrow with much simpler lines and more sports apparel by 1927. Home sewing is evidenced by the number of patterns being offered for children's and adult's clothing. 1929 brought the flapper styles and larger quantities of children's clothes than previously.

Tams and cloches, straight-from-the-shoulder coats, both double-breasted and single-breasted, some with collar capes were seen. Smock and sailor style dresses were shown for little girls. Small boys wore one-piece playsuits while small girls' play costumes were dresses with matching bloomers. Boys proudly wore aviator caps reminiscent of Charles Lindbergh's.

Clothing styles were breaking away from the inconvenience and discomfort of former decades and were moving towards more freedom, better fit, and greater comfort.

These figures from *Needlecraft Magazine,* August, 1924, give clues to construction of the fashions of that day. The simple lines lent themselves admirably to simple construction. These dresses could be finished without a pattern by an experienced seamstress, using only the layouts given.

2120
Emb
706

2118
Emb
718

Emb.
700

1814

2079
Emb
706

Emb
705

2127

2060
Emb
710

1795

2125
Emb
706

2109

2067

2113
Emb. 708

2079

2109   2067   2113

2060

2109   2113   2060

The Fashion Book

For Spring, Illustrating Pictorial Review Fashions

THE PICTORIAL REVIEW COMPANY

Seventh Avenue and Thirty-ninth Street, New York

OFFICERS

WILLIAM P. AHNELT
President and Treasurer

CHAS. W. NELSON
First Vice-President

EVERETT D. TRUMBULL
Second Vice-President

JAY A. WEBER
Secretary

PAUL BLOCK
Advertising Director

MAX HERZBERG
Art Director

BRANCH OFFICES

Pacific Coast Branch—
985 Market Street, San Fran-
cisco, Cal.
Southwestern Branch—
505 North Seventh Street, St.
Louis, Mo.
Southern Branch—82-84 North
Broad Street, Atlanta, Ga.
New England Branch—116 Bed-
ford Street, Boston, 11, Mass.

Western Branch—
200-206 South Market Street,
Chicago, Ill.
Canadian Factory and Sales
Office—
263-267 Adelaide Street, West,
Toronto, Ontario.
European Factory and Sales
Office—163-165 Great Port-
land Street, London, W 1.

HERALDS OF SPRING MODES

SPRING fashions lean towards picturesque expres-
sions, and there are three important silhouettes
that carry out these charming styles: the generally
becoming straight, slender effect, for daytime wear;
the draped silhouette, which clearly defines the figure
and brings with it the longer skirt and a waist-line
low enough to be smart for the individual figure and
the material used; and, finally, there is the slender
silhouette, that is broken by the introduction of godet
plaits and swaying draperies. Circular effects are
added to skirts in various widths, often starting from
the knee-line; these godets and circular movements
appear at the front of a costume, leaving the back
flat. The tight-fitting basque shares honors with the
bloused bodice. Often skirts are entirely plaited, or
there are inserted or floating knife-plaited panels, and
a too tight skirt may add panels of this kind to bring
it up to date. The new shoulder yokes are smart, and
collars, it is rumored, will be round and low. Ribbons finely plaited may be worked into conventional
flower designs. Braided rolls, bias folds, or cordings
are all attractive, used for neck, sleeves, and belt
adornments. Sleeves are tight and long,
flowing or short, according to what the
type of gown demands. Materials are
fascinating, and in silk, satin, crêpe, and
silk-and-wool show Oriental designs, and
in a number of instances blistered, crinkled,
and ratiné surfaces. Double-bordered
effects are lovely, and, with a good pattern,
women may make stunning frocks from
these effects by using the border at
lower skirt for the bodice, and cut
in half to deeply band the sleeves.
Cotton fabrics are quite as smart
for Summer costumes as many of
the more expensive fabrics, and the
new ginghams and voiles, in lovely
colorings in the new, broken
checks, dotted, and lace designs,
make frocks of real distinction.

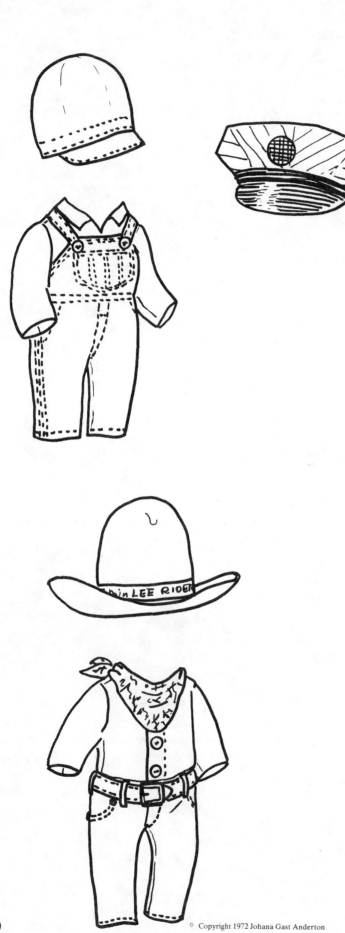

BUDDY LEE DOLLS

The H. D. Lee Company, Inc. originated Buddy Lee dolls in 1920-21 as an advertising piece; the doll was first shown in a Lee price list in 1922.

The first Buddy Lee dolls were dressed in Lee overalls and displayed in the window at Dayton Company Department Store on Nicollet Avenue, Minneapolis, Minnesota.

Engineers Doll — Dressed in bib overalls of blue denim with striped white denim jacket, shop cap and bandanna.

Cowboy Doll — Dressed in denim cowboy pants, plaid shirt, belt, bandanna, cowboy hat, and lariat.

Industrial Dolls — Dressed in many colors of shirts, pants, belts, caps, bow ties, or overhand ties, and Union-Alls (tm).

All-new material may be used for these clothes, or if preferred, worn denims and old, soft workshirts might be utilized. The shirt does not have to be plaid; in advertising photographs furnished this writer by the Company, Buddy Lee wears a shirt with a printed design (see *Twentieth Century Dolls,* p. 32, ADV-L2).

Striped pillow ticking is quite successful in creating the Engineer's outfit. A search of fabric departments will turn up many suitable fabrics for these clothes; however, the look of denim should be considered important in achieving an authentic appearance.

Hats for the Industrial Doll and the Cowboy Doll were buy-outs and there are, therefore, no patterns available for these. The band on the Cowboy hat reads: **"Ride 'Em in Lee Rider Overalls"** and on others: **"Ride 'Em in Lee Copper-Riveted Riders' Overalls"**. Label on Engineers' hat reads **"LEE/UNION MADE"**. Large circles on Industrial uniform are individual company patches; these were made for a wide variety of companies, including Coca Cola.

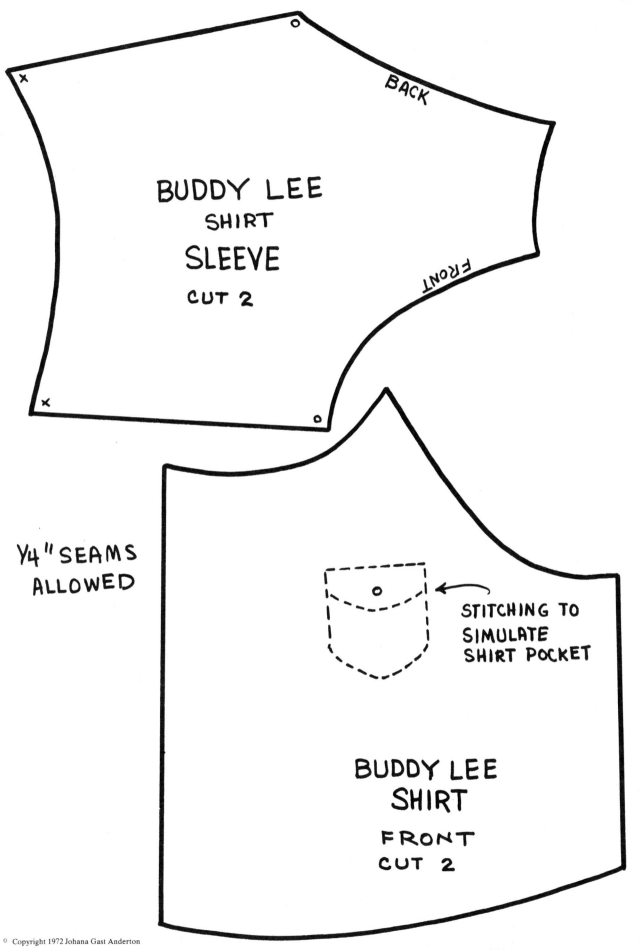

BACK

BUDDY LEE
SHIRT
SLEEVE
CUT 2

FRONT

¼" SEAMS
ALLOWED

o

← STITCHING TO
SIMULATE
SHIRT POCKET

BUDDY LEE
SHIRT

FRONT
CUT 2

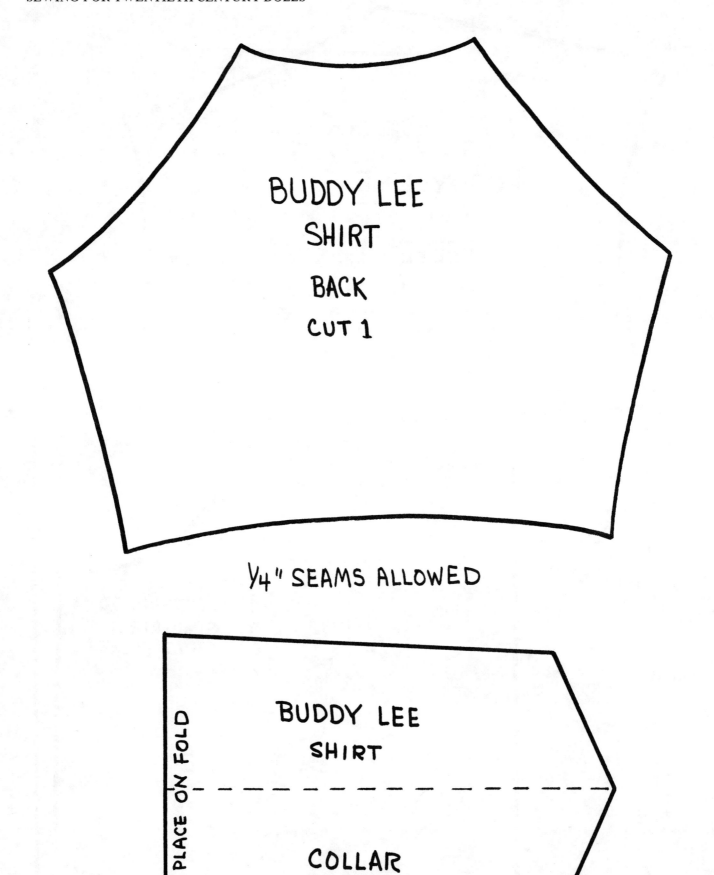

BUDDY LEE
SHIRT

BACK

CUT 1

¼" SEAMS ALLOWED

PLACE ON FOLD

BUDDY LEE
SHIRT

COLLAR
CUT 1 ON FOLD

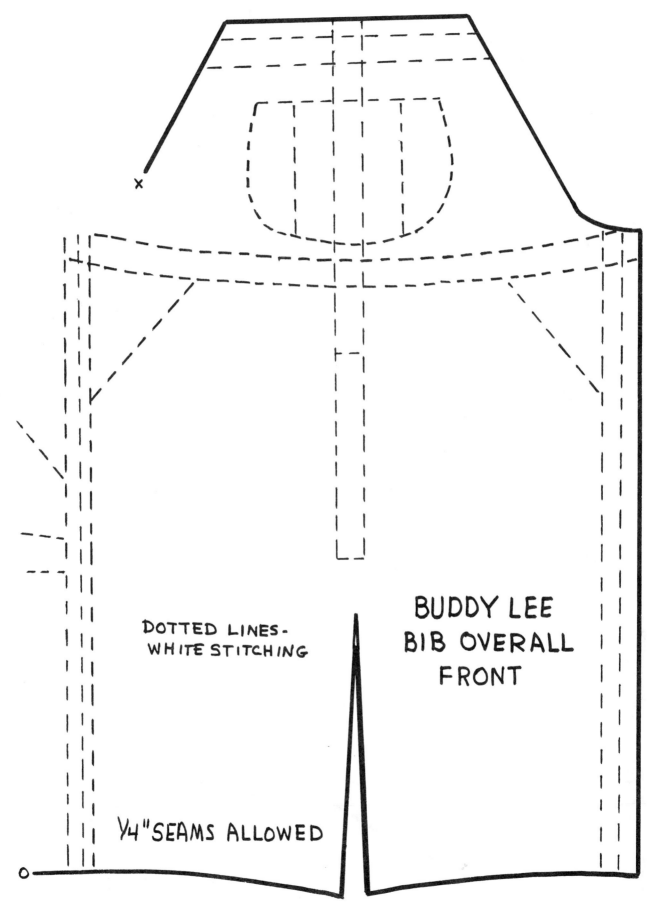

DOTTED LINES-
WHITE STITCHING

BUDDY LEE
BIB OVERALL
FRONT

¼" SEAMS ALLOWED

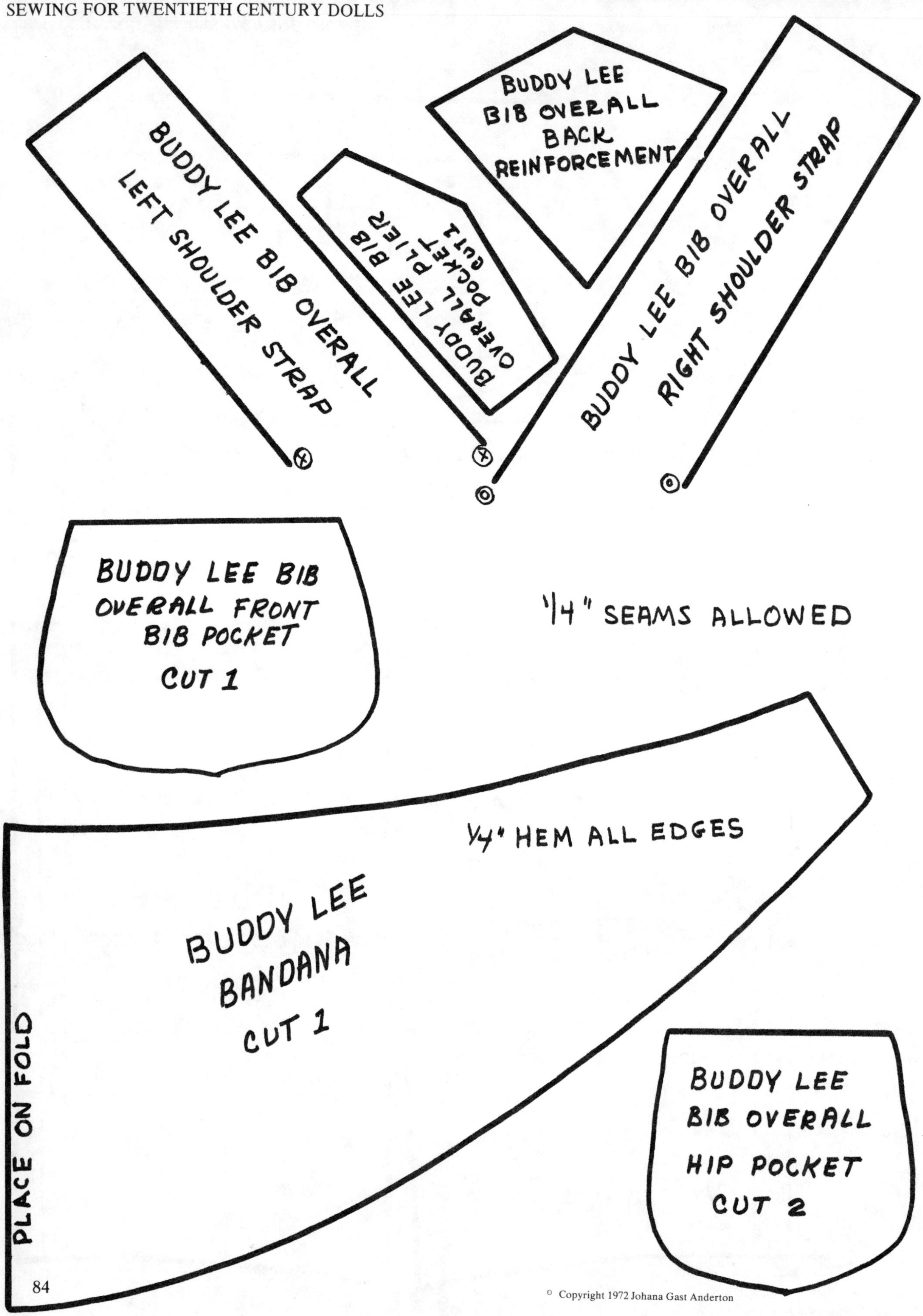

BUDDY LEE BIB OVERALL
LEFT SHOULDER STRAP

BUDDY LEE
BIB OVERALL
BACK
REINFORCEMENT

BUDDY LEE BIB
OVERALL BIB
POCKET
CUT 1

BUDDY LEE BIB OVERALL
RIGHT SHOULDER STRAP

BUDDY LEE BIB
OVERALL FRONT
BIB POCKET
CUT 1

¼" SEAMS ALLOWED

¼" HEM ALL EDGES

BUDDY LEE
BANDANA
CUT 1

PLACE ON FOLD

BUDDY LEE
BIB OVERALL
HIP POCKET
CUT 2

84

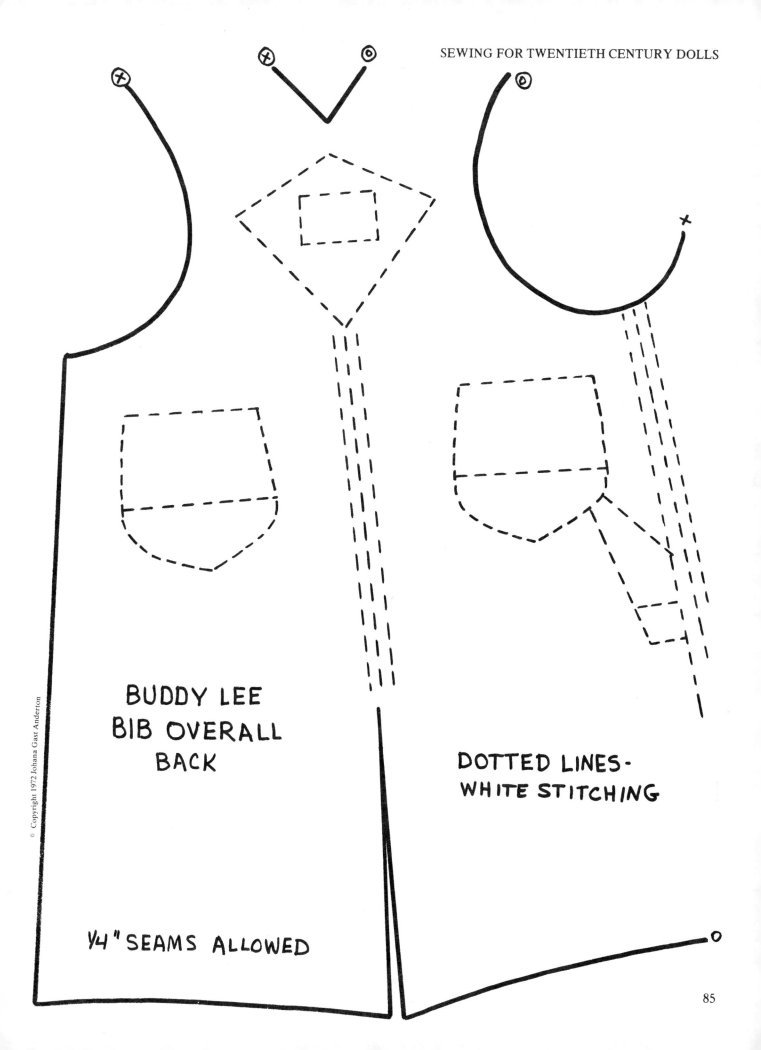

SEWING FOR TWENTIETH CENTURY DOLLS

BUDDY LEE
BIB OVERALL
BACK

DOTTED LINES-
WHITE STITCHING

¼" SEAMS ALLOWED

© Copyright 1972 Johana Gast Anderton

85

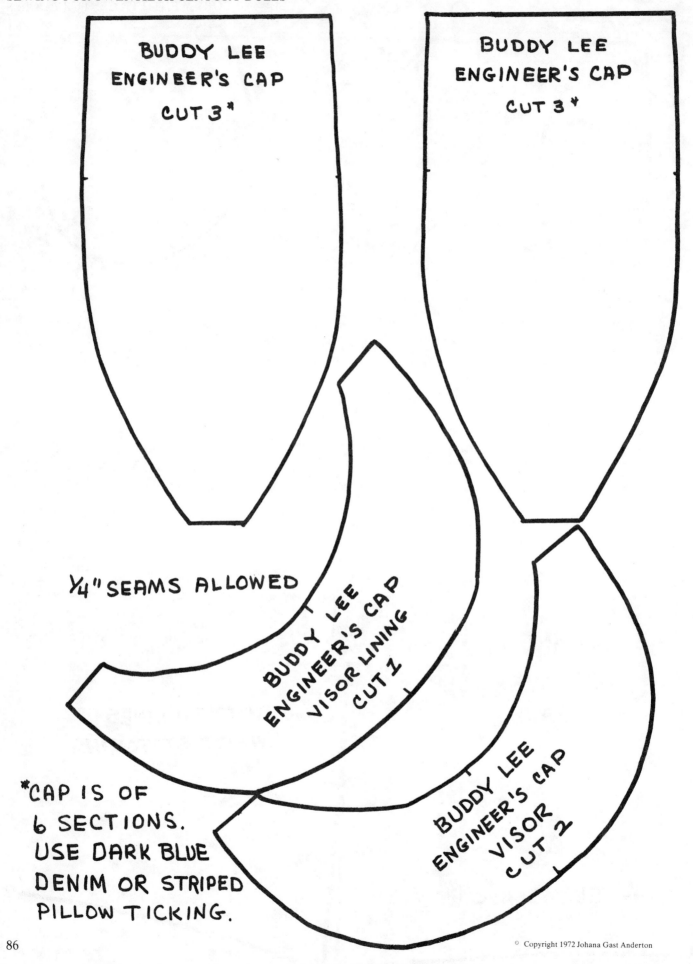

BUDDY LEE
ENGINEER'S CAP
CUT 3*

BUDDY LEE
ENGINEER'S CAP
CUT 3*

¼" SEAMS ALLOWED

BUDDY LEE
ENGINEER'S CAP
VISOR LINING
CUT 1

BUDDY LEE
ENGINEER'S CAP
VISOR
CUT 2

*CAP IS OF
6 SECTIONS.
USE DARK BLUE
DENIM OR STRIPED
PILLOW TICKING.

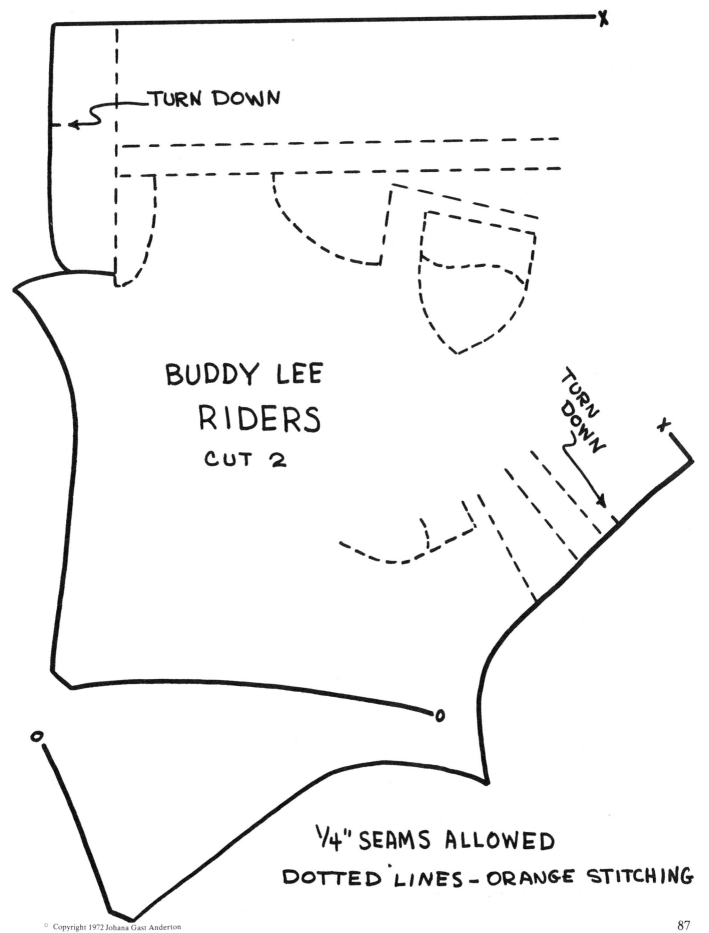

X

TURN DOWN

TURN DOWN

X

BUDDY LEE
RIDERS
CUT 2

O

O

¼" SEAMS ALLOWED
DOTTED LINES – ORANGE STITCHING

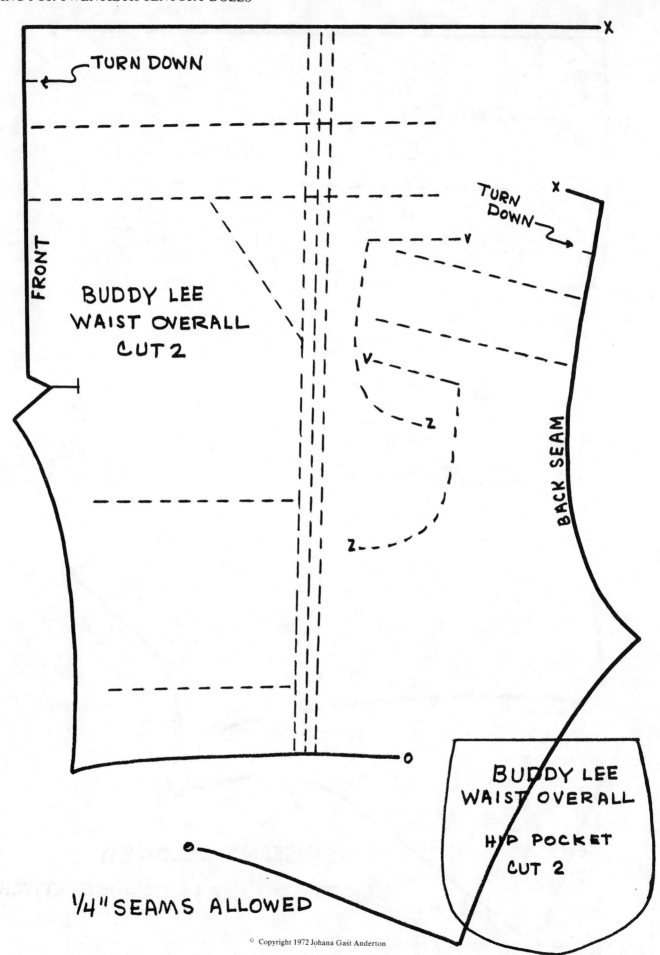

TURN DOWN

FRONT

BUDDY LEE
WAIST OVERALL
CUT 2

TURN DOWN

BACK SEAM

BUDDY LEE
WAIST OVERALL

HIP POCKET

CUT 2

¼" SEAMS ALLOWED

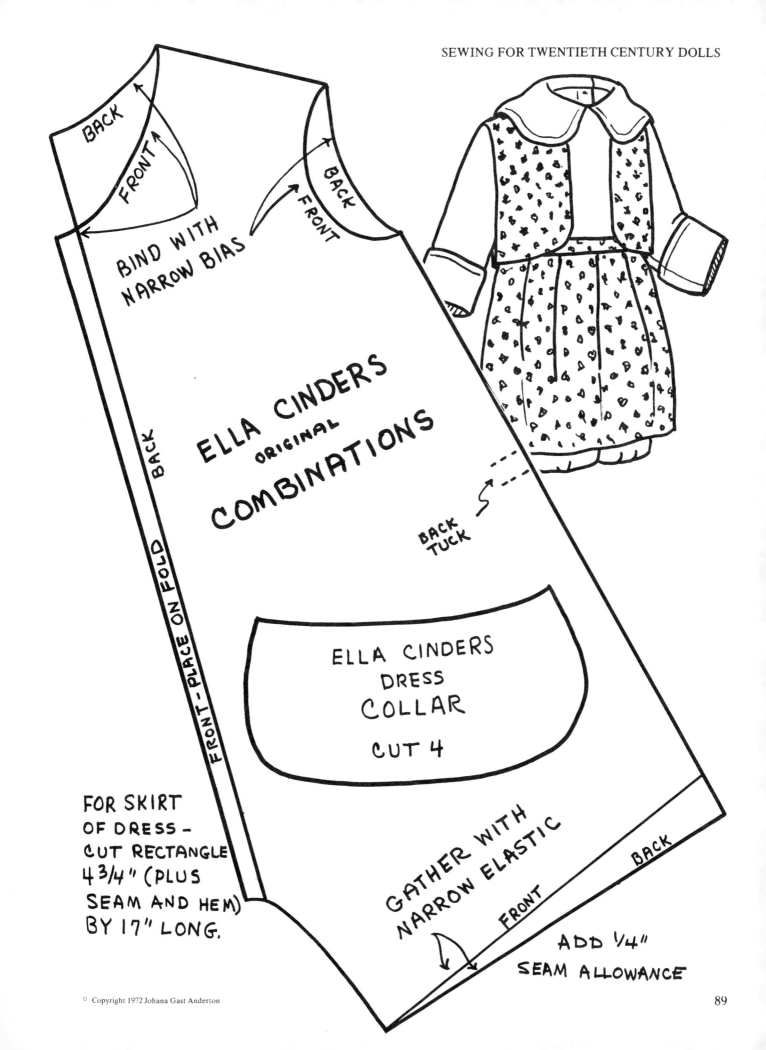

BACK

FRONT

BACK

FRONT

BIND WITH
NARROW BIAS

BACK

FRONT – PLACE ON FOLD

ELLA CINDERS
ORIGINAL
COMBINATIONS

BACK
TUCK

ELLA CINDERS
DRESS
COLLAR

CUT 4

FOR SKIRT
OF DRESS –
CUT RECTANGLE
4 3/4" (PLUS
SEAM AND HEM)
BY 17" LONG.

GATHER WITH
NARROW ELASTIC

BACK

FRONT

ADD 1/4"
SEAM ALLOWANCE

ELLA CINDERS

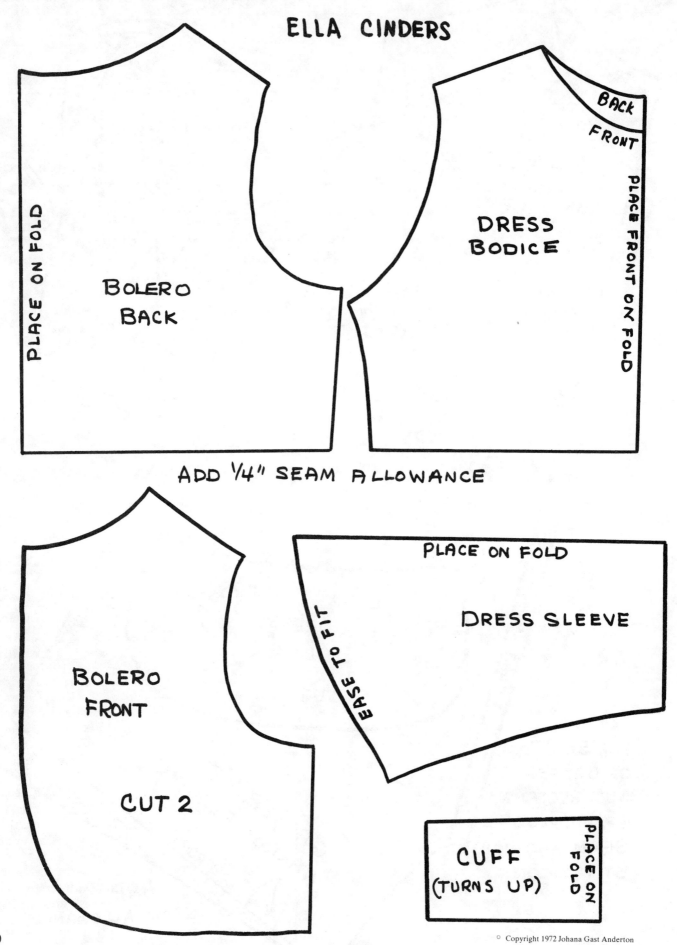

PLACE ON FOLD

BOLERO
BACK

BACK

FRONT

DRESS
BODICE

PLACE FRONT ON FOLD

ADD ¼" SEAM ALLOWANCE

BOLERO
FRONT

CUT 2

EASE TO FIT

PLACE ON FOLD

DRESS SLEEVE

CUFF
(TURNS UP)

PLACE ON FOLD

Layette from pages of *Pictorial Review,* 1913.

ENSEMBLE FOR
10½" BISQUE HEAD BABY

This baby wears all original clothes, although not its own. There is a diaper, a pair of cotton combinations, a cotton short slip (or long shirt, if you will), a long slip, and finally, a long embroidered organdy dress over all.

Fit and complete the underthings beginning with the diaper and working out. This diaper is a strip of flannel cut to fit around the doll and 2 to 2½ inches wide. Attached to this in the center of one long side is a tab measuring 1¼" wide and 4" long. The whole is lace-edged.

The combinations and short slip are cut from a fine-textured cotton and the patterns are self-explanatory.

The long slip is also of this fine cotton, but if desired may be of the organdy used for the dress. The slip hem is edged with ¾ inch lace.

For the skirt of the long baby dress, cut a piece of organdy 13½" wide and 27" long. Turn up a one-half inch hem on one long side, then sew one-half inch lace to bottom edge of this hem. Assemble the bodice, gather top edge of skirt to fit the bodice. Sew waist seam, then top stitch one-fourth inch satin ribbon over seam on right side.

Neck opening and cuffs of sleeves are finished in the same manner as bottom hem of dress. Then satin ribbon is top-stitched over the seam. If desired, the dress may be embroidered with pastel flowers, as is the original. A drawing of the flower design is shown.

91

BACK

FRONT

2 LACE INSERTION
SHORT SLIP

BACK
FRONT

10½" BISQUE
LONG SLIP

BACK
FRONT

PLACE ON FOLD

PLACE ON FOLD

ADD ¼" SEAM
ALLOWANCE

LEAVE BACK
OPEN DOWN
TO HERE.

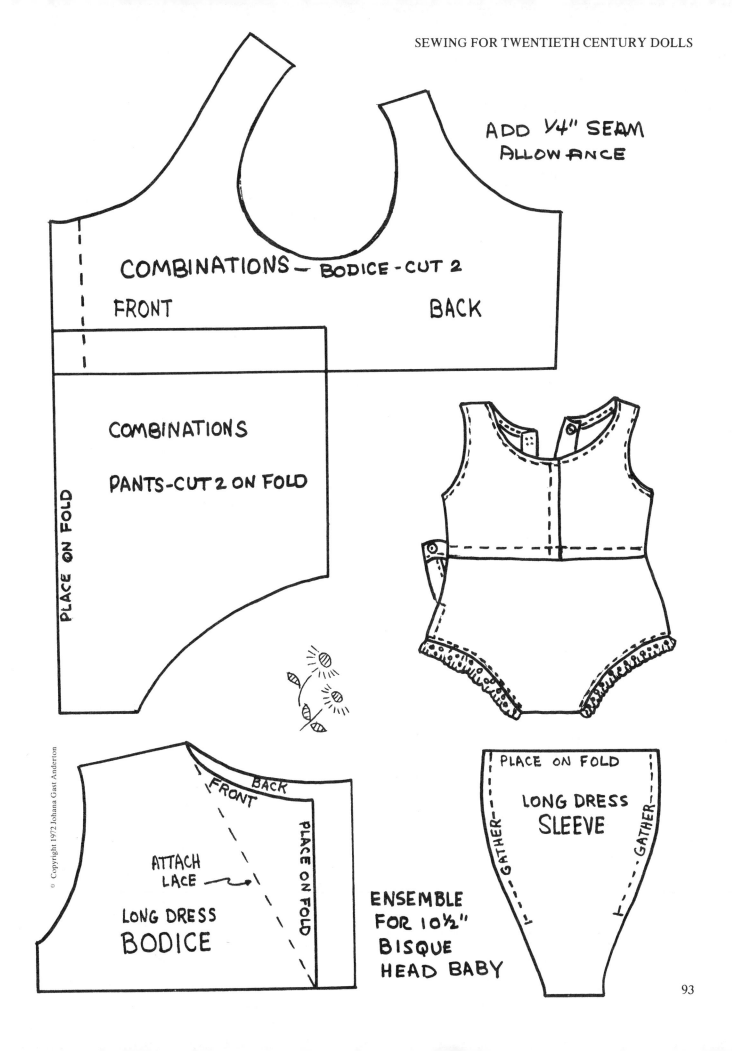

ADD ¼" SEAM
ALLOWANCE

COMBINATIONS — BODICE - CUT 2

FRONT   BACK

COMBINATIONS

PANTS - CUT 2 ON FOLD

PLACE ON FOLD

BACK
FRONT

ATTACH
LACE →

PLACE ON FOLD

LONG DRESS
BODICE

ENSEMBLE
FOR 10½"
BISQUE
HEAD BABY

PLACE ON FOLD

LONG DRESS
SLEEVE

GATHER

GATHER

TUCK

14" BUBBLES DRESS BACK SKIRT CUT 2

BIND NECK WITH BIAS

FINISH WITH DOUBLE RUFFLE

14" BUBBLES DRESS BODICE BACK CUT 2

ATTACH 2½" COTTON EYELET RUFFLE

GATHER — A

B

14" BUBBLES DRESS FRONT SKIRT

PLACE ON FOLD - CENTER FRONT

FINISH WITH DOUBLE RUFFLE

14" BUBBLES DRESS BODICE FRONT

PLACE ON FOLD

B

ATTACH 2½" WIDE COTTON EYELET RUFFLE

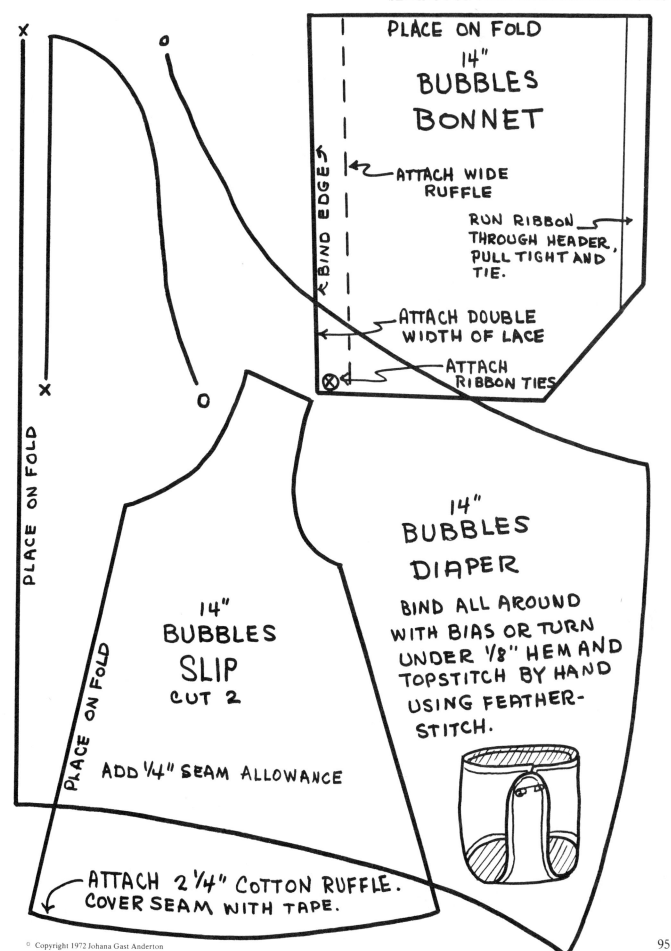

PLACE ON FOLD
14"
BUBBLES
BONNET

← ATTACH WIDE RUFFLE

RUN RIBBON THROUGH HEADER, PULL TIGHT AND TIE.

BIND EDGE

ATTACH DOUBLE WIDTH OF LACE

ATTACH RIBBON TIES

PLACE ON FOLD

14"
BUBBLES
DIAPER

BIND ALL AROUND WITH BIAS OR TURN UNDER 1/8" HEM AND TOPSTITCH BY HAND USING FEATHER-STITCH.

14"
BUBBLES
SLIP
CUT 2

PLACE ON FOLD

ADD 1/4" SEAM ALLOWANCE

ATTACH 2 1/4" COTTON RUFFLE. COVER SEAM WITH TAPE.

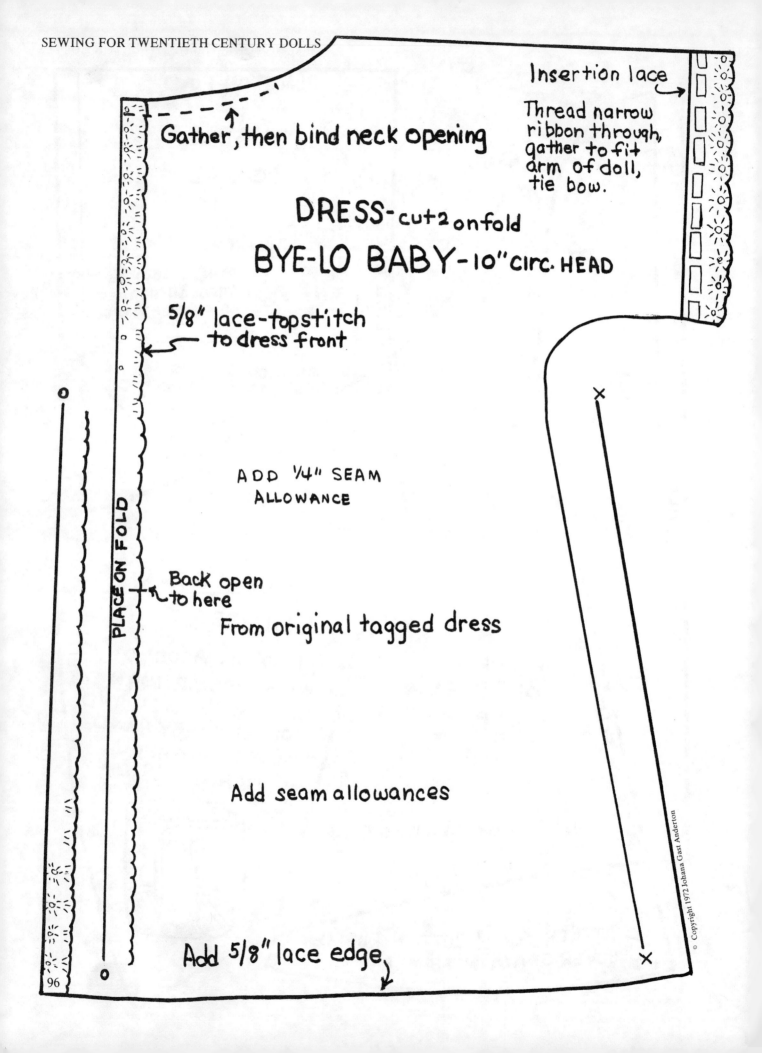

Insertion lace

Thread narrow ribbon through, gather to fit arm of doll, tie bow.

Gather, then bind neck opening

DRESS-cut 2 on fold

BYE-LO BABY-10" circ. HEAD

5/8" lace-topstitch to dress front

ADD ¼" SEAM ALLOWANCE

PLACE ON FOLD

Back open to here
From original tagged dress

Add seam allowances

Add 5/8" lace edge

96

© Copyright 1972 Johana Gast Anderton

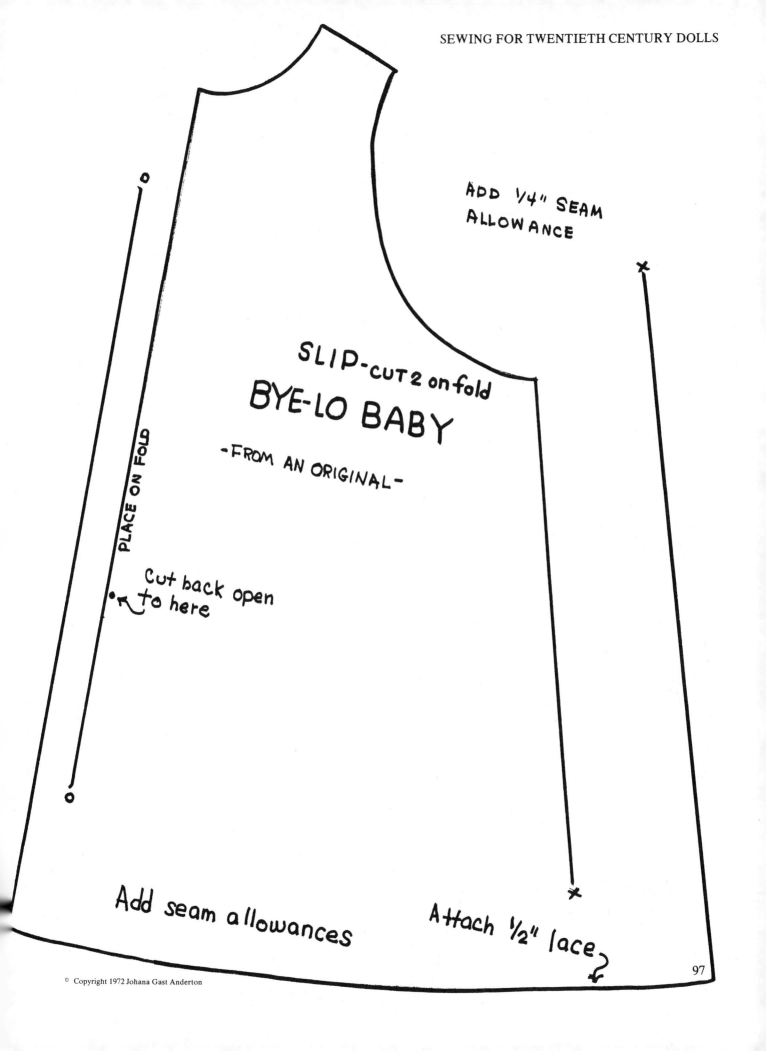

ADD 1/4" SEAM ALLOWANCE

PLACE ON FOLD

SLIP - CUT 2 on fold
BYE-LO BABY
- FROM AN ORIGINAL -

Cut back open to here

Add seam allowances

Attach 1/2" lace

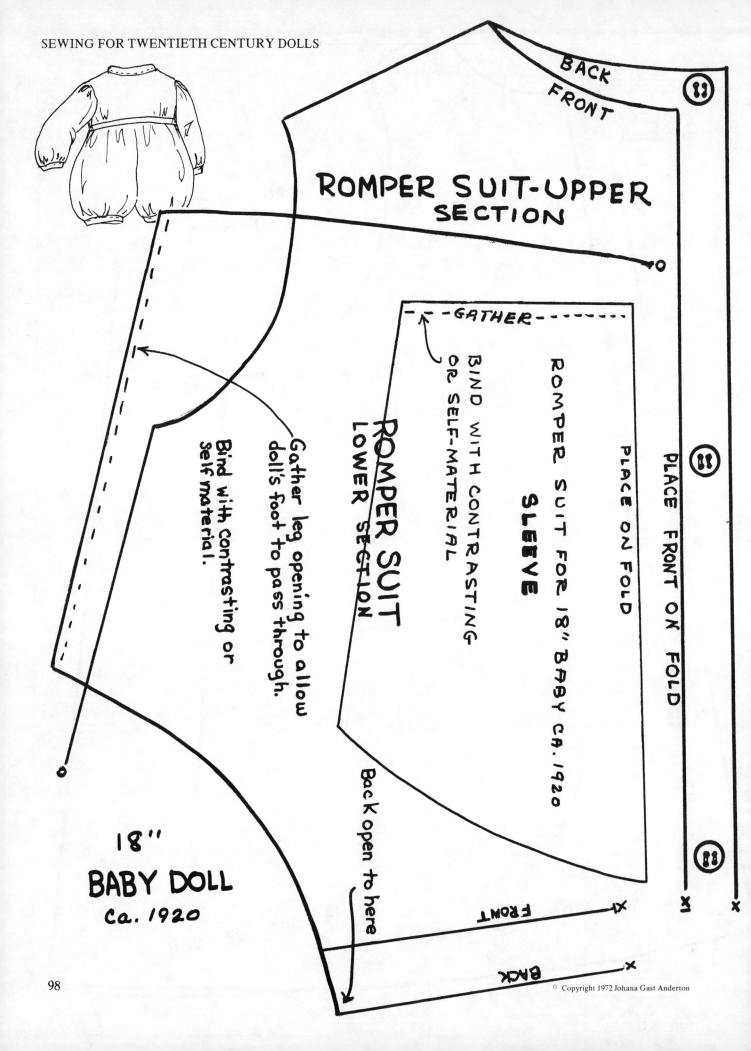

ROMPER SUIT-UPPER
SECTION

BACK
FRONT

GATHER

BIND WITH CONTRASTING
OR SELF-MATERIAL

SLEEVE

ROMPER SUIT FOR 18" BABY CA. 1920

PLACE ON FOLD

PLACE FRONT ON FOLD

ROMPER SUIT
LOWER SECTION

Bind with contrasting or
self material.

Gather leg opening to allow
doll's foot to pass through.

Back open to here

FRONT

BACK

18"
BABY DOLL
Ca. 1920

98

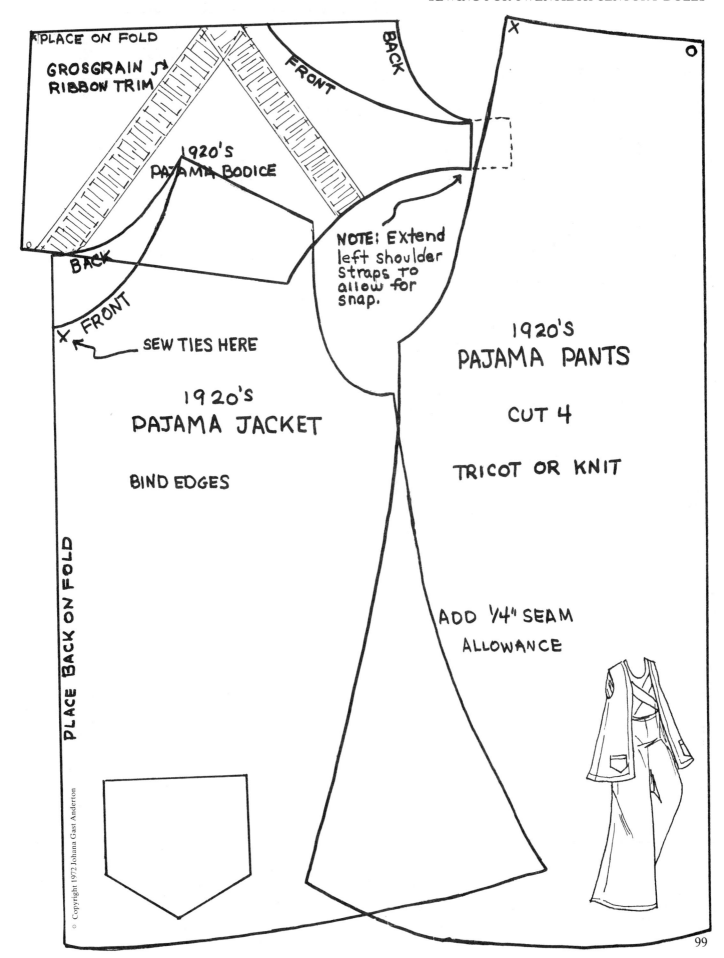

PLACE ON FOLD

GROSGRAIN ↷
RIBBON TRIM

1920'S
PAJAMA BODICE

BACK

FRONT

BACK

FRONT

X FRONT

NOTE: Extend left shoulder straps to allow for snap.

SEW TIES HERE

1920'S
PAJAMA JACKET

BIND EDGES

1920'S
PAJAMA PANTS

CUT 4

TRICOT OR KNIT

PLACE BACK ON FOLD

ADD ¼" SEAM
ALLOWANCE

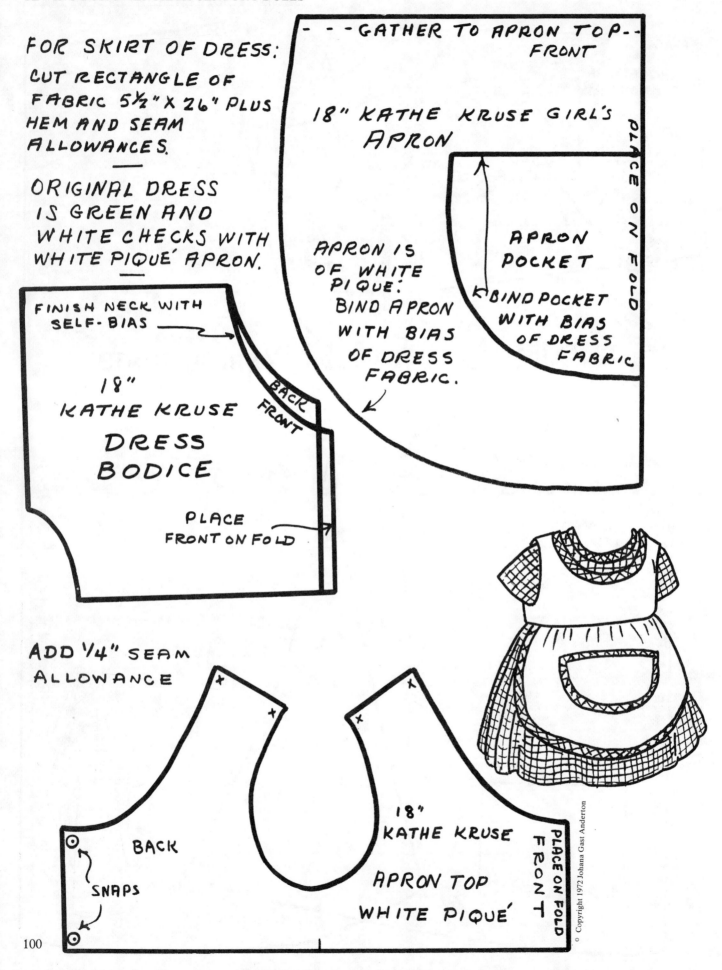

FOR SKIRT OF DRESS:
CUT RECTANGLE OF
FABRIC 5½" X 26" PLUS
HEM AND SEAM
ALLOWANCES.

ORIGINAL DRESS
IS GREEN AND
WHITE CHECKS WITH
WHITE PIQUÉ APRON.

- - - GATHER TO APRON TOP - -
FRONT

18" KATHE KRUSE GIRL'S
APRON

PLACE ON FOLD

APRON IS
OF WHITE
PIQUE:
BIND APRON
WITH BIAS
OF DRESS
FABRIC.

APRON
POCKET
BIND POCKET
WITH BIAS
OF DRESS
FABRIC

FINISH NECK WITH
SELF-BIAS

18"
KATHE KRUSE
DRESS
BODICE

BACK
FRONT

PLACE
FRONT ON FOLD

ADD ¼" SEAM
ALLOWANCE

BACK

SNAPS

18"
KATHE KRUSE
APRON TOP
WHITE PIQUÉ

PLACE ON FOLD
FRONT

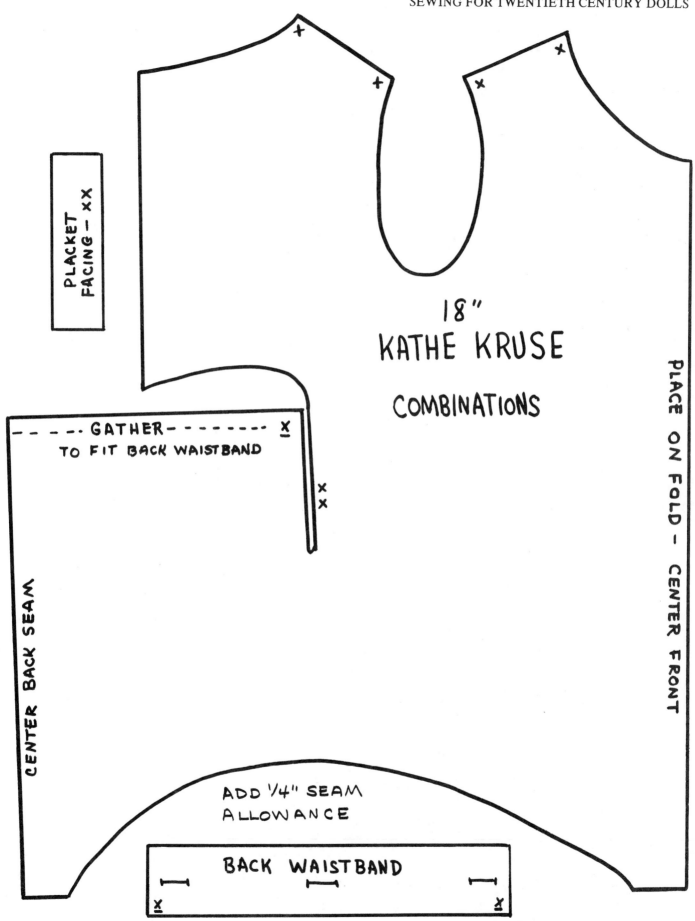

PLACKET FACING — xx

18"
KATHE KRUSE

COMBINATIONS

PLACE ON FOLD — CENTER FRONT

– – – . GATHER – . – – – – – x
TO FIT BACK WAISTBAND

x x

CENTER BACK SEAM

ADD ¼" SEAM
ALLOWANCE

BACK WAISTBAND

1764

1738

1765

1828

1828

No. 1764. Panniers and rosebuds and lace ribbons bedeck this enchanting costume of a typical Southern Belle. You will get a lot of fun out of making it. The patterns for the organdie dress, the velvet hat and the organdie underwear are so perfect to cut by, and the directions so simple. Designed to fit the average 30-inch French doll. Price, 30 cents.

These two pages are taken from the *McCall's Needlework and Decorative Arts Magazine* for Winter 1930-31 and indicate the great amount of industry required to properly dress the bed doll of the period. Complete descriptions have been reproduced including pattern number and price; these patterns are not presently for sale commercially. Fortunate the collector who stumbles across even one of these original patterns in an attic, shop, or auction. The dress, slip, bonnet, and pantalettes patterns were drafted from a doll costume loaned to the author. The Pierrot outfit was designed by the author from a sketch in an old wholesale catalog.

1776

LEADING FASHIONS FOR FRENCH DOLLS

No. 1738. The stately Elizabethan costume of the doll at center top possesses charms very different from those of her fair companion. The close-fitting bodice and voluminous skirt are made of changeable rose taffeta silk, with front panel, collar and cuffs of deep cream lace. The amounts required are—1¼ yards of 35-inch silk for the dress, 1½ yards of 7-inch lace, some insertion, and 12 yards of ruffling. Two more costumes including underwear patterns for all are given. To fit 30-inch long doll with chest measurement, 10½ inches. Price, 35 cents.

No. 1828. Your French doll will be the most charming to grace any boudoir when she appears in one of the fashions from Godey's Lady Book—bonnet and all! The details are fully and perfectly worked out to the last tiny velvet bow or the row of miniature buttons. Changeable taffeta or rayon taffeta are suitable materials. The pattern provides for a fitted bust form to be sewn to the doll and gives all directions, stating amounts of material required. Two Godey costumes for 30-inch doll, including cutting patterns for underwear. Price, 35 cents.

No. 1765. Black lace over a lustrous gold silk dress and a coquettish black satin hat—behold! a Spanish lady enters the scene. The deep 13-inch black lace is skillfully draped over the bodice in mantilla fashion and fully gathered over the skirt. Following the present vogue for things Spanish, your boudoir doll will be very elegant in this costume which is not difficult to make. Patterns and directions for 3 costumes for 30-inch doll, and underwear included. Price, 30 cents.

No. 1776. Imitating the latest pajama fashions worn by her mistress, the boudoir doll at left is seen lounging in smart pajamas of her own, which can be made of flowered silk and trimmed with bands of contrasting silk or velvet, matching the coat. It is surprisingly simple to make, the material you require being 1 yard for coat and pajama bands, and 1⅛ yards for pajama and coat bands. Pattern for Negligee suit also included, both to fit 30-inch doll. Price, 30 cents.

- - GATHER TO FIT ARMHOLE - - -

PLACE ON FOLD

28" BED DOLL
DRESS SLEEVE

RUN ELASTIC THREAD

EDGE WITH LACE

THIS ORIGINAL DRESS
IS OF DOTTED SWISS
WITH FINE COTTON UNDER-
DRESS AND LININGS.

TO MAKE VERY FULL,
THREE-TIERED SKIRT:

5" X 56"
GATHER TO FIT
LOWER EDGE OF BODICE

5" X 104"
GATHER TO FIT LOWER
EDGE OF NEXT TIER

5½" X 136"
GATHER TO FIT LOWER EDGE OF
NEXT TIER

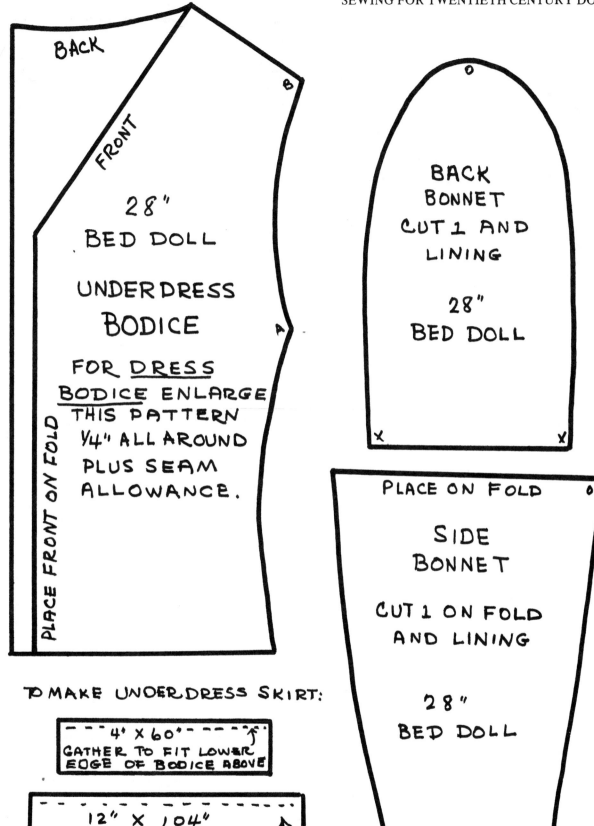

BACK

FRONT

B

A

28"
BED DOLL

UNDERDRESS
BODICE

FOR DRESS
BODICE ENLARGE
THIS PATTERN
¼" ALL AROUND
PLUS SEAM
ALLOWANCE.

PLACE FRONT ON FOLD

BACK
BONNET
CUT 1 AND
LINING

28"
BED DOLL

PLACE ON FOLD

SIDE
BONNET

CUT 1 ON FOLD
AND LINING

28"
BED DOLL

TO MAKE UNDERDRESS SKIRT:

4' X 60"
GATHER TO FIT LOWER
EDGE OF BODICE ABOVE

12" X 104"
GATHER TO FIT LOWER
EDGE OF UPPER TIER

ADD ¼" SEAM ALLOWANCE

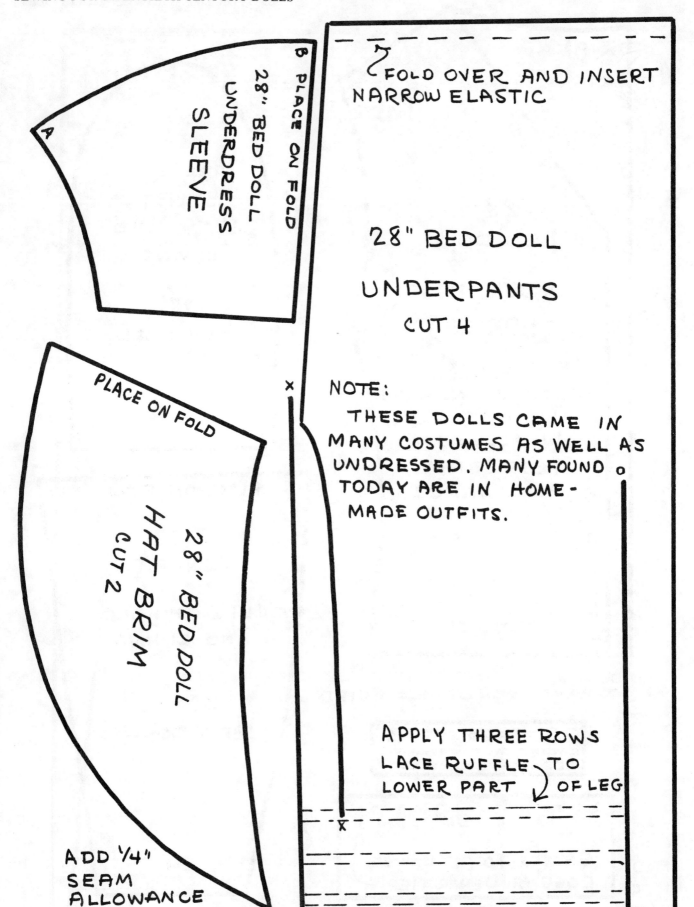

FOLD OVER AND INSERT NARROW ELASTIC

28" BED DOLL

UNDERPANTS

CUT 4

NOTE:

THESE DOLLS CAME IN MANY COSTUMES AS WELL AS UNDRESSED. MANY FOUND TODAY ARE IN HOME-MADE OUTFITS.

APPLY THREE ROWS LACE RUFFLE TO LOWER PART OF LEG

B PLACE ON FOLD

28" BED DOLL UNDERDRESS SLEEVE

A

PLACE ON FOLD

28" BED DOLL HAT BRIM CUT 2

ADD ¼" SEAM ALLOWANCE

FOLD OVER AND INSERT NARROW ELASTIC

28" BED DOLL
PIERROT COSTUME
PANTS
CUT 4

ADD ¼" SEAM ALLOWANCE

GATHER

TO MAKE HAT:
CUT RECTANGLE
TO FIT DOLL'S
HEAD AND
PROCEED AS IN
DIAGRAM.

TRIM WITH COLORFUL DECORATIVE BRAID AND POM-POMS

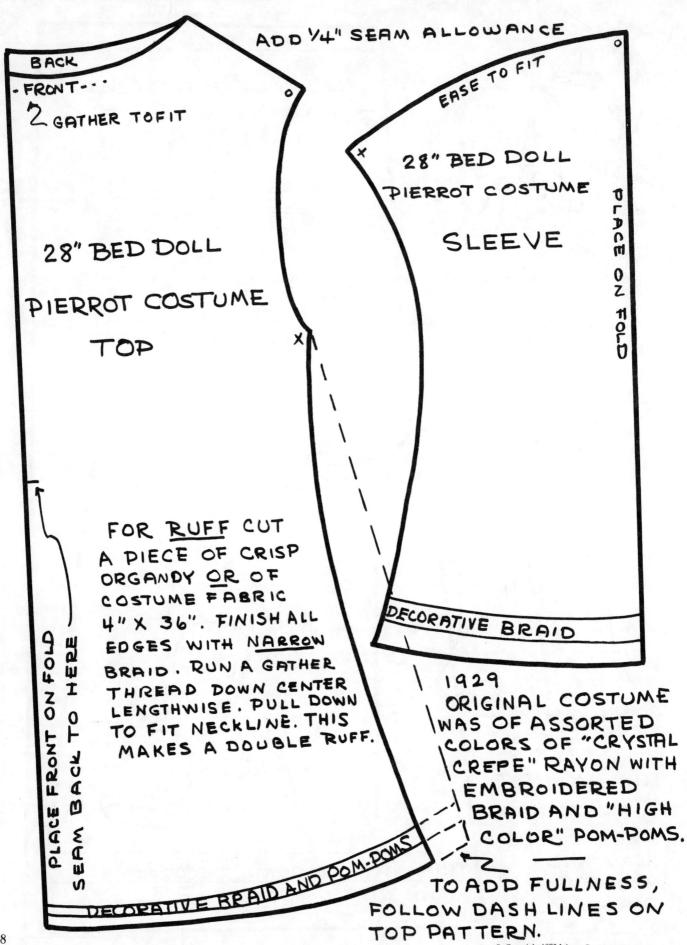

ADD ¼" SEAM ALLOWANCE

BACK

-FRONT---

GATHER TO FIT

28" BED DOLL

PIERROT COSTUME

TOP

EASE TO FIT

28" BED DOLL

PIERROT COSTUME

SLEEVE

PLACE ON FOLD

FOR RUFF CUT A PIECE OF CRISP ORGANDY OR OF COSTUME FABRIC 4" X 36". FINISH ALL EDGES WITH NARROW BRAID. RUN A GATHER THREAD DOWN CENTER LENGTHWISE. PULL DOWN TO FIT NECKLINE. THIS MAKES A DOUBLE RUFF.

PLACE FRONT ON FOLD SEAM BACK TO HERE

DECORATIVE BRAID

DECORATIVE BRAID AND POM-POMS

1929 ORIGINAL COSTUME WAS OF ASSORTED COLORS OF "CRYSTAL CREPE" RAYON WITH EMBROIDERED BRAID AND "HIGH COLOR" POM-POMS.

TO ADD FULLNESS, FOLLOW DASH LINES ON TOP PATTERN.

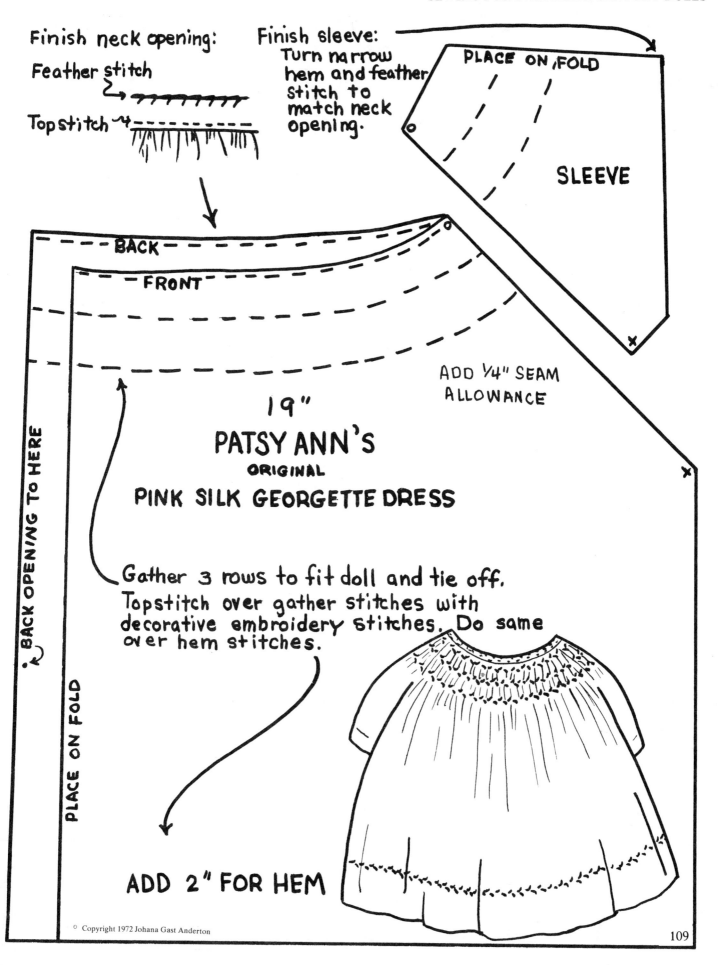

Finish neck opening:

Feather stitch

Topstitch

Finish sleeve:
Turn narrow hem and feather stitch to match neck opening.

PLACE ON FOLD

SLEEVE

BACK

FRONT

ADD ¼" SEAM ALLOWANCE

19"
PATSY ANN'S
ORIGINAL
PINK SILK GEORGETTE DRESS

Gather 3 rows to fit doll and tie off. Topstitch over gather stitches with decorative embroidery stitches. Do same over hem stitches.

BACK OPENING TO HERE

PLACE ON FOLD

ADD 2" FOR HEM

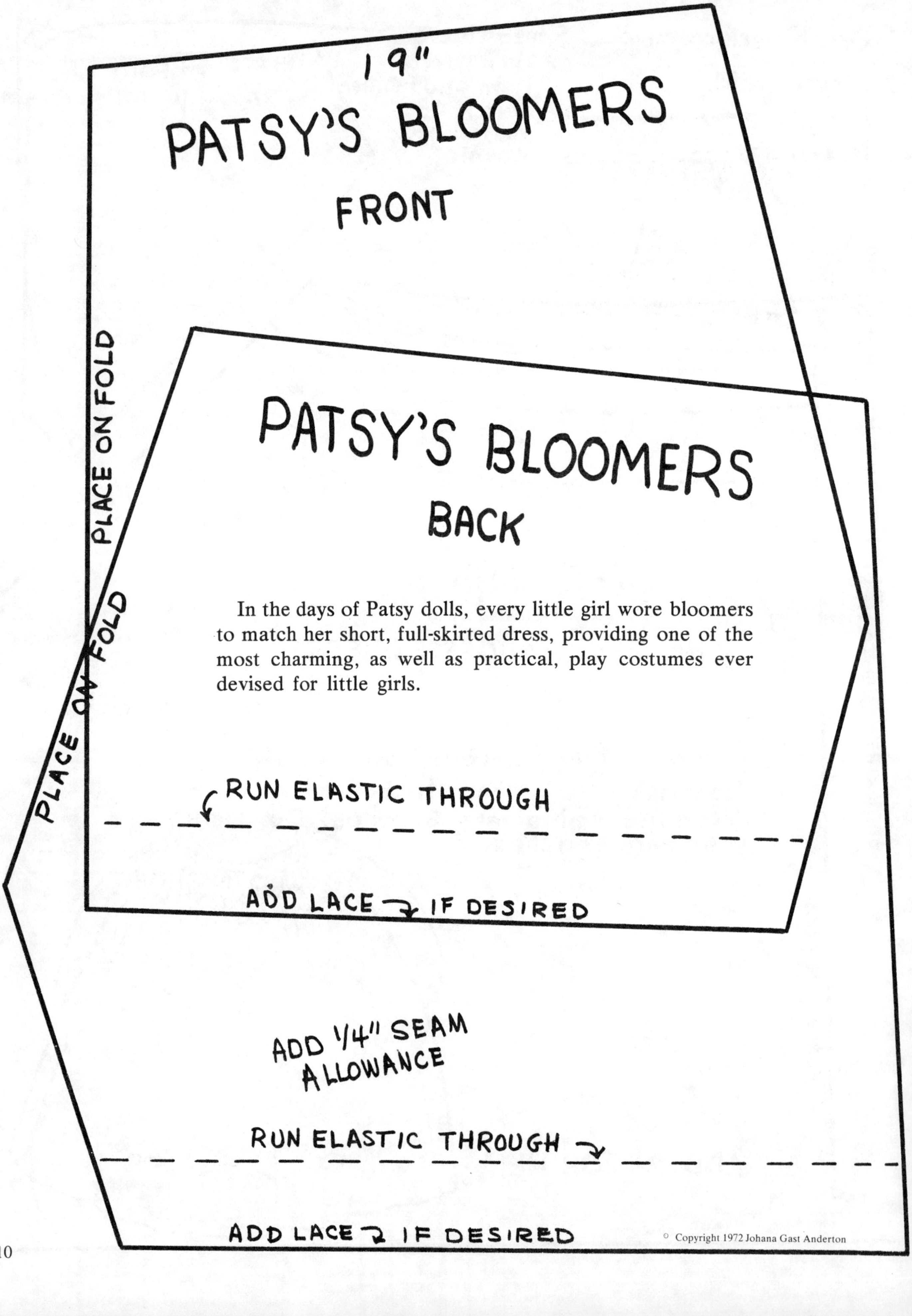

19"

PATSY'S BLOOMERS
FRONT

PLACE ON FOLD

PLACE ON FOLD

PATSY'S BLOOMERS
BACK

In the days of Patsy dolls, every little girl wore bloomers to match her short, full-skirted dress, providing one of the most charming, as well as practical, play costumes ever devised for little girls.

RUN ELASTIC THROUGH

ADD LACE IF DESIRED

ADD 1/4" SEAM ALLOWANCE

RUN ELASTIC THROUGH

ADD LACE IF DESIRED

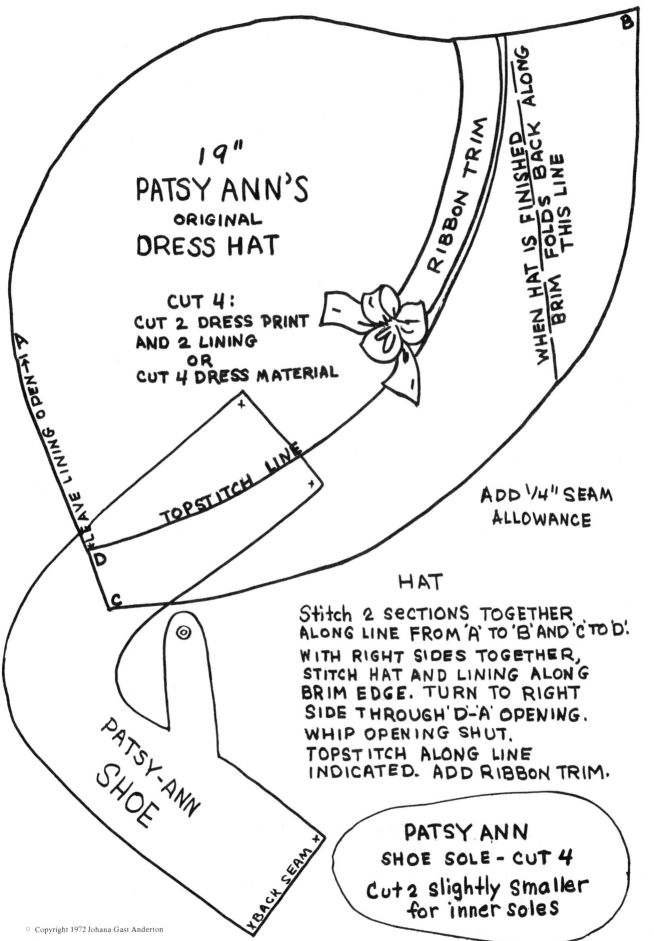

19"

PATSY ANN'S
ORIGINAL
DRESS HAT

CUT 4:
CUT 2 DRESS PRINT
AND 2 LINING
OR
CUT 4 DRESS MATERIAL

RIBBON TRIM

WHEN HAT IS FINISHED
BRIM FOLDS BACK ALONG
THIS LINE

B

A

LEAVE LINING OPEN

TOPSTITCH LINE

ADD 1/4" SEAM
ALLOWANCE

D

C

HAT

Stitch 2 sections together
along line from 'A' to 'B' and 'C' to 'D'.
WITH RIGHT SIDES TOGETHER,
STITCH HAT AND LINING ALONG
BRIM EDGE. TURN TO RIGHT
SIDE THROUGH 'D'-'A' OPENING.
WHIP OPENING SHUT.
TOPSTITCH ALONG LINE
INDICATED. ADD RIBBON TRIM.

PATSY-ANN
SHOE

BACK SEAM

PATSY ANN
SHOE SOLE - CUT 4
Cut 2 slightly smaller
for inner soles

111

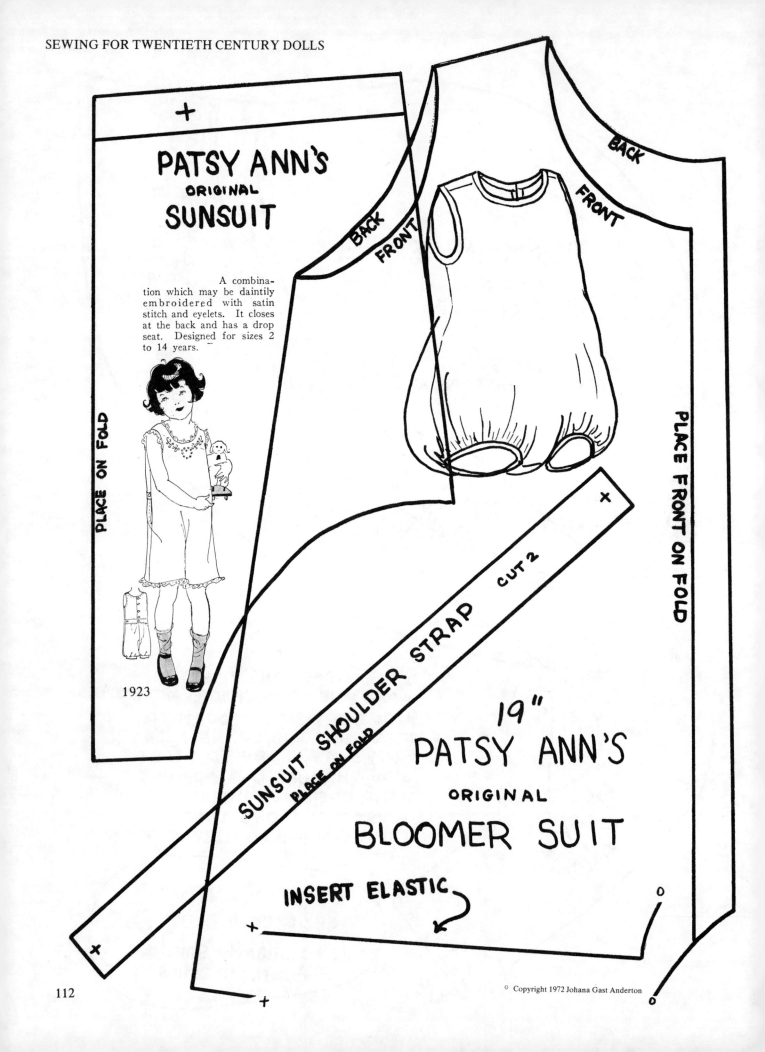

PATSY ANN'S
ORIGINAL
SUNSUIT

A combination which may be daintily embroidered with satin stitch and eyelets. It closes at the back and has a drop seat. Designed for sizes 2 to 14 years.

1923

PLACE ON FOLD

BACK

FRONT

BACK

FRONT

PLACE FRONT ON FOLD

SUNSUIT SHOULDER STRAP   CUT 2
PLACE ON FOLD

19"
PATSY ANN'S
ORIGINAL
BLOOMER SUIT

INSERT ELASTIC

© Copyright 1972 Johana Gast Anderton

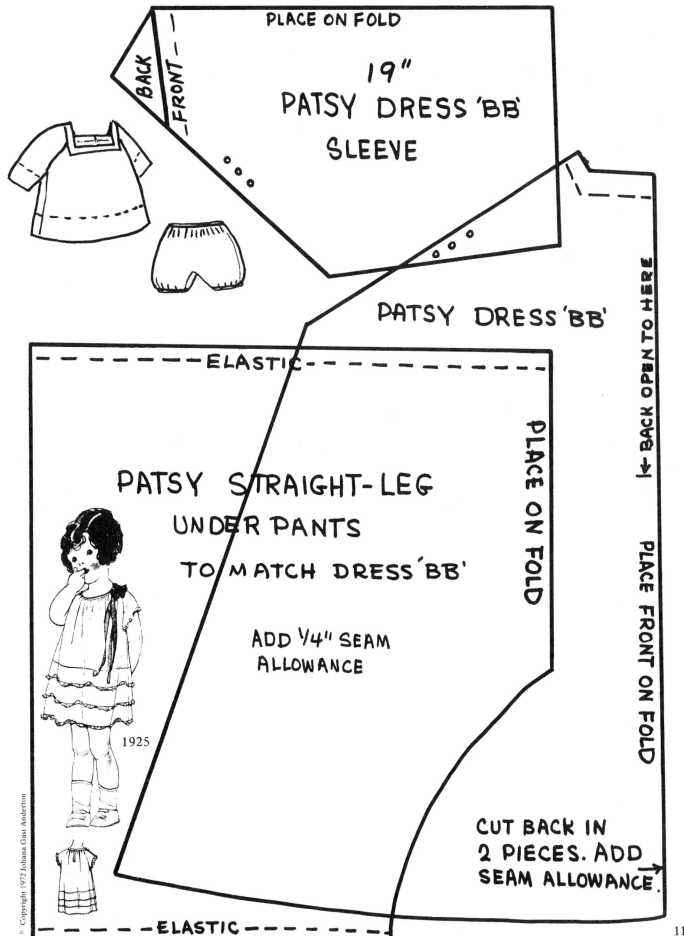

PLACE ON FOLD

BACK

FRONT

19"
PATSY DRESS 'BB'
SLEEVE

PATSY DRESS 'BB'

← BACK OPEN TO HERE

PLACE ON FOLD

PLACE FRONT ON FOLD

ELASTIC

PATSY STRAIGHT-LEG
UNDER PANTS
TO MATCH DRESS 'BB'

ADD ¼" SEAM
ALLOWANCE

1925

CUT BACK IN
2 PIECES. ADD
SEAM ALLOWANCE.

ELASTIC

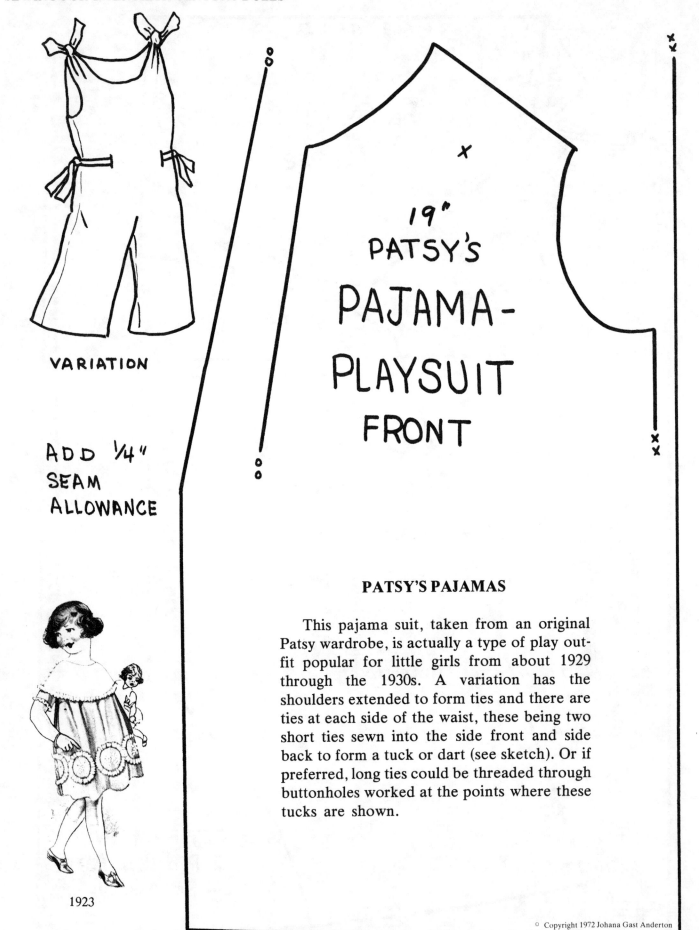

VARIATION

ADD ¼" SEAM ALLOWANCE

19"
PATSY'S
PAJAMA-
PLAYSUIT
FRONT

1923

PATSY'S PAJAMAS

This pajama suit, taken from an original Patsy wardrobe, is actually a type of play out-fit popular for little girls from about 1929 through the 1930s. A variation has the shoulders extended to form ties and there are ties at each side of the waist, these being two short ties sewn into the side front and side back to form a tuck or dart (see sketch). Or if preferred, long ties could be threaded through buttonholes worked at the points where these tucks are shown.

PLACE ON FOLD

I

19"
PATSY'S
PAJAMA-
PLAYSUIT
BACK

ADD 1/4" SEAM ALLOWANCE

1923

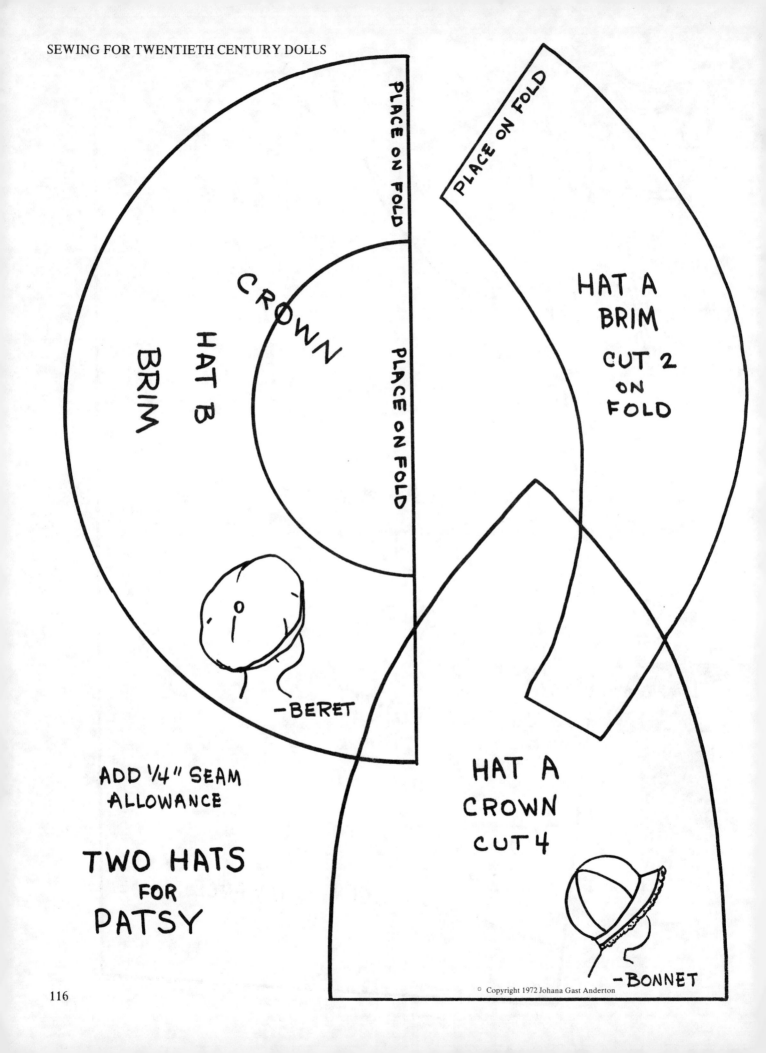

PLACE ON FOLD

PLACE ON FOLD

PLACE ON FOLD

CROWN

HAT B
BRIM

HAT A
BRIM

CUT 2
ON
FOLD

—BERET

HAT A
CROWN
CUT 4

ADD ¼" SEAM
ALLOWANCE

TWO HATS
FOR
PATSY

—BONNET

© Copyright 1972 Johana Gast Anderton

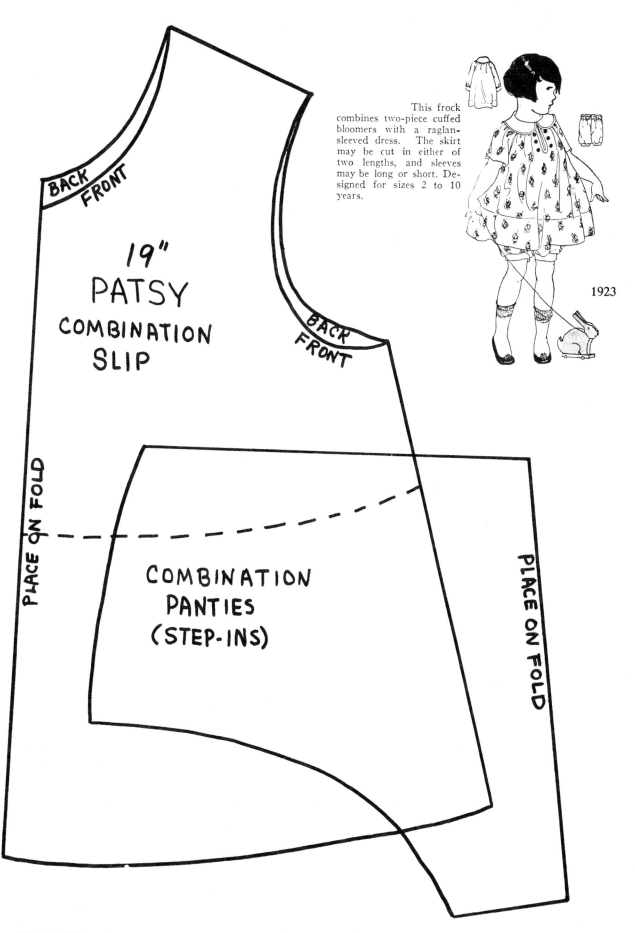

BACK FRONT

19"
PATSY
COMBINATION
SLIP

BACK FRONT

PLACE ON FOLD

COMBINATION
PANTIES
(STEP-INS)

PLACE ON FOLD

This frock combines two-piece cuffed bloomers with a raglan-sleeved dress. The skirt may be cut in either of two lengths, and sleeves may be long or short. Designed for sizes 2 to 10 years.

1923

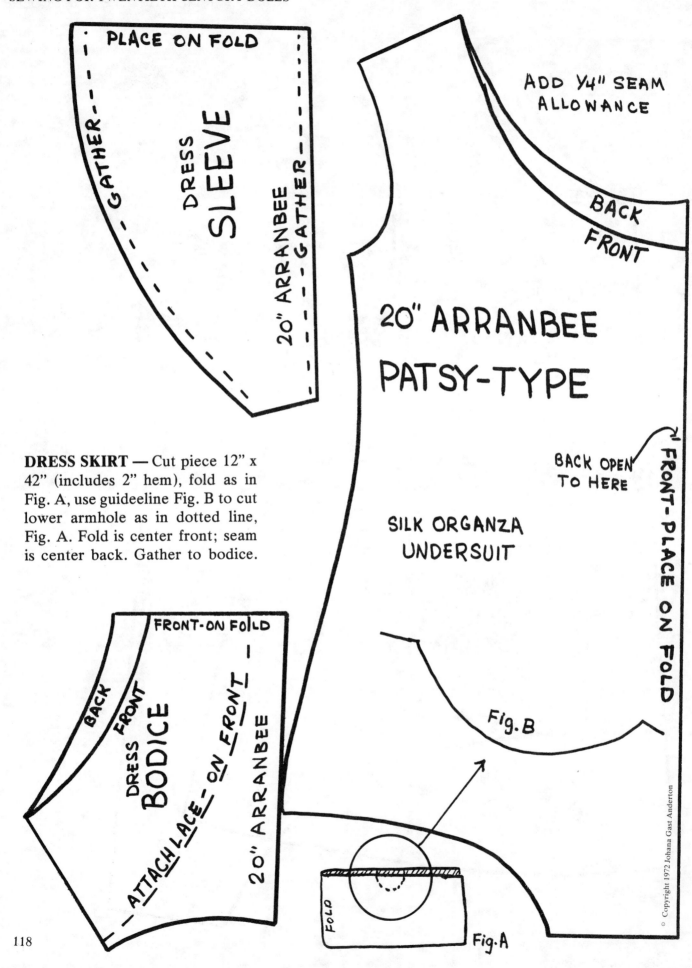

PLACE ON FOLD

DRESS SLEEVE

20" ARRANBEE

GATHER

GATHER

ADD ¼" SEAM ALLOWANCE

BACK

FRONT

20" ARRANBEE PATSY-TYPE

BACK OPEN TO HERE

FRONT-PLACE ON FOLD

SILK ORGANZA UNDERSUIT

DRESS SKIRT — Cut piece 12" x 42" (includes 2" hem), fold as in Fig. A, use guideeline Fig. B to cut lower armhole as in dotted line, Fig. A. Fold is center front; seam is center back. Gather to bodice.

FRONT-ON FOLD

BACK

FRONT

DRESS BODICE

ATTACH LACE — ON FRONT

20" ARRANBEE

Fig. B

FOLD

Fig. A

© Copyright 1972 Johana Gast Anderton

9" PATSY-ETTE

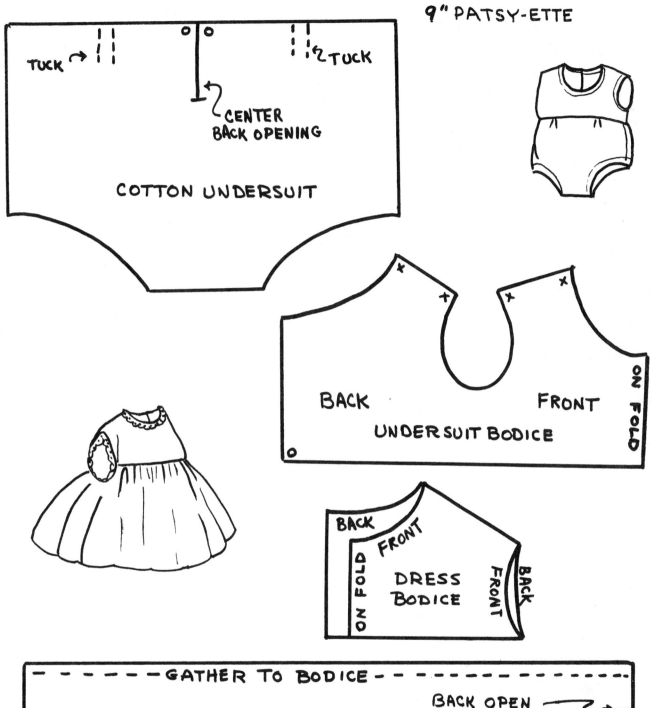

TUCK → | | | | ○ ○ | | | | ²TUCK

CENTER
BACK OPENING

COTTON UNDERSUIT

BACK   FRONT   ON FOLD

UNDERSUIT BODICE

BACK
FRONT
DRESS
BODICE
BACK
FRONT
ON FOLD

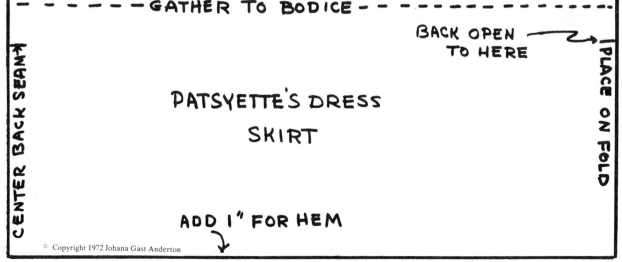

– – – GATHER TO BODICE – – –

BACK OPEN
TO HERE →

CENTER BACK SEAM

PLACE ON FOLD

PATSYETTE'S DRESS
SKIRT

ADD 1" FOR HEM

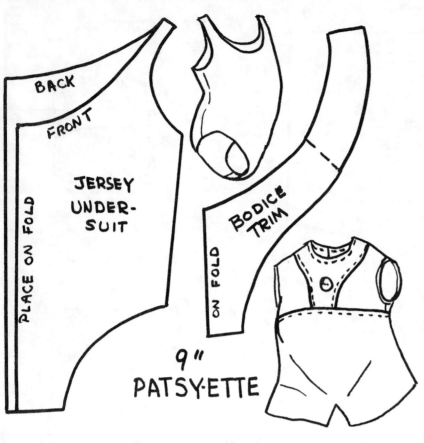

BACK

FRONT

JERSEY UNDER-SUIT

PLACE ON FOLD

BODICE TRIM

ON FOLD

9" PATSY·ETTE

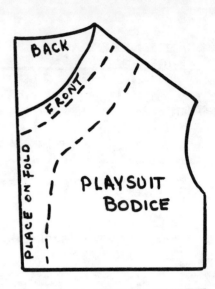

BACK

FRONT

PLAYSUIT BODICE

PLACE ON FOLD

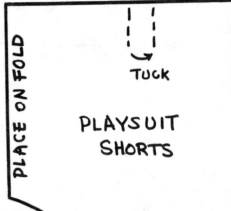

TUCK

PLACE ON FOLD

PLAYSUIT SHORTS

1925

22" E. I. HORSMAN "BABY DIMPLES"
(ORIGINAL LABELED ENSEMBLE)

This costume is resplendent with lace trimming — lace finishes nearly every available edge — so be lavish with your lace. Slip and dress are of good quality organdy; however, lawn may be substituted for making the slip and panties. Sew and fit underclothes first.

PANTIES

Cut of lawn or other fine cotton. Sew side and crotch seams, turn ½" hem at waist and leg openings. Run narrow elastic to fit doll's waist and legs.

DRESS AND SLIP

These are cut from same pattern; cut slip 1" shorter than dress and without sleeves. Cut as shown, sew side seams, attach lace before sewing back seam. Sew only along top edge of lace which may be attached using narrow decorative braid (white). Neckline of dress is finished with lace as are the sleeves.

BONNET

To make bonnet, sew back seam A-A, run gathering thread as indicated, fit to bonnet crown and sew. Stitch lace to bonnet brim and finish edges, then sew brim to bonnet, matching center front dots. Finish face edge of bonnet with lace. Attach ribbon ties.

The little middy dress below may be made of one or two materials. The gathered and plaited skirt is attached to an underbody, and the separate blouse slips on over the head. Designed for sizes 4 to 14 years.

1923

A comfortable pajama suit for little folks, made with a drop seat. Neck may be finished with a front facing, and with or without collar. Sleeves may be long or short. A handkerchief pocket is also provided for. Designed for sizes 2 to 12 years.

A blouse-and-knicker suit, the blouse featuring a back yoke and a patch pocket. The knickers are two-piece and have pockets. Designed for sizes 4 to 12 years.

1923

The blouse of the suit above goes on over the head, and the front is fitted with a shield. The trousers button onto the blouse. Designed for sizes 2 to 8 years.

20" E. I. HORSMAN CHILD CA. 1920

This original dress was made of red and white checked gingham, trimmed with white bias tape. Underclothes were of white cotton trimmed with cotton lace. Lawn is an excellent cotton for the underclothes since it is both fine-textured and inexpensive. Sew and fit underclothes first.

UNDERSUIT

Assemble undersuit skirt, bodice and bloomer separately, then sew together, attaching the three into a single unit at the waist. Finish all seams.

DRESS

Cut a piece of dress fabric 6" long and 24" wide (plus seam and hem allowance) for the skirt front of dress. Gather or pleat to front of bodice (original was pleated).

Make two belts from pieces of dress fabric 8" long and 2" wide. Seam and turn, topstitch. Baste one belt to each side back at X on underarm seam.

Seam back and front sections together at shoulder and side seams. Set in sleeves.

Work buttonhole on end of one belt and sew button to end of remaining belt.

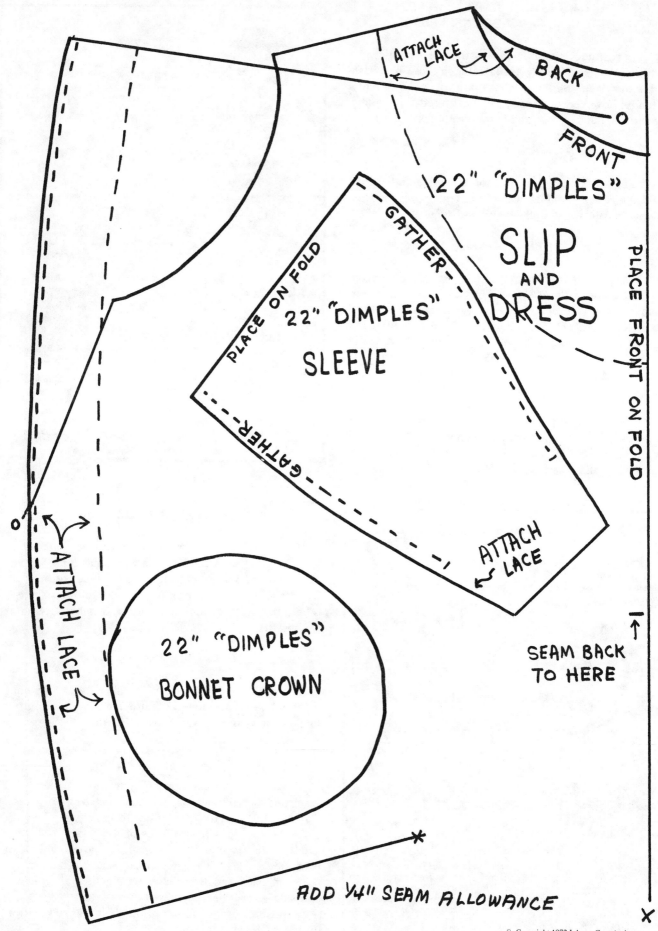

22" "DIMPLES"

ATTACH LACE

BACK

FRONT

SLIP

AND

DRESS

PLACE FRONT ON FOLD

PLACE ON FOLD

GATHER

22" "DIMPLES"

SLEEVE

GATHER

ATTACH LACE

SEAM BACK
TO HERE

ATTACH LACE

22" "DIMPLES"

BONNET CROWN

ADD ¼" SEAM ALLOWANCE

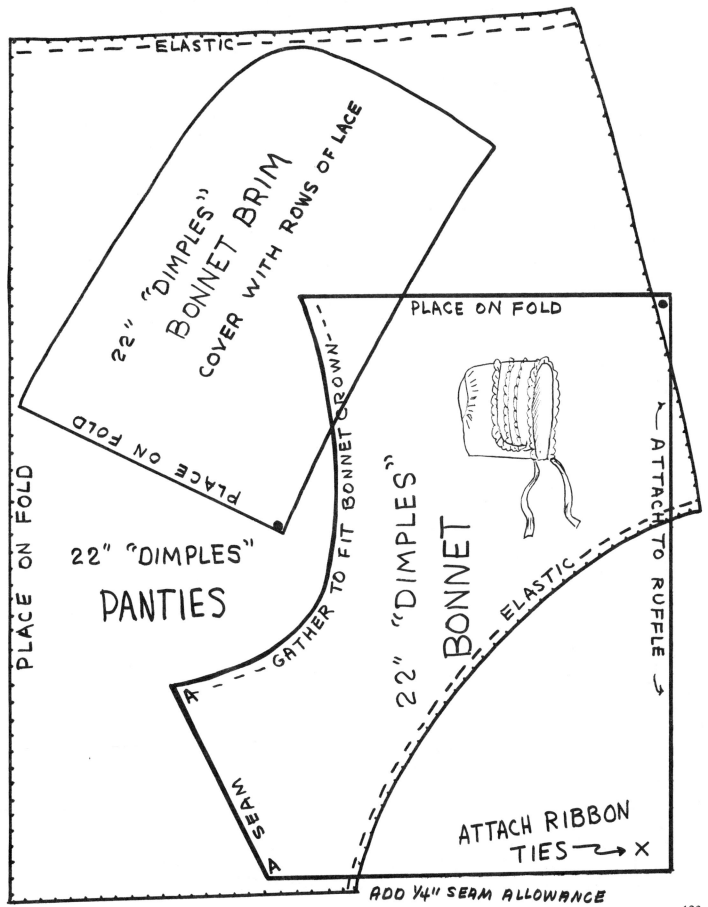

— ELASTIC —

22" "DIMPLES" BONNET BRIM
COVER WITH ROWS OF LACE

PLACE ON FOLD

22" "DIMPLES"
PANTIES

PLACE ON FOLD

GATHER TO FIT BONNET CROWN

PLACE ON FOLD

A

A SEAM

A

22" "DIMPLES" BONNET

ELASTIC

ATTACH TO RUFFLE

ATTACH RIBBON TIES → X

ADD ¼" SEAM ALLOWANCE

123

20" HORSMAN CHILD

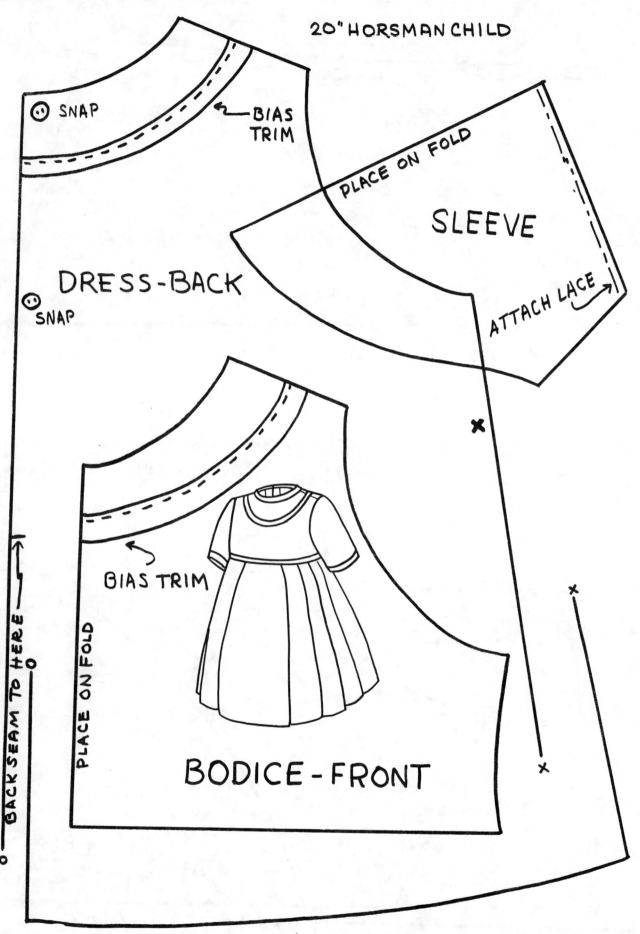

SNAP

BIAS TRIM

PLACE ON FOLD

SLEEVE

DRESS-BACK

SNAP

ATTACH LACE

BIAS TRIM

BACK SEAM TO HERE

PLACE ON FOLD

BODICE-FRONT

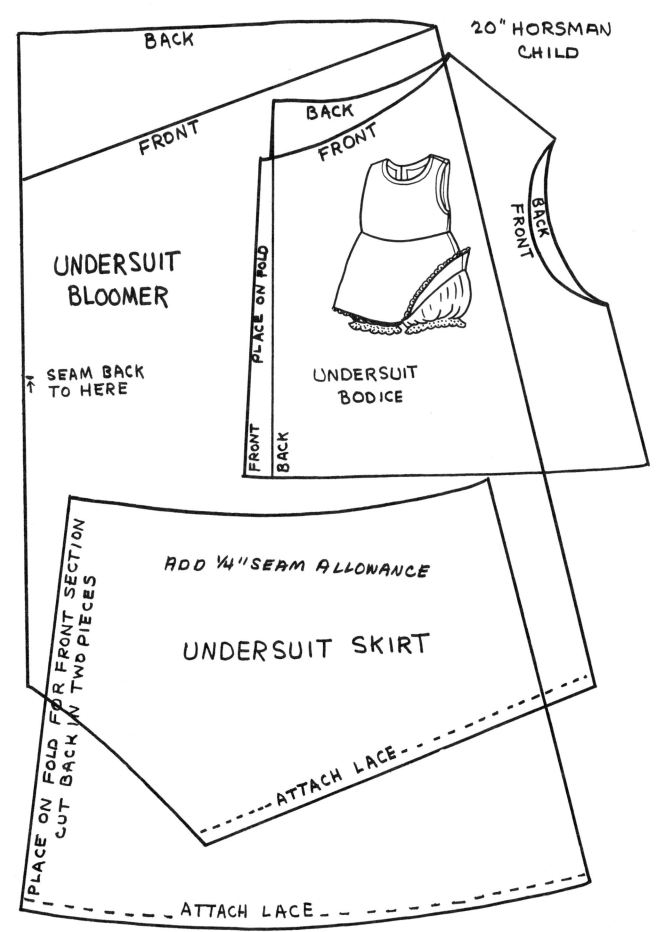

BACK

FRONT

20" HORSMAN
CHILD

BACK

FRONT

UNDERSUIT
BLOOMER

BACK

FRONT

SEAM BACK
TO HERE

PLACE ON FOLD

UNDERSUIT
BODICE

FRONT

BACK

ADD ¼" SEAM ALLOWANCE

UNDERSUIT SKIRT

PLACE ON FOLD FOR FRONT SECTION
CUT BACK IN TWO PIECES

ATTACH LACE

ATTACH LACE

1925

THE 1930s

Silky, slinky pajamas with coats of the same fabric were considered quite chic in 1931. Baby dolls wore moccassin-style shoes of white leather in 1932. Ladies' fashions featured *"Glamorous Hollywood Stars"* in catalogs of 1933 and 1934. Such stars as Claudette Colbert in *"Death Takes a Holiday"*, Marlene Dietrich in *"Song of Songs"*, and Sylvia Sidney in *"World's Fair Favorites"* were posed to display the fashions to advantage. Hollywood was quoted as recommending: *"suit the women with mannish flannels"*.

That same year girls' dresses had puff sleeves and boleros. The fabrics were rayon and cotton blends, percale, organdy, wool jersey and wool and silk blends. Bows trimmed collars and cuffs. Hair was bobbed and sometimes slightly marcelled or Patsy-styled, only fluffier. Cover-all style playsuits were recommended for girls.

Underwear included bloomers, vests, slips, and *"French combinations"* of rayon or cotton. Little boys wore knickers, corduroy Cossack suits, short, banded jackets and trousers, and aviator-style suits.

In ladies' fashions many separate collars were shown in white silk, organdy, and lace. Scarves and belts were recommended to *"perk up that old dress — this is 1933!"* Children's coats reflected adult fashions with double-breasted closings, aviator-style collars, racoon collars, or fur fabric trim. Small girls wore double-breasted, semi-fitted coats with matching tams and fitted leggings with side zipper. Chinchilla cloth was often the choice for both adults and children. *"Autographed fashions"* were the vogue in 1934 and featured *Fay May, Frances Dee,* and *Loretta Young.*

This decade saw a decided change in women's clothing. In 1933 McCall's recommended decorative embroidery on graceful, fluid sleeves. By the end of the decade, shoulders had widened almost without exception to the padded, mannish appearance which was to become a trend lasting into the 1940s.

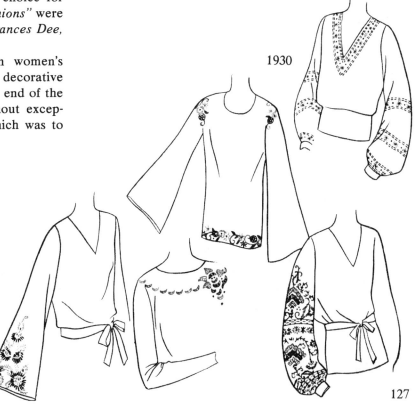

1930

127

Good Count Fast Color Broadcloth

Broadcloth and Linene

Suggested 25c to 29c Retailers
BROADCLOTH AND LINENE—ALL COLORS FAST

1933

Broadcloth

Long Pants Suits

"Mickey Mouse" Fidelity Rib

Children's Anklets

1937

1936

Cable stitching

India Prints

Saw-tooth Trim

Plaiting

Applique

Embroidery

Stitching

Printed Tops

Shirring

1937

EXCLUSIVE shops give proof that trimmings are increasing in importance both for apparel and for home furnishings, and it seems that every kind of fabric is being decorated. Light-weight woolens and firm cottons and linens are smart for short-sleeved, flare-skirted frocks. On these, cable stitching is used as an effective trimming.

Sometimes a bias tubing of the fabric is used and cable-stitched in place with embroidery threads in two or three colors. Some of the peasant skirts have three rows of tubing of the fabric caught down with cable stitches. We see this trim on many sturdy frocks and on beach clothes.

Some good dresses show the tubing covered with the same stitching to make a cord for the waistline. Again, a cord is used for the trim for the neck and the sleeves, and the cord is caught in place with fine hand-stitches.

The very popular saw-tooth trimming of piqué, of linen braid, of bias binding, or of the fabric itself, is ideal because it launders readily. The smartest kind is easy to make with a machine-craft guide. The saw-tooth trimming is made by winding the fabric diagonally on the guide, stitching two rows through the center one-eighth inch apart, and cutting between the rows and in that way obtaining two lengths of trimming.

Turbans, scarfs and blouses of Paisley prints continue everywhere. Many of these are made of medium-sized or large handkerchiefs. Paisley blouses are decidedly smart for beach or sports wear, particularly with plain skirts or with slacks.

1939

1939

1938

1939

1938

1938

1938

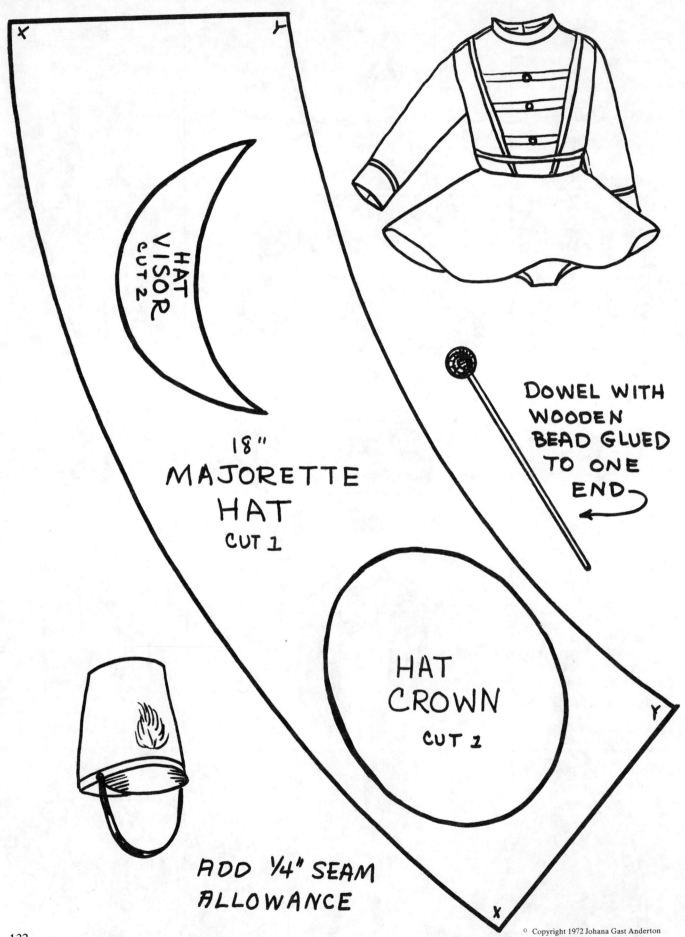

HAT
VISOR
CUT 2

18"
MAJORETTE
HAT
CUT 1

HAT
CROWN
CUT 2

DOWEL WITH
WOODEN
BEAD GLUED
TO ONE
END

ADD ¼" SEAM
ALLOWANCE

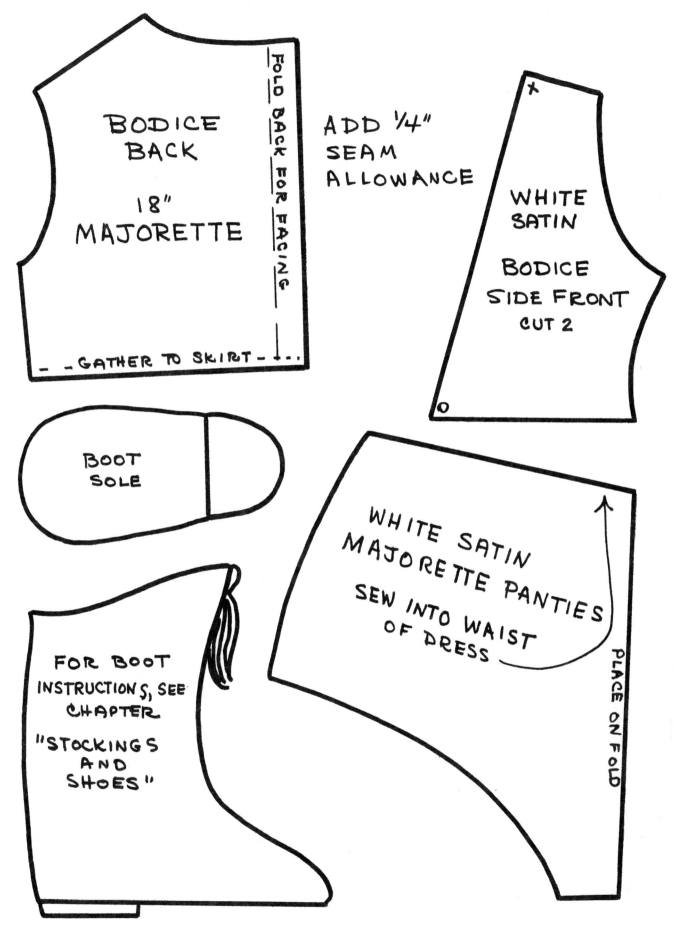

BODICE
BACK

18"
MAJORETTE

FOLD BACK FOR FACING

- _ GATHER TO SKIRT _ _ .

ADD ¼"
SEAM
ALLOWANCE

WHITE
SATIN

BODICE
SIDE FRONT
CUT 2

BOOT
SOLE

WHITE SATIN
MAJORETTE PANTIES
SEW INTO WAIST
OF DRESS

PLACE ON FOLD

FOR BOOT
INSTRUCTIONS, SEE
CHAPTER

"STOCKINGS
AND
SHOES"

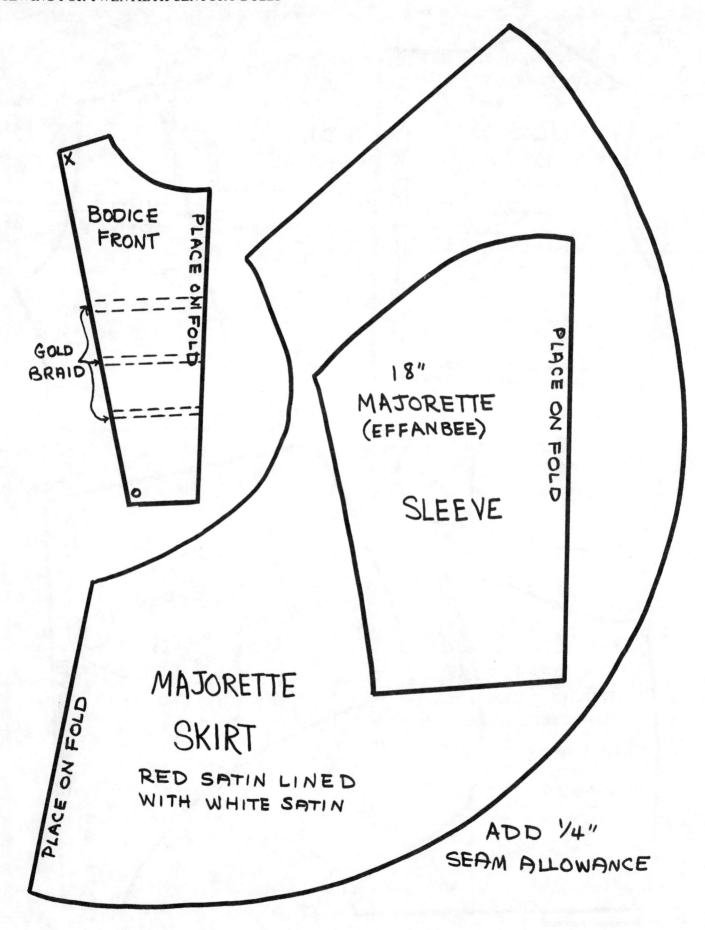

X

BODICE
FRONT

PLACE ON FOLD

GOLD
BRAID

o

18"
MAJORETTE
(EFFANBEE)

PLACE ON FOLD

SLEEVE

PLACE ON FOLD

MAJORETTE

SKIRT

RED SATIN LINED
WITH WHITE SATIN

ADD ¼"
SEAM ALLOWANCE

134

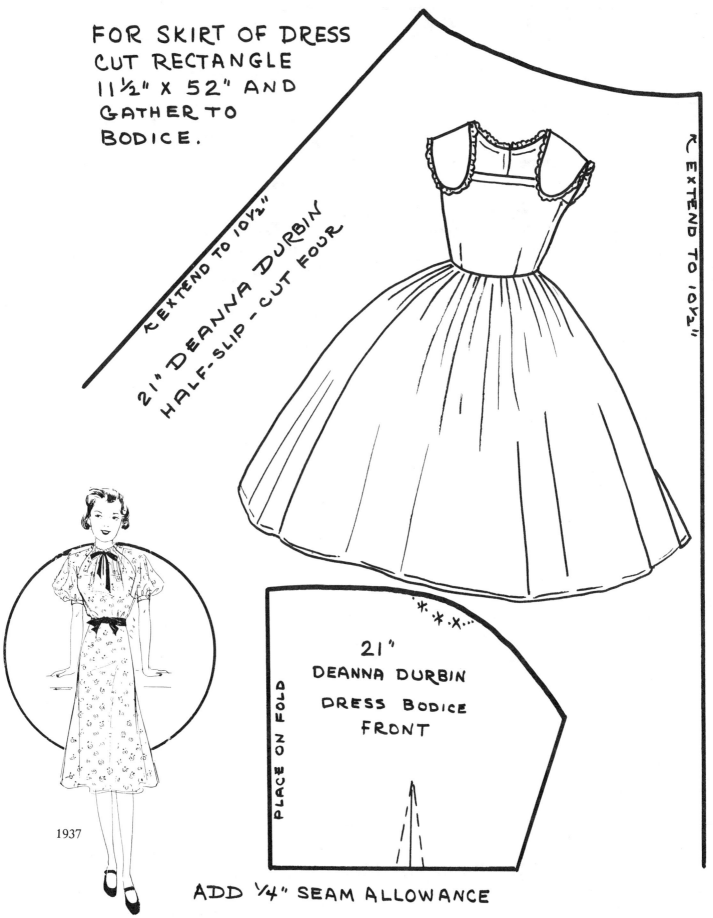

FOR SKIRT OF DRESS
CUT RECTANGLE
11½" X 52" AND
GATHER TO
BODICE.

← EXTEND TO 10½"

EXTEND TO 10½"

21" DEANNA DURBIN
HALF-SLIP – CUT FOUR

1937

21"
DEANNA DURBIN
DRESS BODICE
FRONT

PLACE ON FOLD

ADD ¼" SEAM ALLOWANCE

135

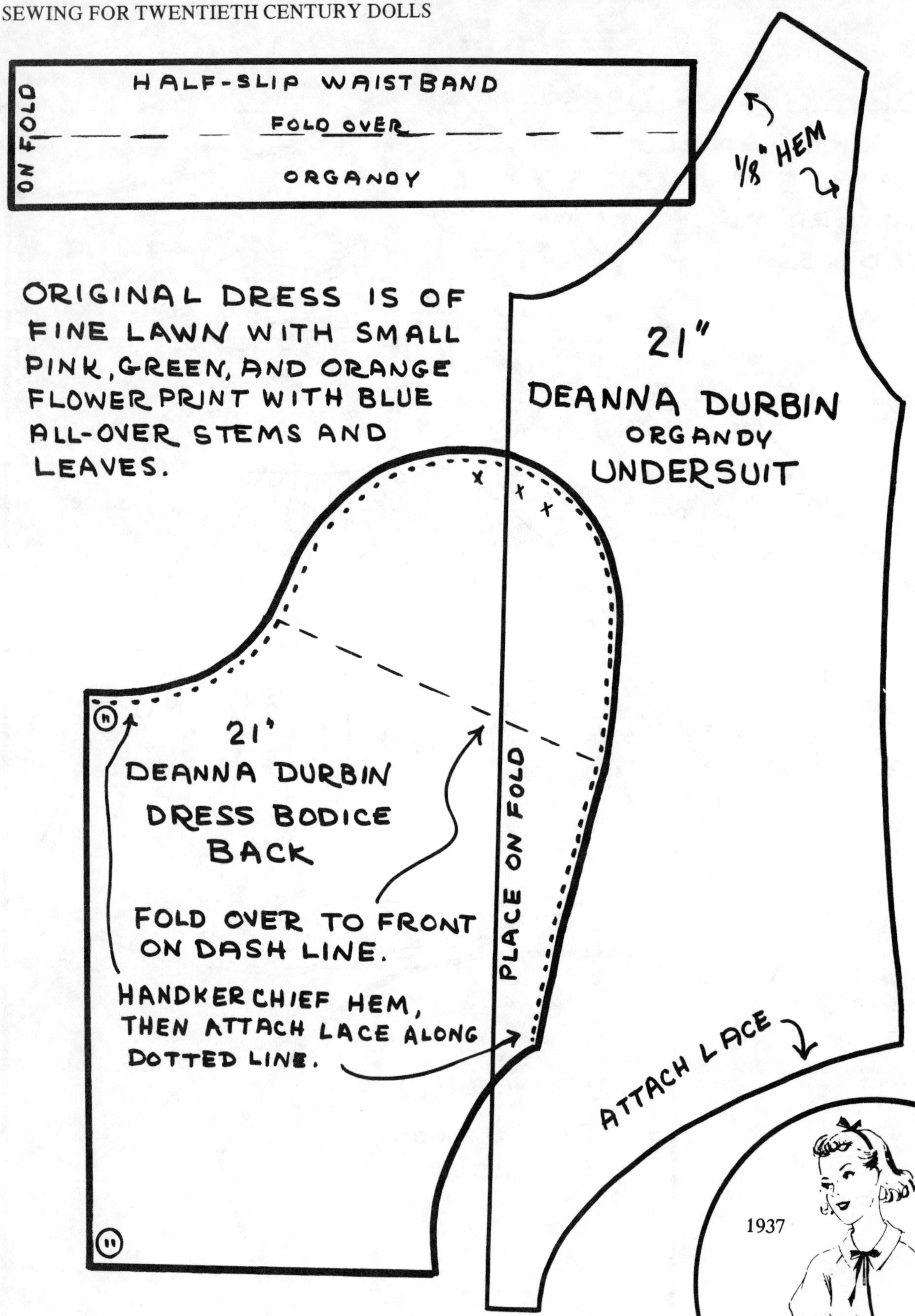

ON FOLD

HALF-SLIP WAISTBAND

FOLD OVER

ORGANDY

ORIGINAL DRESS IS OF
FINE LAWN WITH SMALL
PINK, GREEN, AND ORANGE
FLOWER PRINT WITH BLUE
ALL-OVER STEMS AND
LEAVES.

⅛" HEM

21"
DEANNA DURBIN
ORGANDY
UNDERSUIT

21'
DEANNA DURBIN
DRESS BODICE
BACK

FOLD OVER TO FRONT
ON DASH LINE.

HANDKERCHIEF HEM,
THEN ATTACH LACE ALONG
DOTTED LINE.

PLACE ON FOLD

ATTACH LACE

1937

ADD ¼" SEAM ALLOWANCE

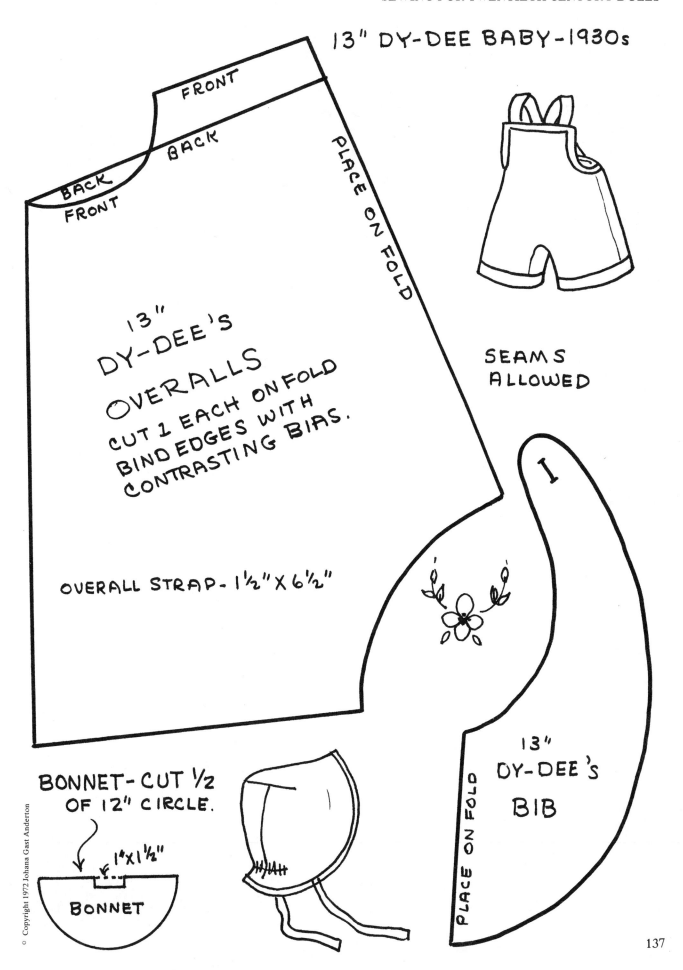

13" DY-DEE BABY-1930s

FRONT

BACK

BACK

FRONT

PLACE ON FOLD

13"
DY-DEE'S
OVERALLS
CUT 1 EACH ON FOLD
BIND EDGES WITH
CONTRASTING BIAS.

SEAMS
ALLOWED

OVERALL STRAP- 1½" X 6½"

I

13"
DY-DEE'S
BIB

PLACE ON FOLD

BONNET- CUT ½
OF 12" CIRCLE.

F. 1"X1½"

BONNET

1936

18" JUDY GARLAND (IDEAL)

Original costume worn by the actress as *Dorothy* in movie, *"The Wizard of Oz"*: blue and white checked rayon with white organdy bodice trimmed with tiny blue ric-rac and organdy underclothes.

Bodice — Cut entire bodice of white organdy, then cut lower (shaded) area of pattern from checked material. Bands on bodice are cut from checked material on bias. Back is finished same as front. Collar is ½ inch ruffle of organdy edged with ric-rac and finished off around neck with another row of ric-rac.

Skirt — Cut three strips of checked fabric as follows:

a) one piece 2¾ inches by 30 inches on straight

b) one piece 1¼ inch by 30 inches on bias

c) one piece 2½ inches by 30 inches on straight

Sew together with bias strip (b) between strips (a) and (c). Turn (c) up one inch for hem and finish. Set aside.

Make organdy petticoat of strip of fabric 3½ inches by 24 inches, edge one long edge with lace, baste other long edge to upper edge of (a) on skirt unit.

Gather as one to fit bodice and seam to bodice. Seam up back to within 2 inches of waist seam.

Shoes — See chapter "STOCKINGS AND SHOES".

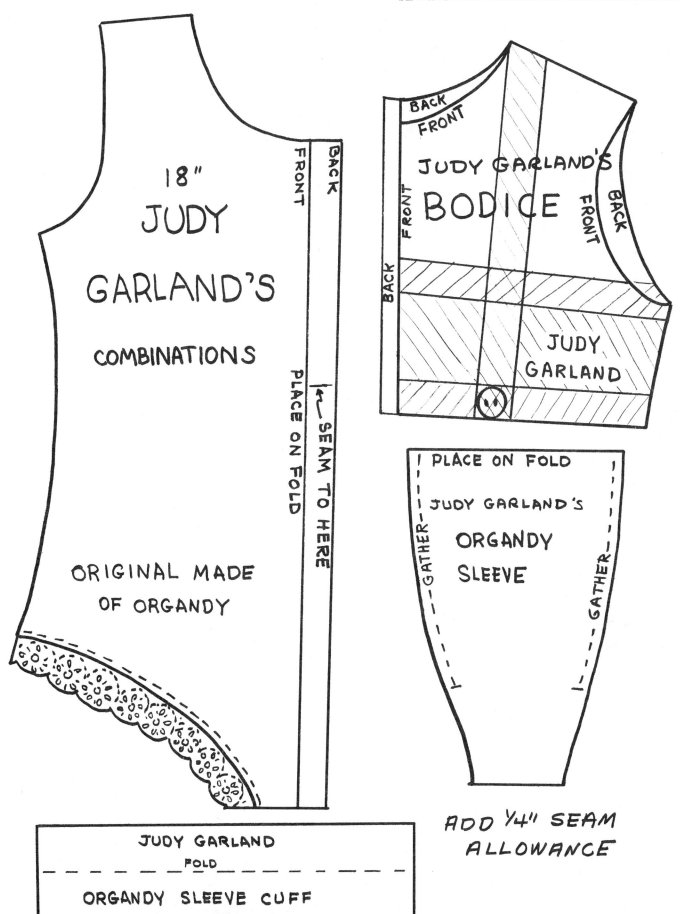

18"
JUDY
GARLAND'S
COMBINATIONS

FRONT BACK

PLACE ON FOLD

← SEAM TO HERE

ORIGINAL MADE
OF ORGANDY

JUDY GARLAND
FOLD
ORGANDY SLEEVE CUFF

BACK
FRONT

JUDY GARLAND'S
BODICE

FRONT BACK

BACK

JUDY
GARLAND

PLACE ON FOLD

JUDY GARLAND'S
ORGANDY
SLEEVE

GATHER

GATHER

ADD ¼" SEAM
ALLOWANCE

BACK

FRONT

FRONT ON FOLD

BODICE

24" COMPOSITION GIRL DOLL 1930s

ADD ¼" SEAM ALLOWANCE

1937

THIS DRESS WAS FOUND ON A 24" 1930s COMPOSITION HEAD AND LIMBS WITH CLOTH BODY.

DRESS IS OF FINE PINK LAWN AS IS THE RUFFLE ON THE BIG COLLAR.

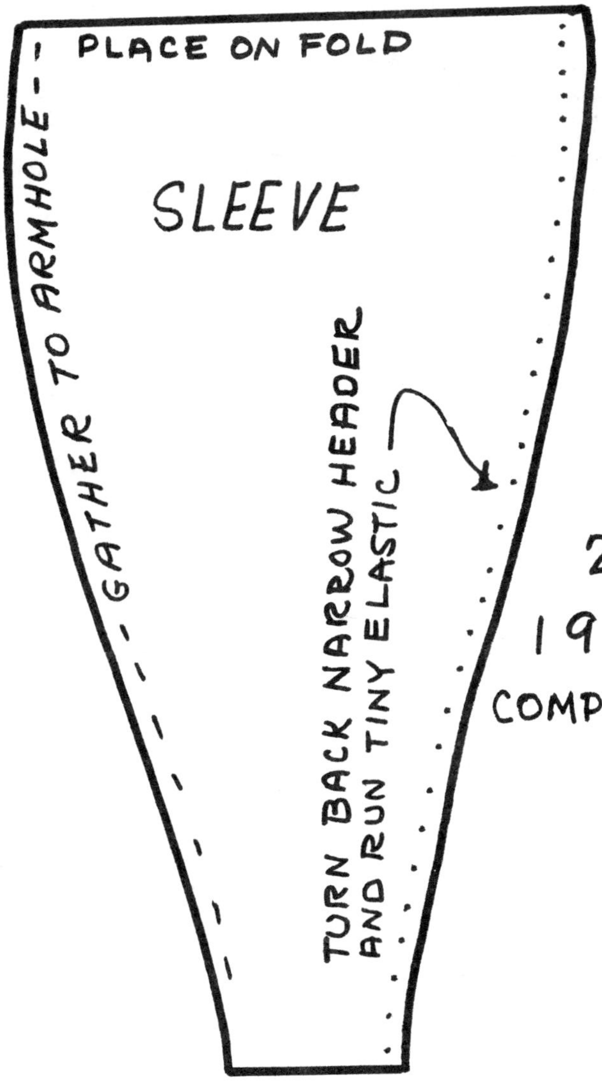

PLACE ON FOLD

SLEEVE

-- GATHER TO ARMHOLE --

TURN BACK NARROW HEADER AND RUN TINY ELASTIC

24"
1930s
COMPOSITION

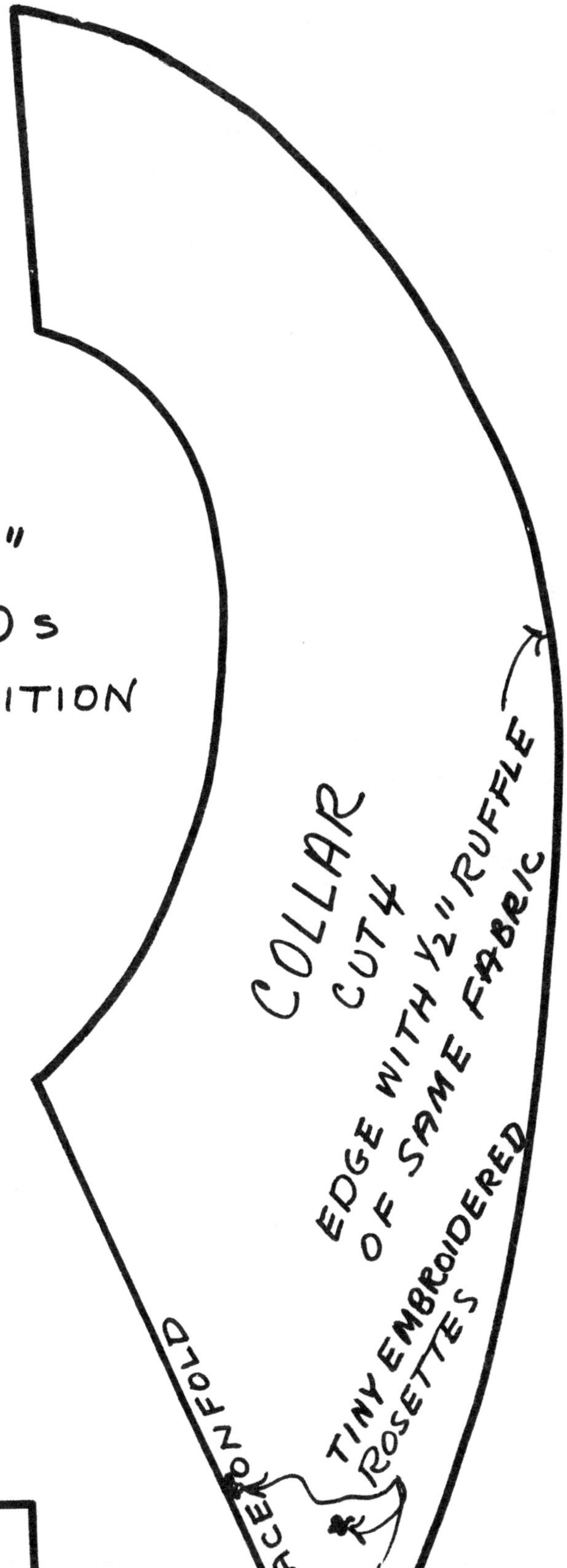

COLLAR
CUT 4

EDGE WITH ½" RUFFLE OF SAME FABRIC

TINY EMBROIDERED ROSETTES

PLACE ON FOLD

TO MAKE SKIRT, CUT FOLLOWING SECTIONS:

2½" X 32"

2½" X 60"

2½" X 96"

ABOVE FOR SKIRT TIERS ALLOWS ¼"
SEAM AND ¼" HEM ON EACH TIER.
BEGIN AT LOWER TIER HEM, GATHER
TO NEXT, ETC. FINALLY, GATHER TO BODICE.

141

SHIRLEY TEMPLE DOLL
OUTFITS

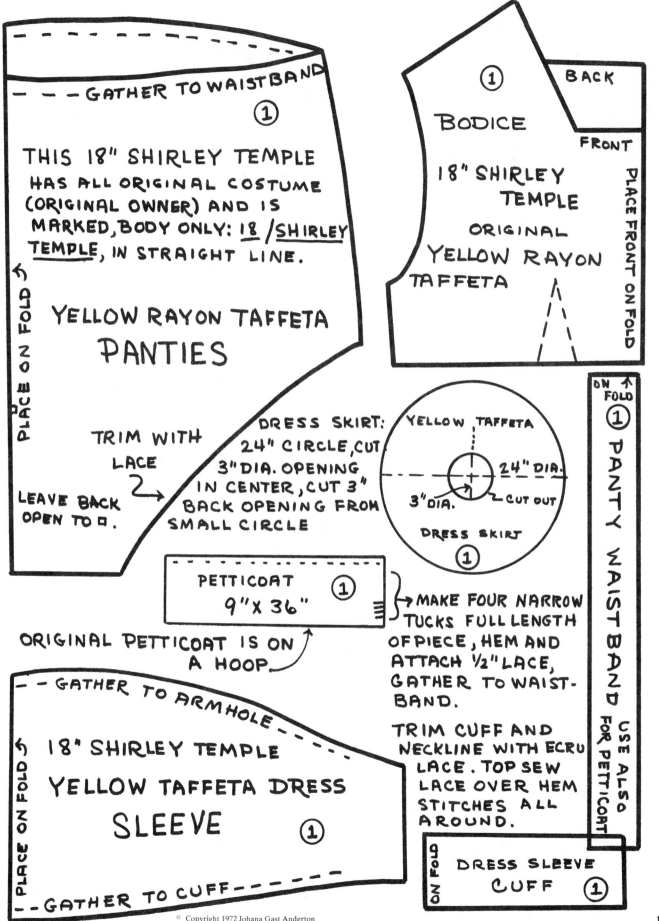

GATHER TO WAISTBAND ①

THIS 18" SHIRLEY TEMPLE HAS ALL ORIGINAL COSTUME (ORIGINAL OWNER) AND IS MARKED, BODY ONLY: 18 /SHIRLEY TEMPLE, IN STRAIGHT LINE.

YELLOW RAYON TAFFETA
PANTIES

PLACE ON FOLD

TRIM WITH LACE

LEAVE BACK OPEN TO □.

BODICE ①
BACK
FRONT

18" SHIRLEY TEMPLE
ORIGINAL
YELLOW RAYON TAFFETA

PLACE FRONT ON FOLD

DRESS SKIRT: 24" CIRCLE, CUT 3" DIA. OPENING IN CENTER, CUT 3" BACK OPENING FROM SMALL CIRCLE

YELLOW TAFFETA
24" DIA.
3" DIA.
CUT OUT
DRESS SKIRT ①

ON FOLD ①
PANTY WAISTBAND
USE ALSO FOR PETTICOAT

PETTICOAT ①
9" X 36"

ORIGINAL PETTICOAT IS ON A HOOP.

MAKE FOUR NARROW TUCKS FULL LENGTH OF PIECE, HEM AND ATTACH ½" LACE, GATHER TO WAIST-BAND.

TRIM CUFF AND NECKLINE WITH ECRU LACE. TOP SEW LACE OVER HEM STITCHES ALL AROUND.

GATHER TO ARMHOLE

18" SHIRLEY TEMPLE
YELLOW TAFFETA DRESS
SLEEVE ①

PLACE ON FOLD

GATHER TO CUFF

ON FOLD
DRESS SLEEVE
CUFF ①

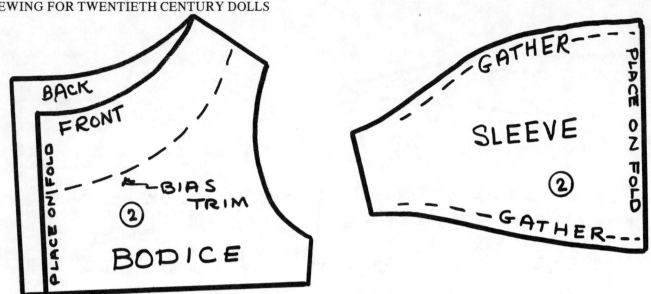

18" SHIRLEY TEMPLE ORIGINAL DRESS

SKIRT OF DRESS:

CUT RECTANGLE 5½" X 30", CUT SCALLOPS ALONG ONE LONG SIDE USING PROFILE BELOW. BIND SCALLOP EDGE WITH VERY NARROW BIAS IN SAME COLOR AS DOTS ON DRESS FABRIC.*

MAKE PETTICOAT OF WHITE ORGANDY PIECE 4½" X 24". HEM, THEN GATHER SKIRT AND PETTICOAT AS ONE AND ATTACH TO BODICE

THIS SHIRLEY WEARS AN UNDER-GARMENT IDENTICAL TO THAT WORN BY JUDY GARLAND, WHICH SEE.

ADD ¼" SEAM ALLOWANCE

PROFILE OF SCALLOPS

*USING SAME NARROW BIAS, STITCH TWO ROWS OF TRIM ONE INCH APART AND ONE INCH FROM HEM.

③

BRASS BUTTON

UNIFORM
JACKET
FRONT-CUT 2

TAN TWILL

18" SHIRLEY TEMPLE

③

18" SHIRLEY TEMPLE

UNIFORM
JACKET

BACK

PLACE ON FOLD

BELT: 1½" TWILL TAPE
13½" LONG. FOLD TO
MAKE BELT ¾" WIDE,
TOPSTITCH ALL EDGES.

PLACE ON FOLD

18" SHIRLEY TEMPLE
SLEEVE-CUT 2

③

③

FOLD

BRASS BUTTON

COLLAR ③

FOLD OVER → CUT 2 ON FOLD

ON FOLD

ADD ¼" SEAM ALLOWANCE

145

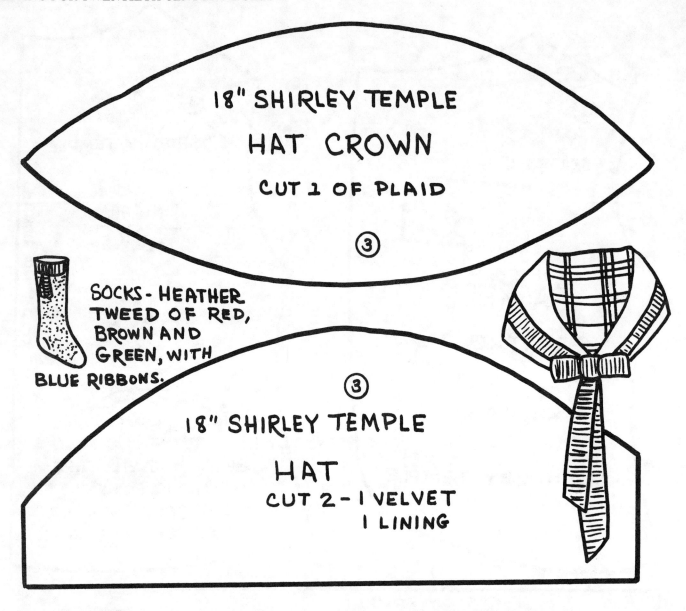

18" SHIRLEY TEMPLE
HAT CROWN
CUT 1 OF PLAID
③

SOCKS - HEATHER TWEED OF RED, BROWN AND GREEN, WITH BLUE RIBBONS.

③
18" SHIRLEY TEMPLE
HAT
CUT 2 - 1 VELVET
1 LINING

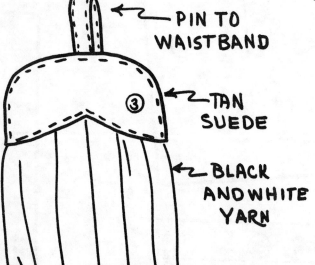

→ PIN TO WAISTBAND

③
→ TAN SUEDE

→ BLACK AND WHITE YARN

TO MAKE KILT:

CUT RECTANGLE 5½" X 24" PLUS HEM AND SEAM ALLOWANCE. PLEAT EVENLY TO WAISTBAND.

WAISTBAND OF SKIRT (KILT):

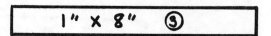

1" X 8"   ⑤

ADD ¼" SEAM ALLOWANCE

146

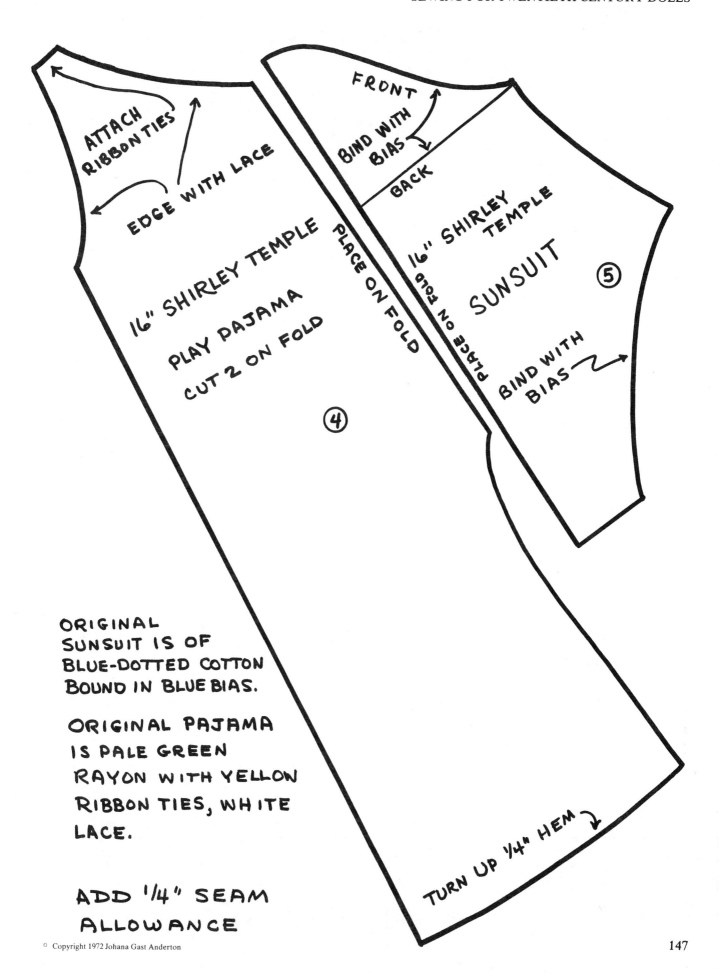

ATTACH RIBBON TIES

EDGE WITH LACE

16" SHIRLEY TEMPLE
PLAY PAJAMA
CUT 2 ON FOLD

④

PLACE ON FOLD

FRONT

BIND WITH BIAS

BACK

16" SHIRLEY TEMPLE
SUNSUIT

⑤

PLACE ON FOLD

BIND WITH BIAS

ORIGINAL
SUNSUIT IS OF
BLUE-DOTTED COTTON
BOUND IN BLUE BIAS.

ORIGINAL PAJAMA
IS PALE GREEN
RAYON WITH YELLOW
RIBBON TIES, WHITE
LACE.

ADD ¼" SEAM
ALLOWANCE

TURN UP ¼" HEM

147

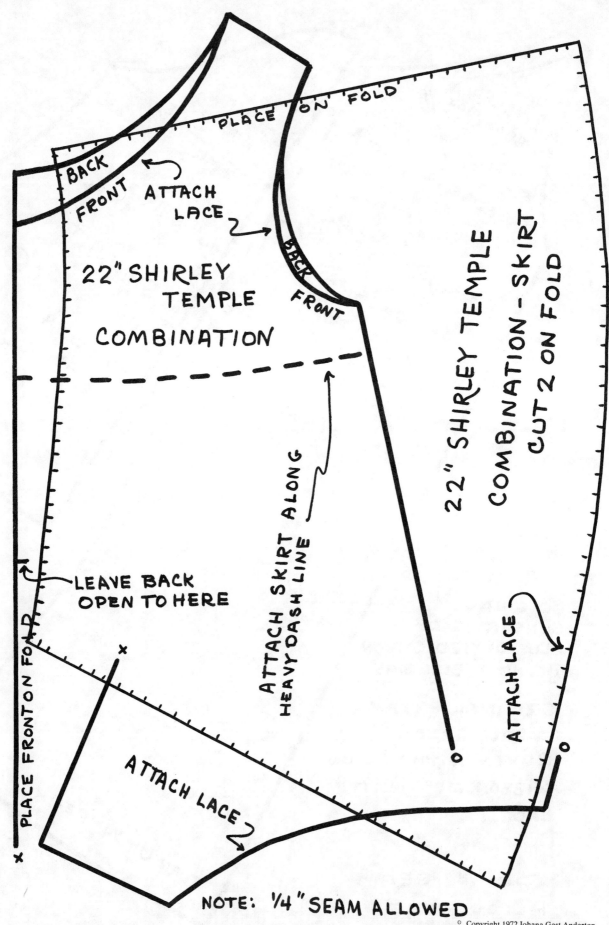

BACK

FRONT

ATTACH LACE

PLACE ON FOLD

22" SHIRLEY TEMPLE COMBINATION

BACK

FRONT

22" SHIRLEY TEMPLE COMBINATION - SKIRT CUT 2 ON FOLD

ATTACH SKIRT ALONG HEAVY DASH LINE

LEAVE BACK OPEN TO HERE

PLACE FRONT ON FOLD

ATTACH LACE

ATTACH LACE

NOTE: ¼" SEAM ALLOWED

148

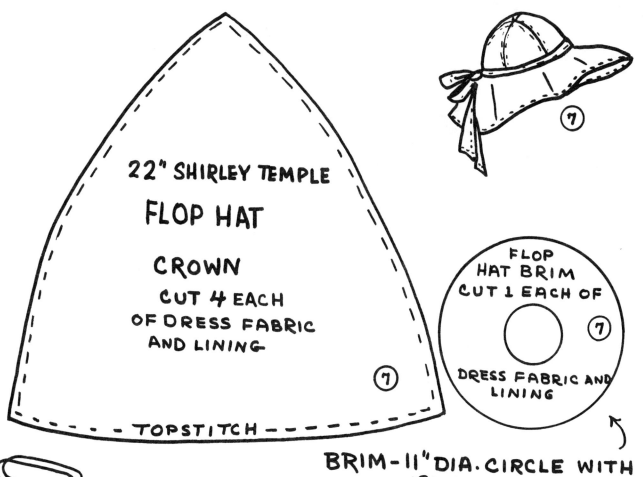

22" SHIRLEY TEMPLE

FLOP HAT

CROWN

CUT 4 EACH
OF DRESS FABRIC
AND LINING

⑦

— TOPSTITCH —

FLOP
HAT BRIM
CUT 1 EACH OF
⑦

DRESS FABRIC AND
LINING

HAT TIE - CUT PIECE
OF DRESS FABRIC
2" X 36", SEAM,
TURN AND TOPSTITCH.

BRIM - 11" DIA. CIRCLE WITH
4 3/4" DIA. CIRCLE CUT
OUT FOR CROWN. LINE
WITH CONTRASTING
FABRIC OR USE DRESS
FABRIC IF DESIRED.

NOTE:
1/4" SEAMS
ALLOWED.

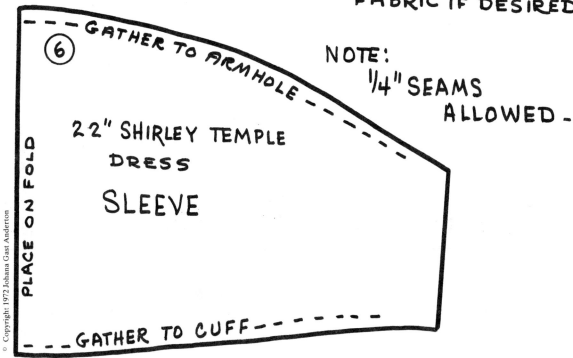

⑥ GATHER TO ARMHOLE

22" SHIRLEY TEMPLE
DRESS
SLEEVE

PLACE ON FOLD

GATHER TO CUFF

149

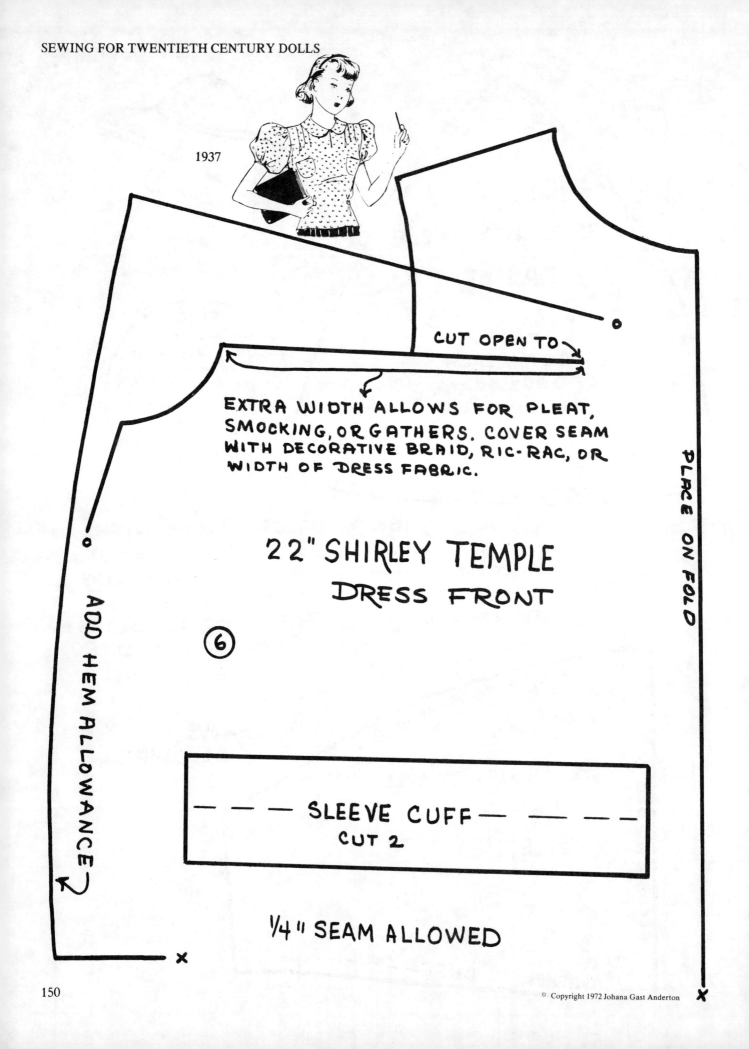

1937

CUT OPEN TO

EXTRA WIDTH ALLOWS FOR PLEAT,
SMOCKING, OR GATHERS. COVER SEAM
WITH DECORATIVE BRAID, RIC-RAC, OR
WIDTH OF DRESS FABRIC.

PLACE ON FOLD

22" SHIRLEY TEMPLE
DRESS FRONT

⑥

ADD HEM ALLOWANCE

— — — SLEEVE CUFF — — — —
CUT 2

¼" SEAM ALLOWED

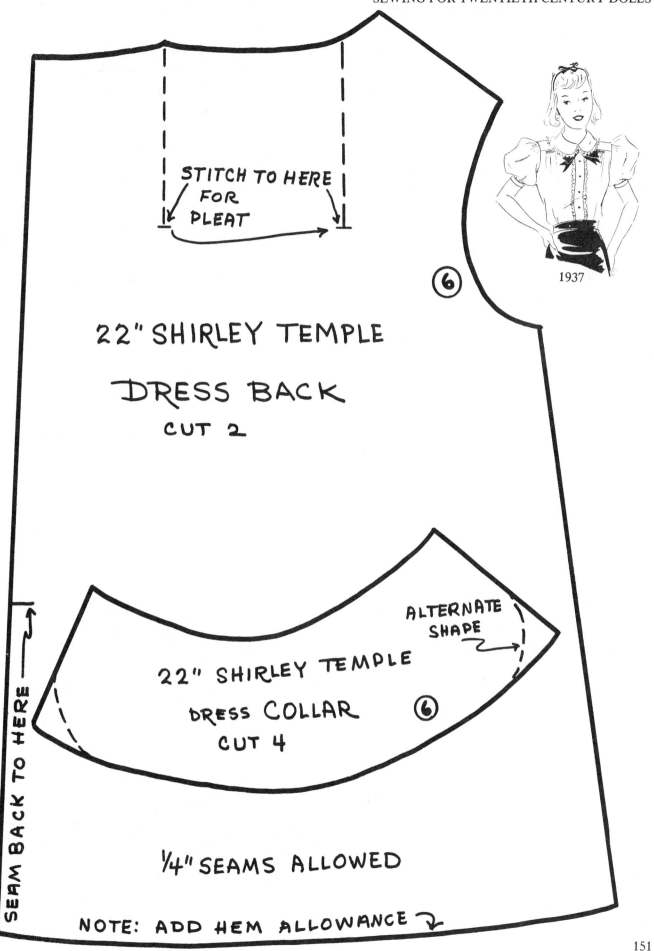

STITCH TO HERE
FOR
PLEAT

⑥

1937

22" SHIRLEY TEMPLE

DRESS BACK

CUT 2

ALTERNATE
SHAPE

22" SHIRLEY TEMPLE

DRESS COLLAR   ⑥

CUT 4

SEAM BACK TO HERE

¼" SEAMS ALLOWED

NOTE: ADD HEM ALLOWANCE

19" EMELIE DIONNE BY MADAME ALEXANDER

Tiny lavendar flowers and leaves, narrow lace and soft white cotton make up this original *Dionne* costume by *Madame Alexander*. Fit and sew undergarments first; fit dress over completed underwear on doll.

COMBINATIONS

Cut from lawn or other fine white cotton. Cut a rectangle 20 inches long and 5 inches wide (plus hem and seam allowances) for skirt of this combination panty-slip. Hem and attach 3 / 8 inch lace on one long side, gather remaining long side and fit to undersuit along broken line on pattern.

DRESS

For skirt front cut a rectangle of dress fabric 20 inches long and 5½ inches wide (plus hem and seam allowances). Gather and fit to bodice on one long side, seam bodice-skirt unit to dress back at shoulder, insert sleeves and stitch side seams, continuing through sleeve underarm seam. Finish neck opening with tiny ric-rac; sew narrow insertion lace around waist over seam; insert narrow black satin ribbon and tie bow in front.

BONNET

Seam bonnet together at back seam, sew side A to bonnet crown. Seam two pieces of bonnet brim, right sides together, turn and attach to side B of bonnet. Finish edges and attach black satin ribbon ties.

SHOES

For Emelie's shoes, see chapter "STOCKINGS AND SHOES".

EMELIE DIONNE -

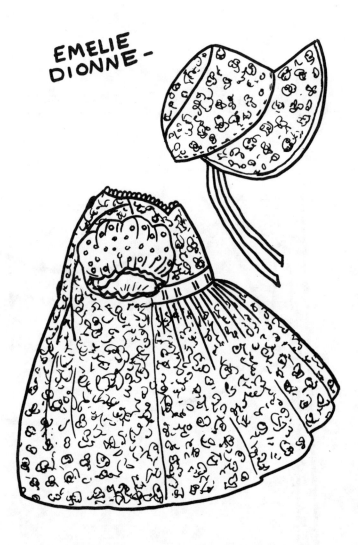

152

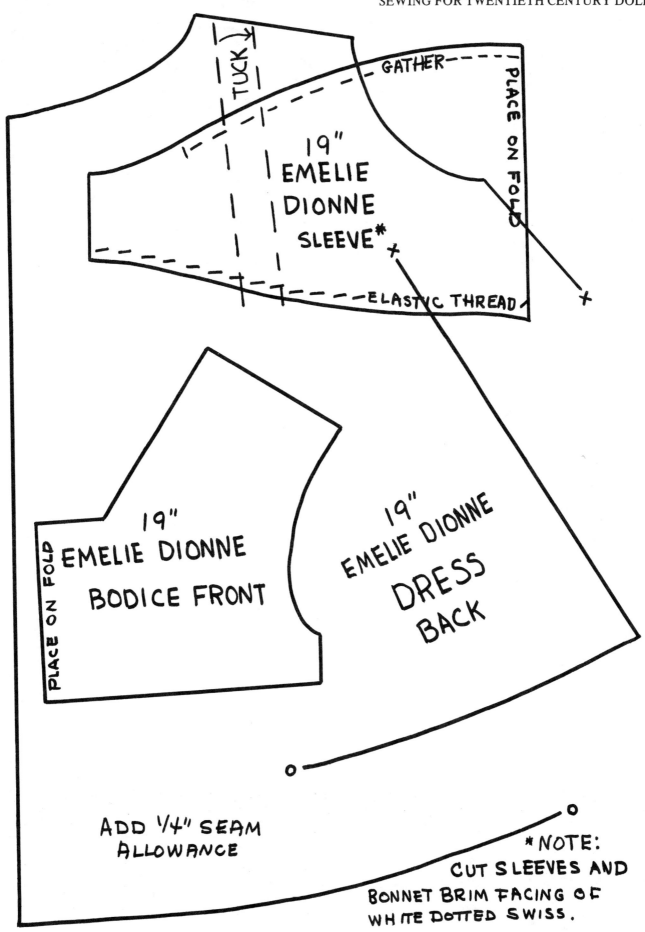

TUCK

GATHER

PLACE ON FOLD

19"
EMELIE
DIONNE
SLEEVE*

ELASTIC THREAD

19"
EMELIE DIONNE
BODICE FRONT

PLACE ON FOLD

19"
EMELIE DIONNE
DRESS
BACK

ADD ¼" SEAM
ALLOWANCE

*NOTE:
CUT SLEEVES AND
BONNET BRIM FACING OF
WHITE DOTTED SWISS.

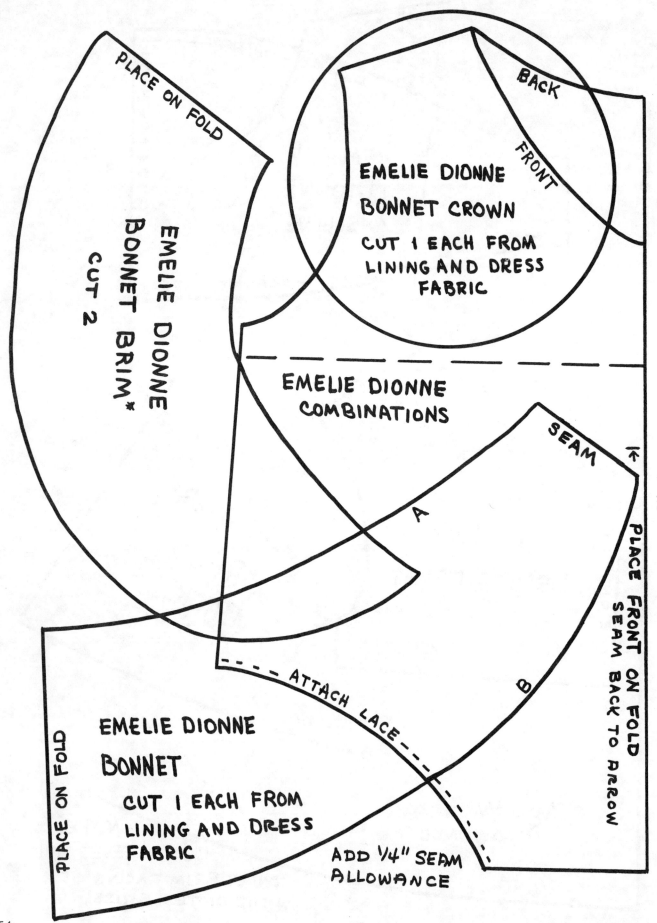

PLACE ON FOLD

EMELIE DIONNE
BONNET BRIM*
CUT 2

BACK

FRONT

EMELIE DIONNE
BONNET CROWN
CUT 1 EACH FROM
LINING AND DRESS
FABRIC

EMELIE DIONNE
COMBINATIONS

SEAM

A

B

ATTACH LACE

PLACE FRONT ON FOLD SEAM BACK TO ARROW

PLACE ON FOLD

EMELIE DIONNE
BONNET
CUT 1 EACH FROM
LINING AND DRESS
FABRIC

ADD ¼" SEAM
ALLOWANCE

THE 1940s

Styles for women and girls were still soft and feminine in 1940, with large puffed sleeves and wide skirts. With the advent of World War II, the sleeves and shoulders took on a grim, mannish appearance and skirts narrowed into more conservative lines. Work clothes for women gave designers the challenge of providing attractive fashions for all the *"Rosie Riveters"* and *"Victory Gardeners"* who rushed into jobs formerly held by men.

Dirndl skirts and peasant blouses were a must in every wardrobe of 1942. More and more slacks for girls and women were shown in 1943. These were of woven plaids, rayons, spun rayon, and in the lighter fabrics, linen weave rayon and striped seersucker. One-piece sleepers, called *Dr. Dentons,* were a must for the young set. Jumpers for little girls had circular skirts, dresses were along *Princess* lines. School clothes, 1943, included long, long sweaters in sets with plaid skirts in coordinated colors. Skirts had four, six, or eight gores or were pleated all around. Jodphurs were a classic for small girls and boys.

Tailored, two-piece suits with fitted jackets and four-gored "swing" skirts in woven plaids and herringbone tweeds for young girls were shown in 1943. Dresses that year were two-piece, tailored with short sleeves and six-gore skirts in striped cotton, chambray, striped chambray, and checked seersucker. Tailored sportswear consisted of wide-legged slacks suits and overalls for victory farmers. The 1944 pinafore had wide shoulder ruffles although the skirts were not so full as in pre-war years.

Later styles of the decade are illustrated with patterns and sketches.

-1943-

MOTHER-AND-DAUGHTER FASHIONS. In the 1850's, there was a great vogue for mothers and daughters to dress exactly alike. That fashion has been bobbing up for recognition every season for several years. Now it is important in all types of merchandise, especially in cotton frocks and smocks, aprons, and housecoats. We show you some of the smartest of such fashions because early in the year is the time to make wash frocks for spring and summer — to have time to make them nicely — to do nice finishing, make nice buttonholes, and have such ready for wear when the crocuses come.

GINGHAM FROCKS. · Short sleeves, bias-cut waists, and peasant skirts, finished with Peter Pan collars and center-front buttons or slide-fasteners, are a popular type of gingham dress. The brighter the plaid, the smarter the frock.

DENIM OR BROADCLOTH SMOCKS. Long sleeves and roomy pockets are an essential part of the new smocks. All have wide hems and ample fabric throughout. The length of the new smocks varies from the top of the hip to the bottom of the skirt. Many have large pearl buttons and bound buttonholes for fastening. Grand for maternity wear.

WAISTLINE APRONS. Something new in aprons! The fitted waistline, gathered skirts, halter neck, and wide rick-rack trimming make aprons gay — without disturbing their functional quality. Blue with red stripes and white rick-rack, or red and white stripes with blue rick-rack make a *patriotic affair* of these aprons — popular with mothers and daughters the country across.

1940

156

1940

PINAFORES. The movie version of THE WIZARD OF OZ may be responsible for the new vogue for pinafores. They are young and smart and practical. Many women make a little chemise dress; the skirt of which serves as a slip, and then the pinafore for wear over this. Notice the surplus back which laps, and strings that come around and tie at the center-front. Pinafore opens out, making the ironing easy.

PRINCESS FROCKS. Make these for dress-up of fine wool, silk, rayon, or cotton, or make them for home wear. The dresses shown are of a rayon print in brightest color, with velvet bows for accent. Use slide-fasteners at the center-front to make them easy to get in and out of.

HOUSECOATS. Make them of velveteen, corduroy, flannel, seersucker, or unbleached muslin, but style them smartly. Put "dash" in the silhouette, and "umph" in the trimming, and the fabric can be inexpensive because the smartness will balance the result for you.

BRAID, BRAID, AND *MORE* BRAID. Perhaps it is the military influence, perhaps it is the acceptance of decoration — anyway, braid is everywhere. Middy and soutache braids are the most popular. Some is put on with beads to simulate necklaces; some straight; some in designs; others to form a fringe. Anyway, use braid with beads or without to decorate a new frock, or to revive an old one. Fashion likes it and so will you.

1943

5376

5377

5373

5325

5360

5361

5347

SCHOOL Days

1943

5342

5341

5349

5316

5315

The brisk boxy coat with velvet collar is as mannish as Dad's, with its fly pleat closing. No. 5315.

The double-breasted coat, cut nice and boxy, is for Brother. He has a velvet collar, too. No. 5316.

The shorts button to the shirt in this two-piece suit. Everything is *very* correct here. No. 5325.

The feminine half of the brother-and-sister set, above center, buttons all the way down. No. 5341.

Scalloped edging outlines the tucks on Brother's suit. His pants button to his blouse. No. 5342.

The grey flannel school suit is pretty snappy! And done in the very best tailored tradition. No. 5347.

The green coat is beautifully fitted with princess seams at back. The best one for best. No. 5349.

A red jacket, suspender skirt, and a crisp blouse for the smaller half of this sister pair. No. 5360.

The same three-piece suit for Big Sister, with important pleats in the bias plaid skirt. No. 5361.

The best of all school dresses is the jumper in pinafore style, with its own beige blouse. No. 5373.

The sailor dress buttons all the way down. She will love the white buttons and the braid. No. 5376.

Last but not least, a blue shirtfrock made just like Mother's shown on a preceding page. No. 5377.

> The illustrations on these two pages are taken from McCall pattern listings of 1943, and give a good resume of the styles of the war years.

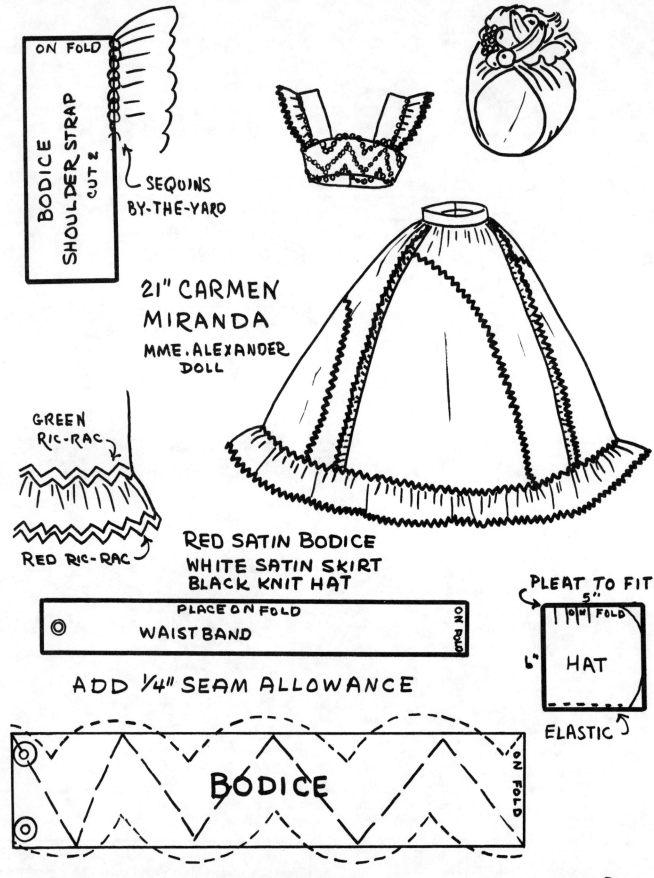

ON FOLD

BODICE SHOULDER STRAP CUT 2

SEQUINS BY-THE-YARD

21" CARMEN MIRANDA

MME. ALEXANDER DOLL

GREEN RIC-RAC

RED RIC-RAC

RED SATIN BODICE
WHITE SATIN SKIRT
BLACK KNIT HAT

PLACE ON FOLD
WAIST BAND
ON FOLD

ADD ¼" SEAM ALLOWANCE

PLEAT TO FIT
5"
ON FOLD
6"
HAT

ELASTIC

BODICE
ON FOLD

ATTACH SEQUINS-BY-THE-YARD FOLLOWING DOTTED AND DASHED LINES ON PATTERN.

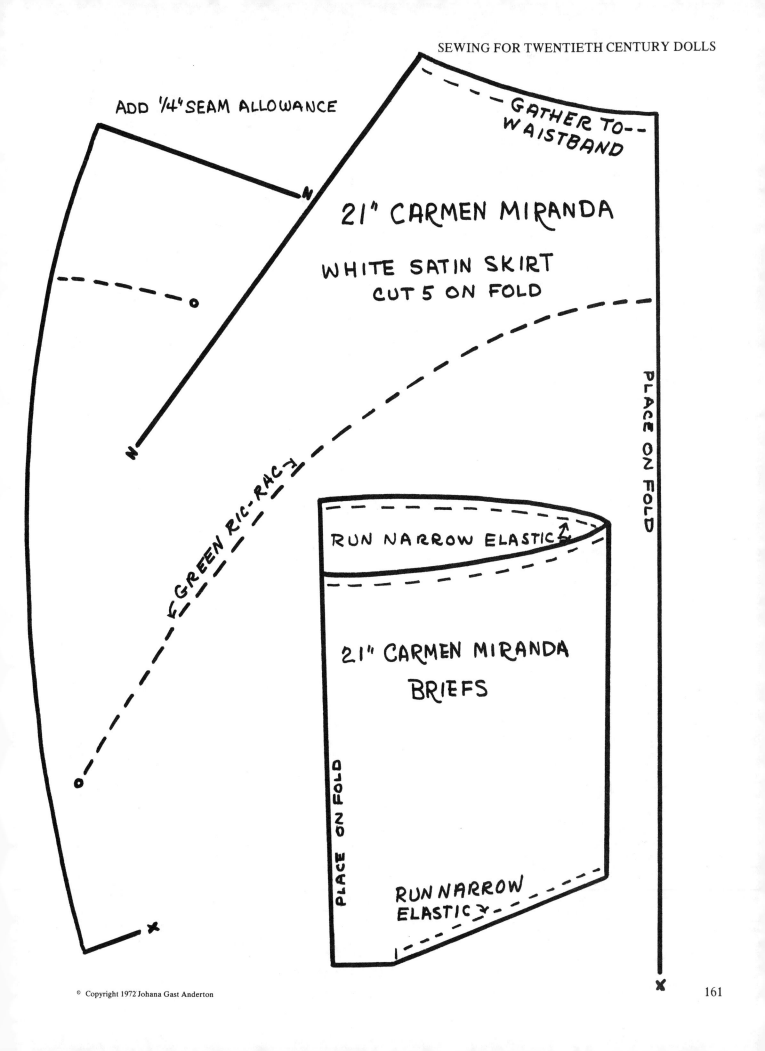

ADD ¼" SEAM ALLOWANCE

GATHER TO-- WAISTBAND

21" CARMEN MIRANDA

WHITE SATIN SKIRT
CUT 5 ON FOLD

PLACE ON FOLD

←GREEN RIC-RAC→

RUN NARROW ELASTIC

21" CARMEN MIRANDA
BRIEFS

PLACE ON FOLD

RUN NARROW
ELASTIC →

SKI COSTUME
14" SONJA HENIE

Pale beige, fine-wale corduroy fashions this original ski costume. The hood was edged about the face with white fur, probably rabbit. This material may be purchased in larger fabric shops in a narrow strip sold by the yard. The ski-pants bodice is of plain tan cotton.

Ski Pants — Sew inside leg seam between O's and turn one leg to right side. Insert this leg inside the other, right sides together, matching seams, and sew crotch seam, leaving opening in back from waist to X.

Skis — Skis may be made of thin balsa wood strips, following pattern and contour sketch, or by laminating three thicknesses of cardboard and shaping as glue dries. Paint and glue on black elastic straps.

Ski Poles — Insert 7 and ½ inch pieces of dowel into cardboard circles, paint, add black elastic wrist straps.

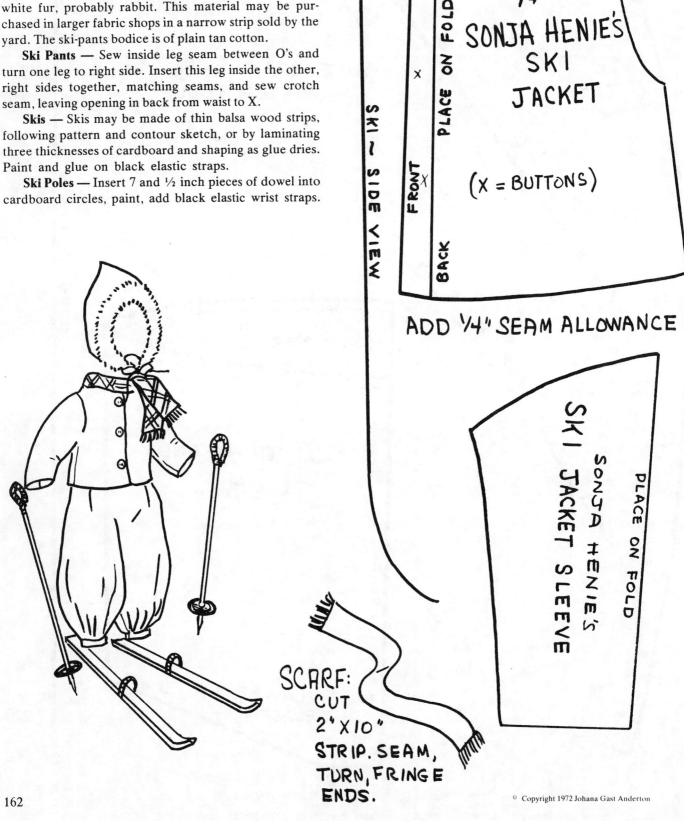

SKI ~ SIDE VIEW

BACK   FRONT

14" SONJA HENIE'S SKI JACKET

PLACE ON FOLD

FRONT

BACK

(X = BUTTONS)

ADD ¼" SEAM ALLOWANCE

SONJA HENIE'S SKI JACKET SLEEVE

PLACE ON FOLD

SCARF: CUT 2" X 10" STRIP. SEAM, TURN, FRINGE ENDS.

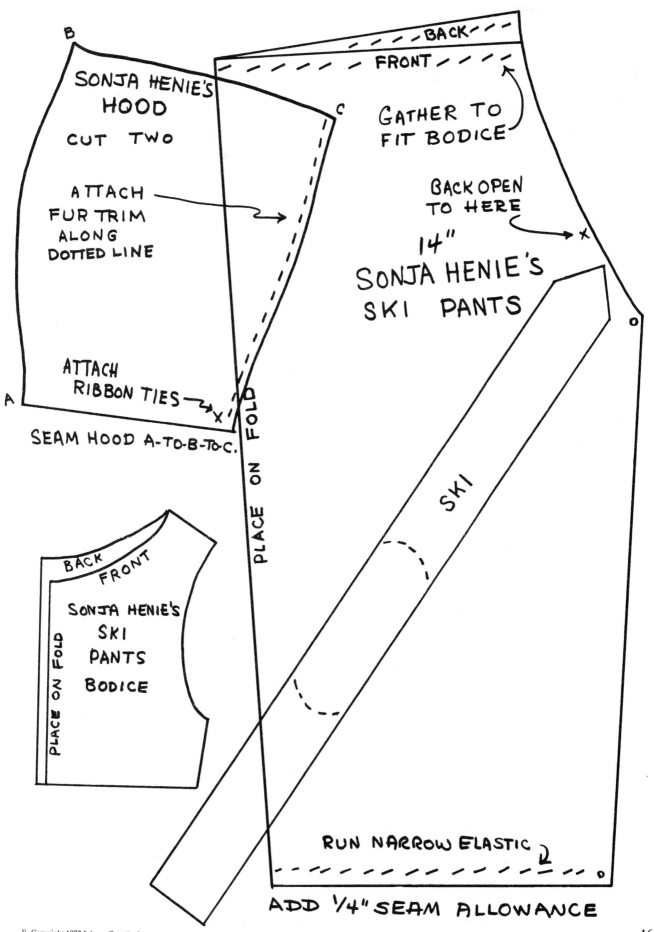

SONJA HENIE'S
HOOD

CUT TWO

ATTACH
FUR TRIM
ALONG
DOTTED LINE

ATTACH
RIBBON TIES

SEAM HOOD A-TO-B-TO-C.

BACK
FRONT

GATHER TO
FIT BODICE

BACK OPEN
TO HERE

14"
SONJA HENIE'S
SKI PANTS

PLACE ON FOLD

SKI

SONJA HENIE'S
SKI
PANTS
BODICE

BACK
FRONT

PLACE ON FOLD

RUN NARROW ELASTIC

ADD 1/4" SEAM ALLOWANCE

163

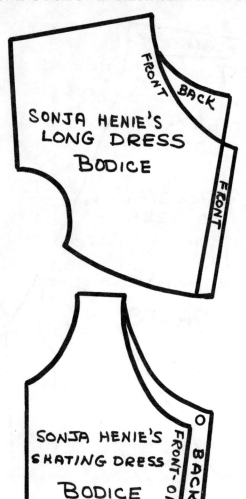

SONJA HENIE'S
LONG DRESS
BODICE

FRONT BACK
FRONT

**SKATING COSTUME
14" SONJA HENIE**

This original skating costume is of pale pink satin, with a taffeta skirt trimmed with one-inch band of satin, and a satin flower on the bodice.

SONJA HENIE'S
SKATING DRESS
BODICE

FRONT-ON FOLD
BACK

SKATING DRESS SKIRT—3" X 26"

LONG DRESS SKIRT—6¼" X 30"

ADD ¼" SEAM ALLOWANCE

GATHER WITH
ELASTIC

SONJA HENIE'S
SATIN PANTIES
CUT 2 ON FOLD

THESE ARE NOT
SHAPED-ONLY
FINISHED THEN
CAUGHT WITH
A STITCH AT
CENTER FOR
CROTCH.

PLACE ON FOLD

**LONG DRESS
14" SONJA HENIE**

Dress is of pale blue silk crepe with ecru lace overskirt. Bodice is covered with ecru lace net, trimmed with narrow lace.

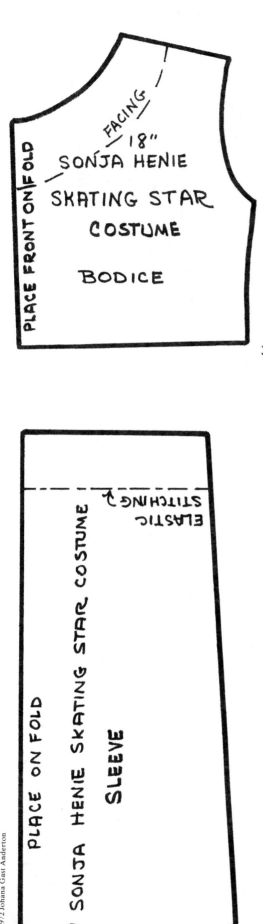

18" SONJA HENIE

SKATING STAR COSTUME

HAT — Cardboard circle 3½ inches in diameter for crown, sides 1 inch cardboard, glued together with tabs. Cover entirely with rabbit fur or fake fur.

MUFF — Piece of fabric 3 inches by 5 inches, folded over and stitched; this also is covered with fur. Wrist strap gold elastic.

BELT — Piece of dress fabric 9 inches long by 1 inch, folded over with gold decorative braid topstitched the length, finished off with gold bow, could be piece of jewelry or child's hair barrette.

NECK RUFF — This is separate from dress: Piece of rabbit fur 7 inches long, tied with gold elastic.

DRESS — White taffeta, trimmed about the skirt with rabbit fur. Skirt is 10 inch diameter circle, with waist circle cut out. Bottom of skirt is folded to right side and glued, then rabbit fur strip is glued over that, giving finished underside to hem. Glue often darkens fabric; therefore you may wish to stitch this hem and catchstitch the fur to hem.

165

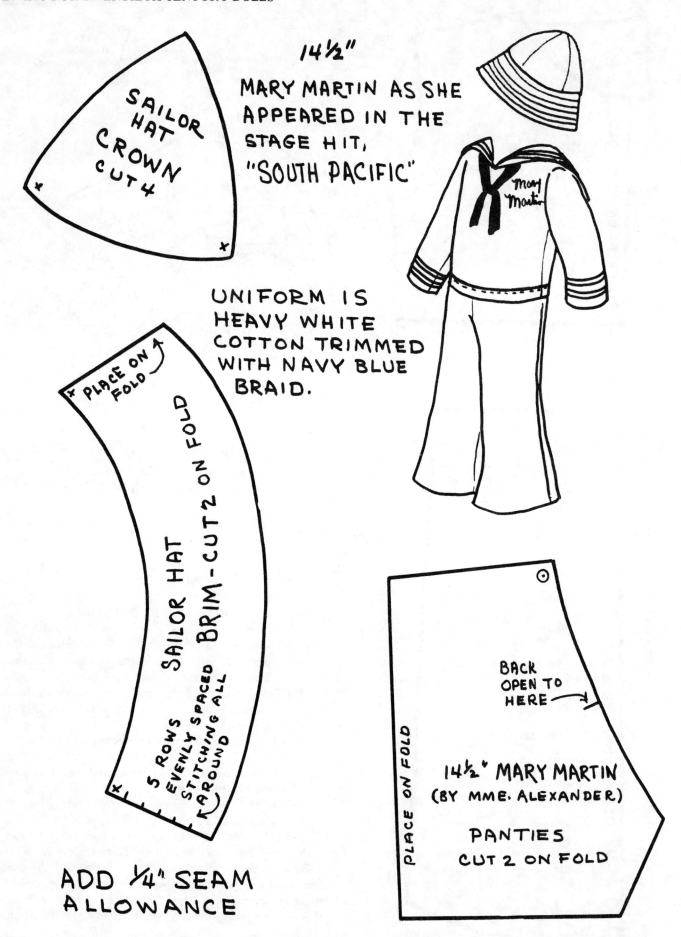

SAILOR
HAT
CROWN
CUT 4

14½"
MARY MARTIN AS SHE
APPEARED IN THE
STAGE HIT,
"SOUTH PACIFIC"

Mary
Martin

UNIFORM IS
HEAVY WHITE
COTTON TRIMMED
WITH NAVY BLUE
BRAID.

PLACE ON
FOLD

SAILOR HAT
BRIM — CUT 2 ON FOLD

5 ROWS
EVENLY SPACED
STITCHING ALL
AROUND

ADD ¼" SEAM
ALLOWANCE

BACK
OPEN TO
HERE

PLACE ON FOLD

14½" MARY MARTIN
(BY MME. ALEXANDER)

PANTIES
CUT 2 ON FOLD

166

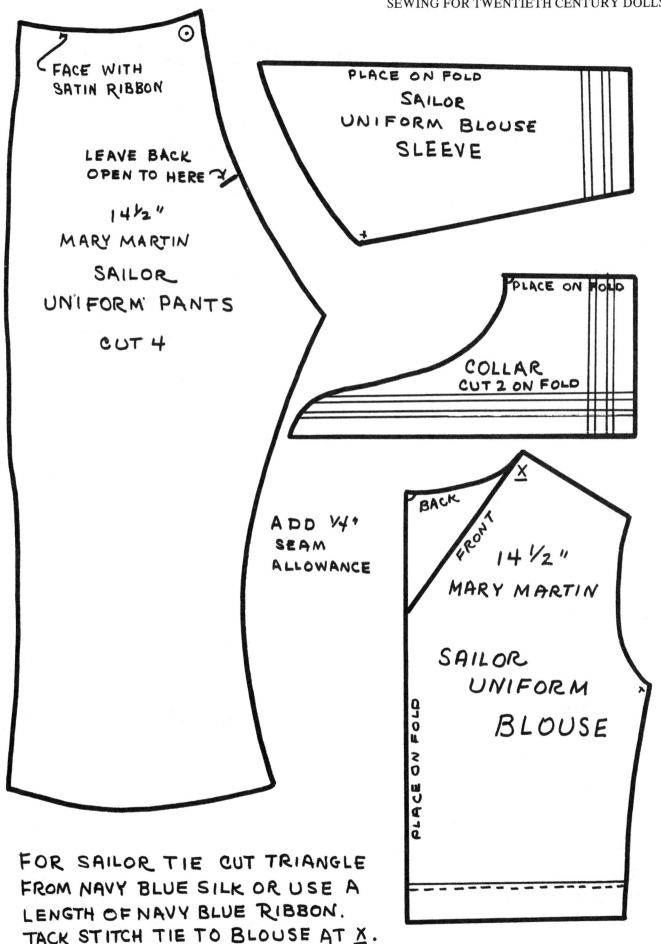

FACE WITH
SATIN RIBBON

LEAVE BACK
OPEN TO HERE

14½"
MARY MARTIN

SAILOR

UNIFORM PANTS

CUT 4

PLACE ON FOLD
SAILOR
UNIFORM BLOUSE
SLEEVE

PLACE ON FOLD

COLLAR
CUT 2 ON FOLD

ADD ¼"
SEAM
ALLOWANCE

BACK

FRONT

X

14½"
MARY MARTIN

SAILOR
UNIFORM
BLOUSE

PLACE ON FOLD

FOR SAILOR TIE CUT TRIANGLE
FROM NAVY BLUE SILK OR USE A
LENGTH OF NAVY BLUE RIBBON.
TACK STITCH TIE TO BLOUSE AT X.

167

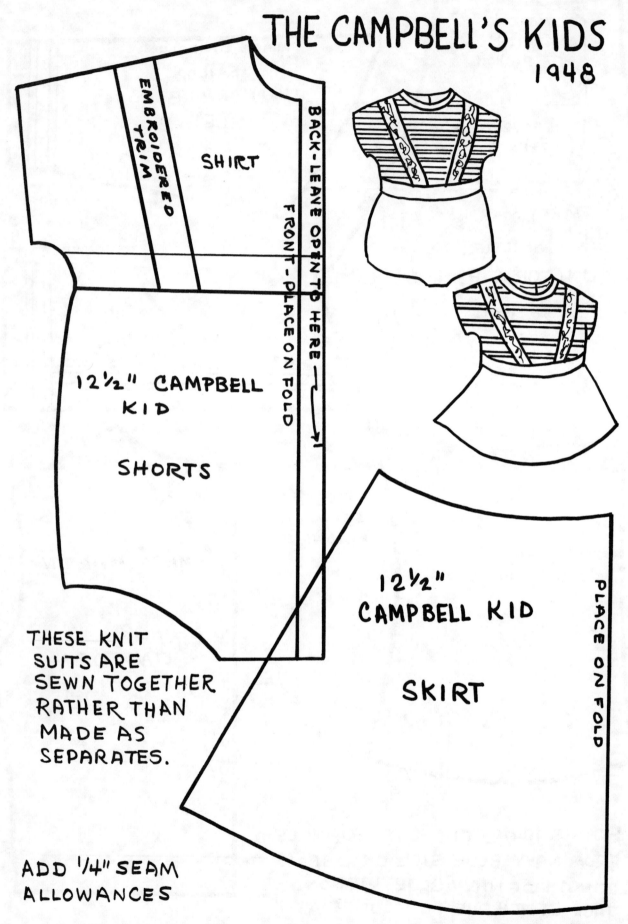

THE CAMPBELL'S KIDS
1948

EMBROIDERED TRIM

SHIRT

BACK - LEAVE OPEN TO HERE

FRONT - PLACE ON FOLD

12½" CAMPBELL KID

SHORTS

THESE KNIT SUITS ARE SEWN TOGETHER RATHER THAN MADE AS SEPARATES.

12½" CAMPBELL KID

SKIRT

PLACE ON FOLD

ADD ¼" SEAM ALLOWANCES

BACK

12 3/4" MANNEQUIN
"JUST LIKE THOSE IN
THE STORE WINDOWS
OF THE 1940s AND
EARLY 1950s."

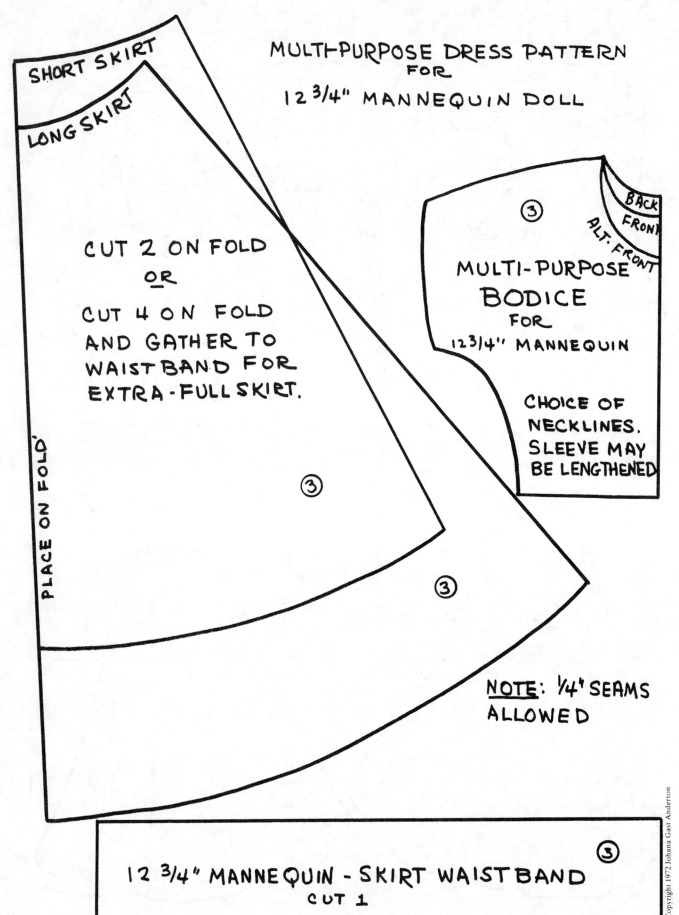

SHORT SKIRT

LONG SKIRT

MULTI-PURPOSE DRESS PATTERN
FOR
12 3/4" MANNEQUIN DOLL

CUT 2 ON FOLD
OR
CUT 4 ON FOLD
AND GATHER TO
WAISTBAND FOR
EXTRA-FULL SKIRT.

PLACE ON FOLD

③

BACK
FRONT
ALT. FRONT

③

MULTI-PURPOSE
BODICE
FOR
12 3/4" MANNEQUIN

CHOICE OF
NECKLINES.
SLEEVE MAY
BE LENGTHENED

③

NOTE: 1/4" SEAMS
ALLOWED

③

12 3/4" MANNEQUIN - SKIRT WAISTBAND
CUT 1

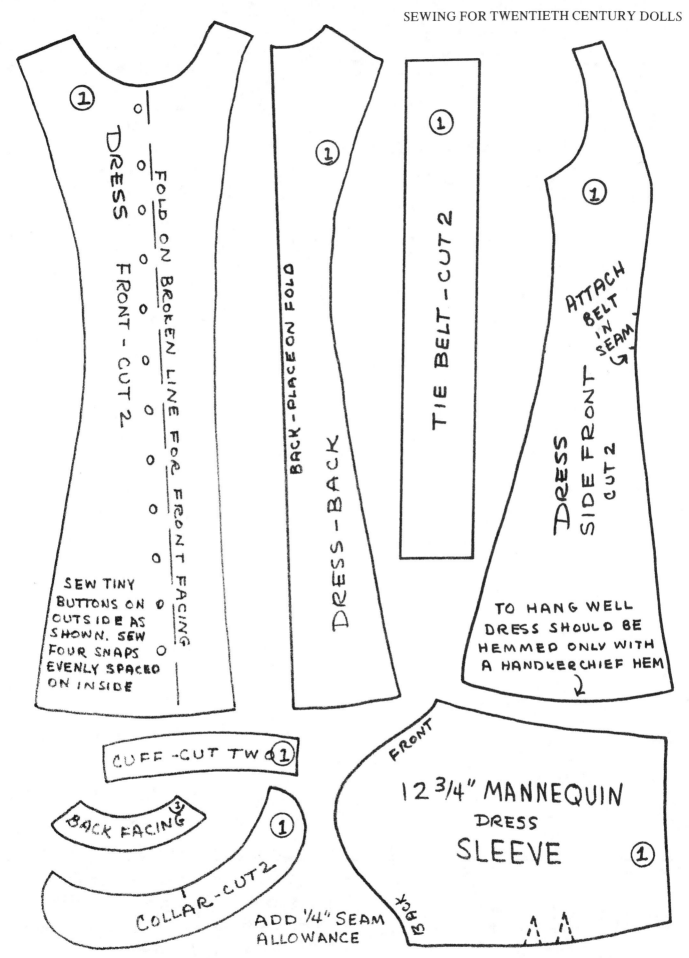

DRESS FRONT - CUT 2

DRESS

FOLD ON BROKEN LINE FOR FRONT FACING

① SEW TINY BUTTONS ON OUTSIDE AS SHOWN. SEW FOUR SNAPS EVENLY SPACED ON INSIDE

BACK - PLACE ON FOLD

DRESS - BACK

TIE BELT - CUT 2

ATTACH BELT IN SEAM

DRESS SIDE FRONT CUT 2

TO HANG WELL DRESS SHOULD BE HEMMED ONLY WITH A HANDKERCHIEF HEM

CUFF - CUT TWO ①

BACK FACING

COLLAR - CUT 2

ADD ¼" SEAM ALLOWANCE

FRONT

12 ¾" MANNEQUIN DRESS SLEEVE

BACK

171

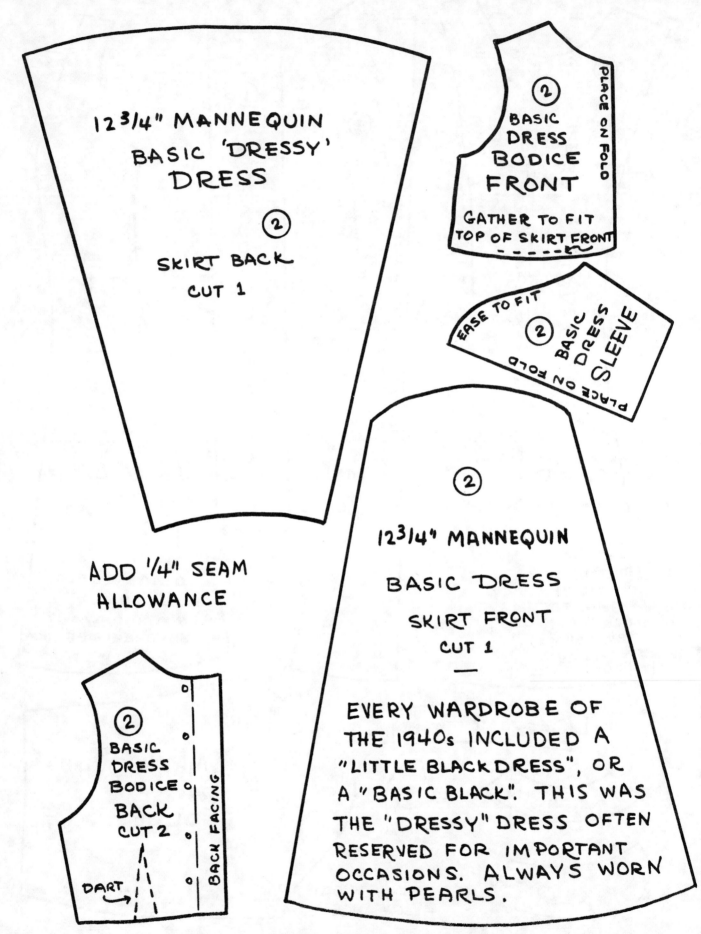

12³/4" MANNEQUIN

BASIC 'DRESSY' DRESS

② SKIRT BACK CUT 1

② BASIC DRESS BODICE FRONT

PLACE ON FOLD

GATHER TO FIT TOP OF SKIRT FRONT

EASE TO FIT

② BASIC DRESS SLEEVE

PLACE ON FOLD

ADD '/4" SEAM ALLOWANCE

② BASIC DRESS BODICE BACK CUT 2

DART

BACK FACING

② 12³/4" MANNEQUIN

BASIC DRESS SKIRT FRONT CUT 1

EVERY WARDROBE OF THE 1940s INCLUDED A "LITTLE BLACK DRESS", OR A "BASIC BLACK". THIS WAS THE "DRESSY" DRESS OFTEN RESERVED FOR IMPORTANT OCCASIONS. ALWAYS WORN WITH PEARLS.

THE 1950s

Embossed cottons, polished cottons, wool jersey, cottons with gold metallic overprint, and corduroy were a few of the varied fabrics of the '50s. Man-made fibres were becoming more available and blends of cotton, wool were being created. Skirts were long and hair was short. he Italian cut, a short, curly, little-boy hair-do could easily be styled to the individual face and figure. The effect was that of a pyramid, with the tiny head and flared skirt.

The full, full skirts were held triumphantly bouffant with the aid of at least two petticoats. A new material, nylon, furnished excellent net petticoats which remained stiff and bouncy through countless washings.

Raglan sleeves, batwing sleeves, big collars on blouses, and wide waistbands were all marks of the 1950s. Suits often had boxy jackets and straight skirts. These were buttoned high to a stand-up collar.

In the doll world, several fashionable misses were introduced, including *Toni, Betsy McCall, Terri Lee, Miss Revlon, Cissy,* and *Sweet Sue.* It is these charming style setters who will review for us the fashions of the 1950s since their wardrobes were so extensive as to include nearly every whim and nuance of that elusive thing called *style.*

On the following three pages are reprints from a booklet packed with a *Toni* doll, showing the various outfits available for *Betsy McCall* and *Toni.* These are the American Character versions of the two dolls; there are also Ideal *Toni* and *Betsy McCall* dolls. Style numbers and prices of the costumes appear with each outfit; a lucky find in old store stock may yield several of these fashions. These clothes are ca. 1959-1960.

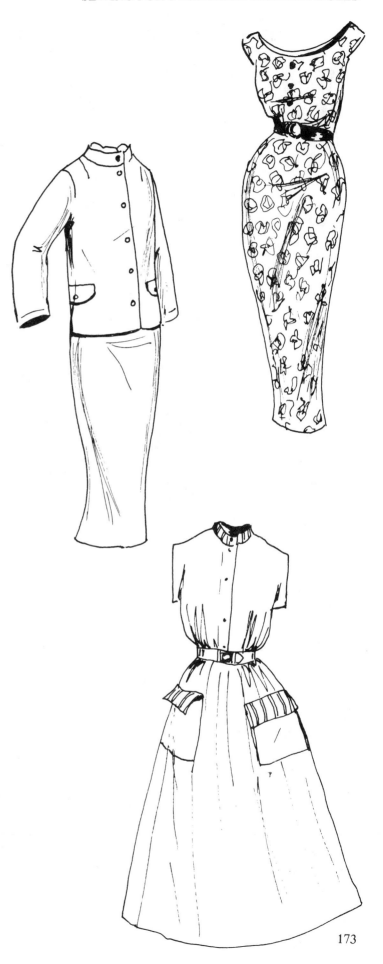

HERE ARE YOUR EXTRA OUTFITS FOR THE 8½″ BETSY McCALL DOLL

B 100—Doll Dressed in
Chemise, Shoes and Socks
$2.25

B 29
April Showers
$1.50

B 49
Riding Habit
$1.50

B 39
Ballerina
$1.50

B 19
Schoolgirl
$1.50

HERE ARE YOUR EXTRA OUTFITS FOR THE 8½″ BETSY McCALL DOLL

B 79
Coat and Hat
$2.00

B 129
Sugar & Spice
$3.00

B 99
Sunday Best
$2.50

B 69
On the Ice
$2.00

HERE ARE YOUR EXTRA OUTFITS FOR THE 8½″ BETSY McCALL DOLL

B 119
Bride
$3.00

B 109
Town and Country
$2.50

B 89
Sweet Dreams
$2.50

B 59
Holiday.
$2.00

HERE ARE YOUR EXTRA OUTFITS FOR THE 10½" TONI DOLL

A 95
Coat and Hat
$2.50

A 98
Bon Soir
$3.00

A 96
Shopping Time
$2.50

A 911
Bride
$4.00

HERE ARE YOUR EXTRA OUTFITS FOR THE 10½" TONI DOLL

A 99
Suburbanite
$3.00

A 97
High Society
$2.50

A 912
American Beauty
$4.00

A 910
Sunday Best
$3.00

These illustrations are from a booklet packed with a *Betsy McCall* doll.

HERE ARE YOUR EXTRA OUTFITS FOR THE 10½" TONI DOLL

A 92
Brunch Time
$2.00

A 93
Tea Time
$2.00

A 91
Collegiate
$2.00

A 94
At the Beach
$2.00

A 300
$2.98

TONI with Toni Playwave Set
Dressed in Brassalette
and High Heel Shoes

175

BETSY McCALL DOLL 14" TALL COMPLETE WITH COSTUME

#414
Holiday
$8.98

#614.
Bride
$9.98

#214
Schooldays
$7.98

#914
Doll in Chemise with
Trunk and Three Outfits
$12.98

TONI DOLL 20″ TALL COMPLETE WITH COSTUME AND TONI PLAYWAVE SET

She walks, wears high
heels, has wavy hair
and rolls her eyes.

204
Bride
$17.98

201
Sunday Best
$12.98

203
American Beauty
$17.98

BETSY McCALL DOLL 20″ TALL COMPLETE WITH COSTUME

220
Sunday Best
$11.98

320
Ensemble
$12.98

520
Sugar & Spice
$12.98

176

16" TERRI LEE DRESS

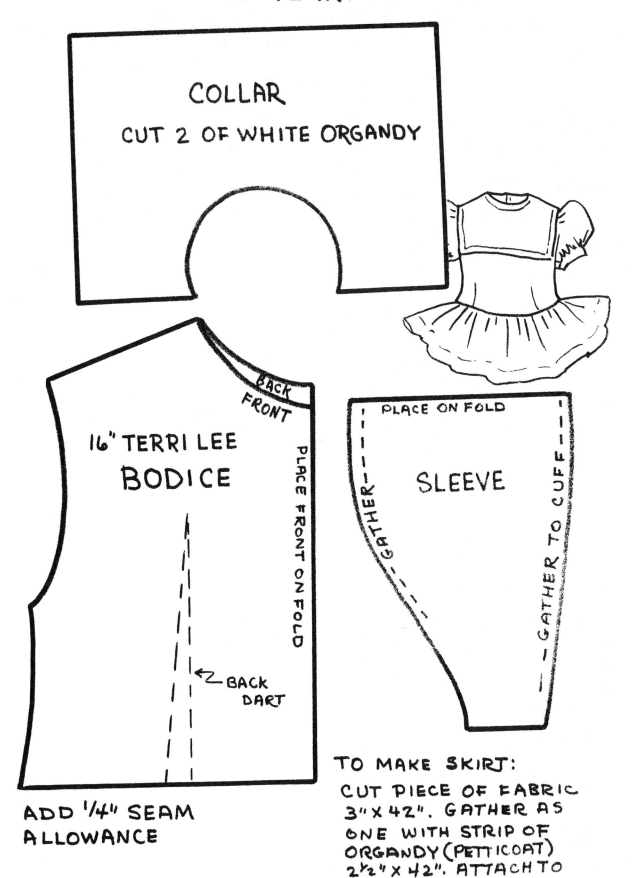

COLLAR

CUT 2 OF WHITE ORGANDY

16" TERRI LEE
BODICE

BACK
FRONT

PLACE FRONT ON FOLD

← BACK
DART

PLACE ON FOLD

GATHER

SLEEVE

GATHER TO CUFF

ADD ¼" SEAM
ALLOWANCE

TO MAKE SKIRT:
CUT PIECE OF FABRIC
3" X 42". GATHER AS
ONE WITH STRIP OF
ORGANDY (PETTICOAT)
2½" X 42". ATTACH TO
BODICE.

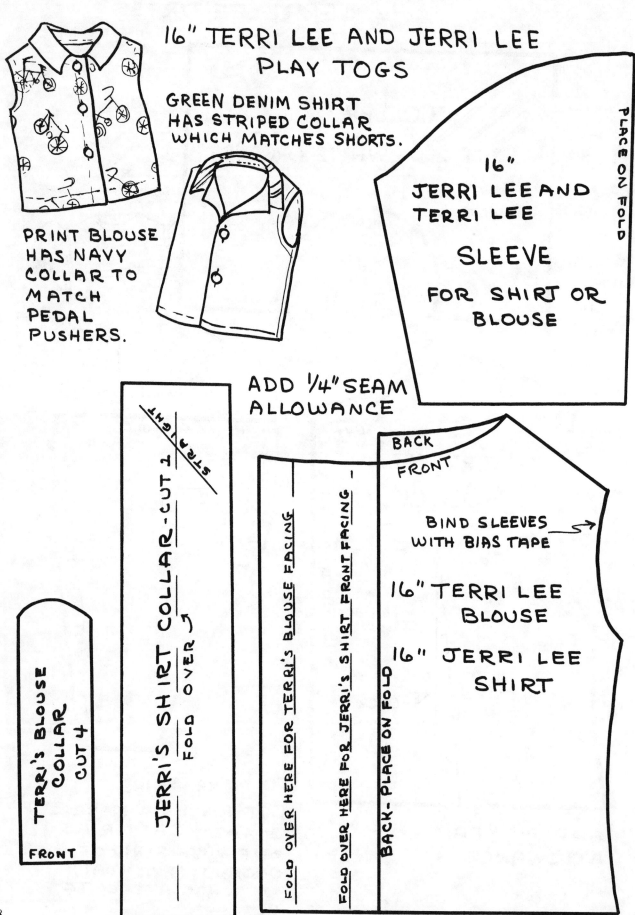

16" TERRI LEE AND JERRI LEE PLAY TOGS

GREEN DENIM SHIRT HAS STRIPED COLLAR WHICH MATCHES SHORTS.

PRINT BLOUSE HAS NAVY COLLAR TO MATCH PEDAL PUSHERS.

16" JERRI LEE AND TERRI LEE

SLEEVE

FOR SHIRT OR BLOUSE

PLACE ON FOLD

ADD ¼" SEAM ALLOWANCE

BACK
FRONT

BIND SLEEVES WITH BIAS TAPE

16" TERRI LEE BLOUSE

16" JERRI LEE SHIRT

JERRI'S SHIRT COLLAR - CUT 1

FOLD OVER

STRAIGHT

FOLD OVER HERE FOR TERRI'S BLOUSE FACING

FOLD OVER HERE FOR JERRI'S SHIRT FRONT FACING

BACK - PLACE ON FOLD

TERRI'S BLOUSE COLLAR CUT 4

FRONT

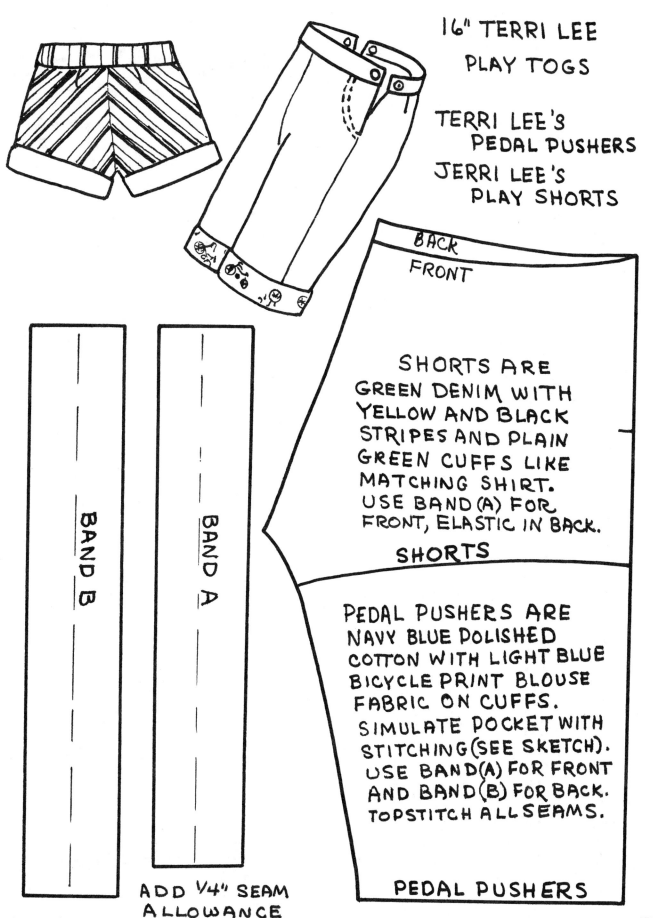

16" TERRI LEE
PLAY TOGS

TERRI LEE'S
    PEDAL PUSHERS
JERRI LEE'S
    PLAY SHORTS

BACK
FRONT

SHORTS ARE
GREEN DENIM WITH
YELLOW AND BLACK
STRIPES AND PLAIN
GREEN CUFFS LIKE
MATCHING SHIRT.
USE BAND (A) FOR
FRONT, ELASTIC IN BACK.

SHORTS

BAND B

BAND A

PEDAL PUSHERS ARE
NAVY BLUE POLISHED
COTTON WITH LIGHT BLUE
BICYCLE PRINT BLOUSE
FABRIC ON CUFFS.
SIMULATE POCKET WITH
STITCHING (SEE SKETCH).
USE BAND (A) FOR FRONT
AND BAND (B) FOR BACK.
TOPSTITCH ALL SEAMS.

ADD 1/4" SEAM
ALLOWANCE

PEDAL PUSHERS

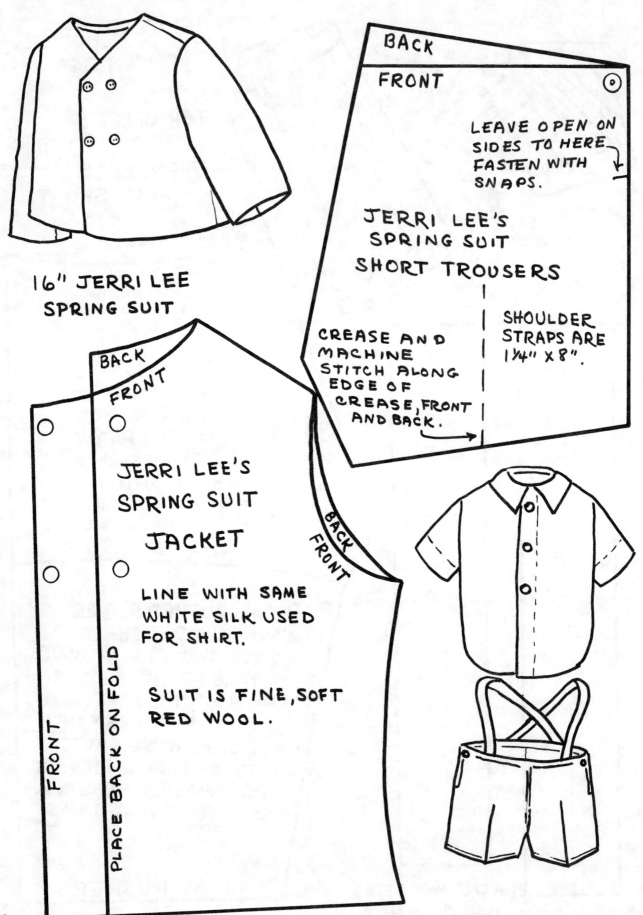

16" JERRI LEE
SPRING SUIT

BACK
FRONT

LEAVE OPEN ON
SIDES TO HERE
FASTEN WITH
SNAPS.

JERRI LEE'S
SPRING SUIT
SHORT TROUSERS

CREASE AND
MACHINE
STITCH ALONG
EDGE OF
CREASE, FRONT
AND BACK.

SHOULDER
STRAPS ARE
1¼" X 8".

BACK
FRONT

JERRI LEE'S
SPRING SUIT
JACKET

LINE WITH SAME
WHITE SILK USED
FOR SHIRT.

SUIT IS FINE, SOFT
RED WOOL.

BACK
FRONT

FRONT

PLACE BACK ON FOLD

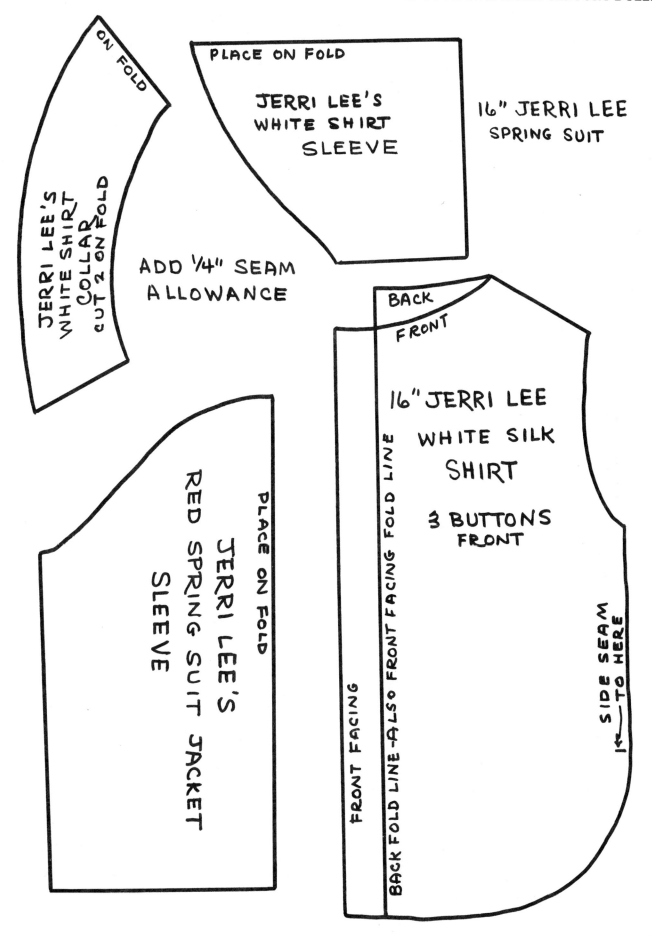

ON FOLD

PLACE ON FOLD

JERRI LEE'S
WHITE SHIRT
SLEEVE

16" JERRI LEE
SPRING SUIT

JERRI LEE'S
WHITE SHIRT
COLLAR
CUT 2 ON FOLD

ADD ¼" SEAM
ALLOWANCE

BACK

FRONT

16" JERRI LEE
WHITE SILK
SHIRT

3 BUTTONS
FRONT

PLACE ON FOLD

JERRI LEE'S
RED SPRING SUIT JACKET
SLEEVE

FRONT FACING

BACK FOLD LINE-ALSO FRONT FACING FOLD LINE

SIDE SEAM
TO HERE

BLUEBIRD WHITE SHIRT

FOLD OVER

COLLAR

PLACE ON STRAIGHT OF FABRIC

10" TINY TERRI LEE
BLUE BIRD

10" TINY TERRI LEE

BLUE BIRD
CAMPFIRE GIRL
WHITE SHIRT

BACK-PLACE ON FOLD
FRONT-TURN BACK ⅛"

ADD ¼" SEAM
ALLOWANCE

BEANIE BRIM

BLUE
BIRD
CAMP
FIRE
GIRL
BEANIE
CUT 4

CUT BEANIE
OF NAVY BLUE
FELT,
BLUEBIRD
EMBLEM OF
LIGHT BLUE
FELT.

BACK

FRONT

PLACE ON FOLD

• FRONT

RED TWILL
BLUE BIRD VEST

ON FRONT:
2 WHITE PEARL
BUTTONS OVER
2 SNAPS

×

10" TINY TERRI LEE

NAVY BLUE TWILL
BLUE BIRD
CAMPFIRE GIRL SKIRT

CUT 4

WAISTBAND IS BIAS TAPE.
SEW SNAP FASTENER.

16" TERRI LEE GIRL SCOUT

PLACE ON FOLD

GIRL SCOUT UNIFORM
SLEEVE

GIRL SCOUT
UNIFORM
SKIRT BACK
CUT 1

ADD 1/4" SEAM
ALLOWANCE

GIRL SCOUT
UNIFORM
SKIRT FRONT
CUT 2

FOLD OVER FOR FRONT FACING

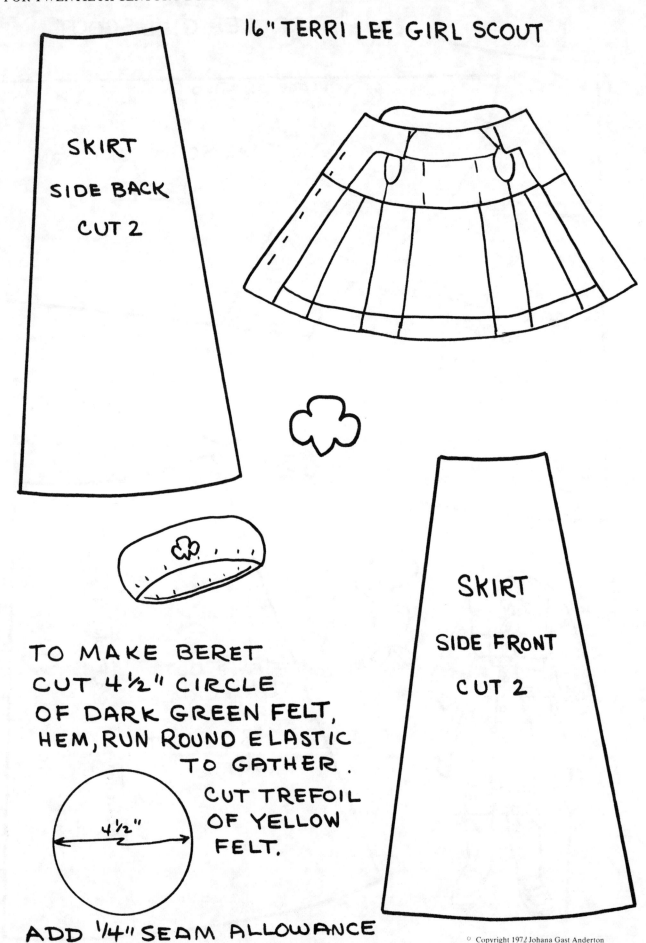

16" TERRI LEE GIRL SCOUT

SKIRT

SIDE BACK

CUT 2

SKIRT

SIDE FRONT

CUT 2

TO MAKE BERET
CUT 4½" CIRCLE
OF DARK GREEN FELT,
HEM, RUN ROUND ELASTIC
TO GATHER.
CUT TREFOIL
OF YELLOW
FELT.

4½"

ADD ¼" SEAM ALLOWANCE

184

16" TERRI LEE GIRL SCOUT

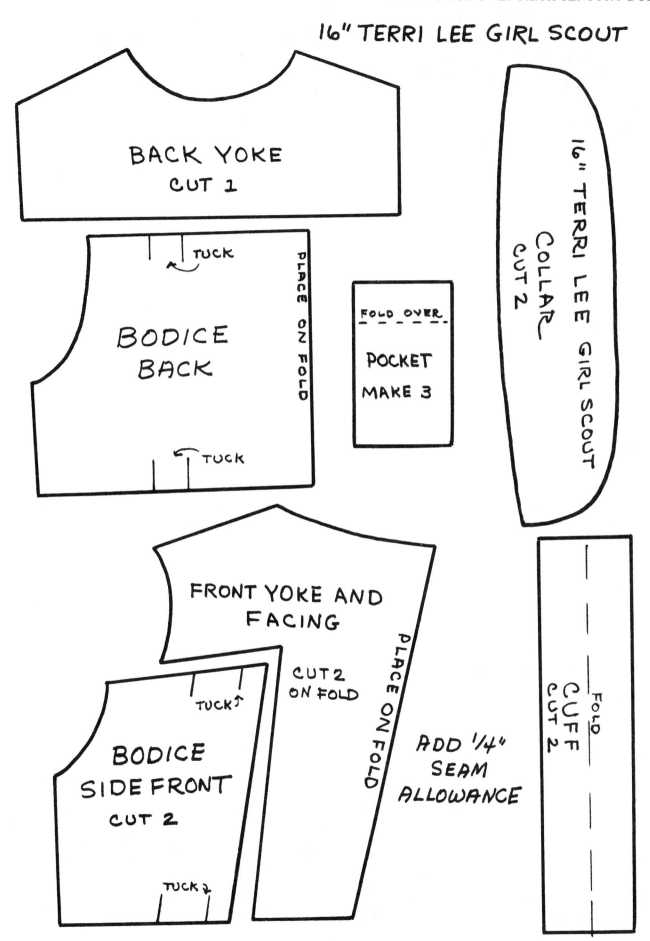

BACK YOKE
CUT 1

TUCK

BODICE
BACK

PLACE ON FOLD

TUCK

FOLD OVER

POCKET
MAKE 3

16" TERRI LEE GIRL SCOUT
COLLAR
CUT 2

FRONT YOKE AND
FACING

CUT 2
ON FOLD

TUCK

BODICE
SIDE FRONT
CUT 2

TUCK

PLACE ON FOLD

ADD 1/4"
SEAM
ALLOWANCE

FOLD
CUFF
CUT 2

TUCK

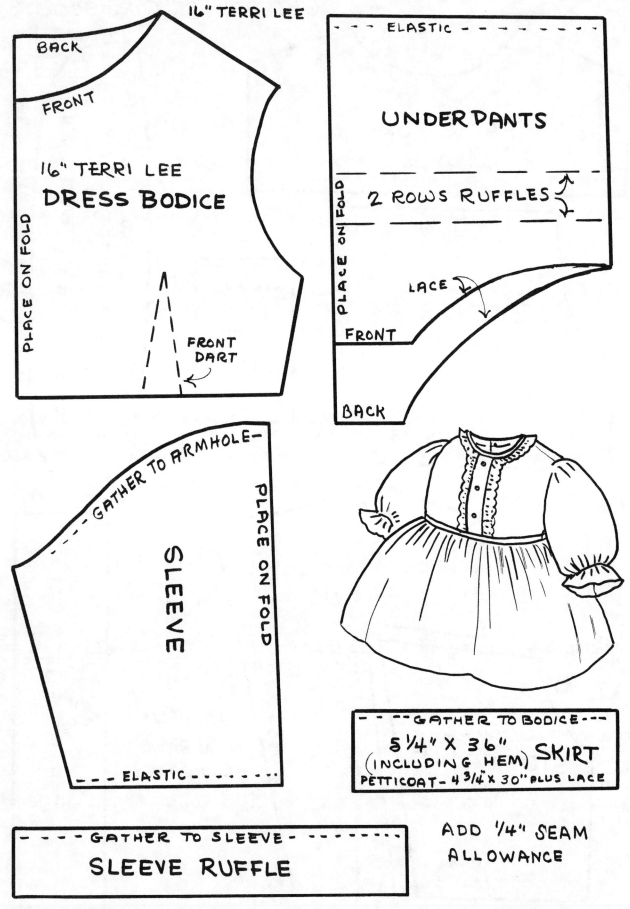

16" TERRI LEE

BACK

FRONT

16" TERRI LEE
DRESS BODICE

PLACE ON FOLD

FRONT
DART

— ELASTIC —

UNDERPANTS

PLACE ON FOLD

2 ROWS RUFFLES

LACE

FRONT

BACK

GATHER TO ARMHOLE

SLEEVE

PLACE ON FOLD

ELASTIC

GATHER TO SLEEVE
SLEEVE RUFFLE

GATHER TO BODICE
5¼" x 36"
(INCLUDING HEM) SKIRT
PETTICOAT- 4¾" x 30" PLUS LACE

ADD ¼" SEAM
ALLOWANCE

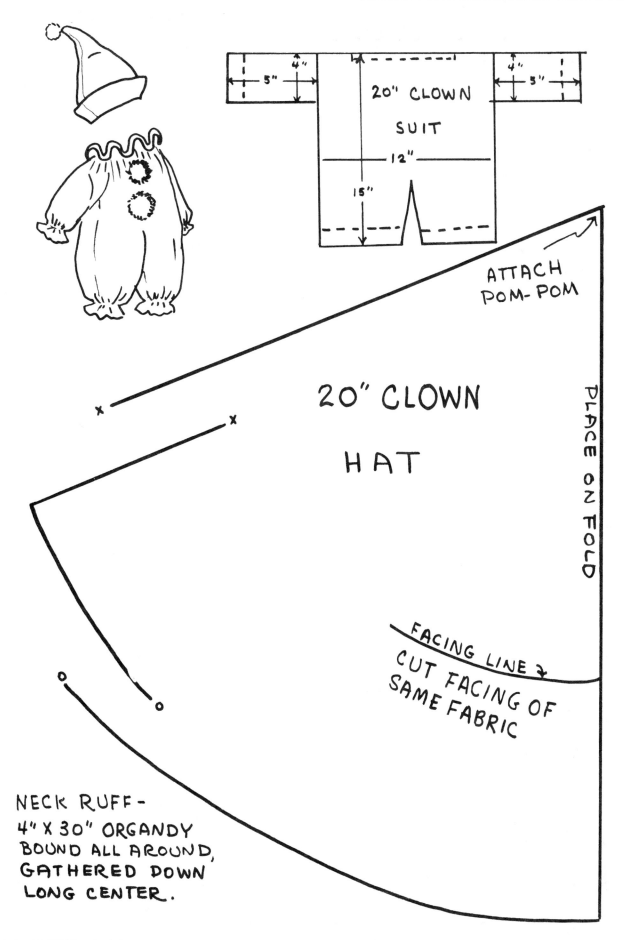

20" CLOWN
SUIT

4"

5"

4"

5"

12"

15"

ATTACH
POM- POM

PLACE ON FOLD

20" CLOWN

HAT

FACING LINE

CUT FACING OF
SAME FABRIC

NECK RUFF-
4" X 30" ORGANDY
BOUND ALL AROUND,
GATHERED DOWN
LONG CENTER.

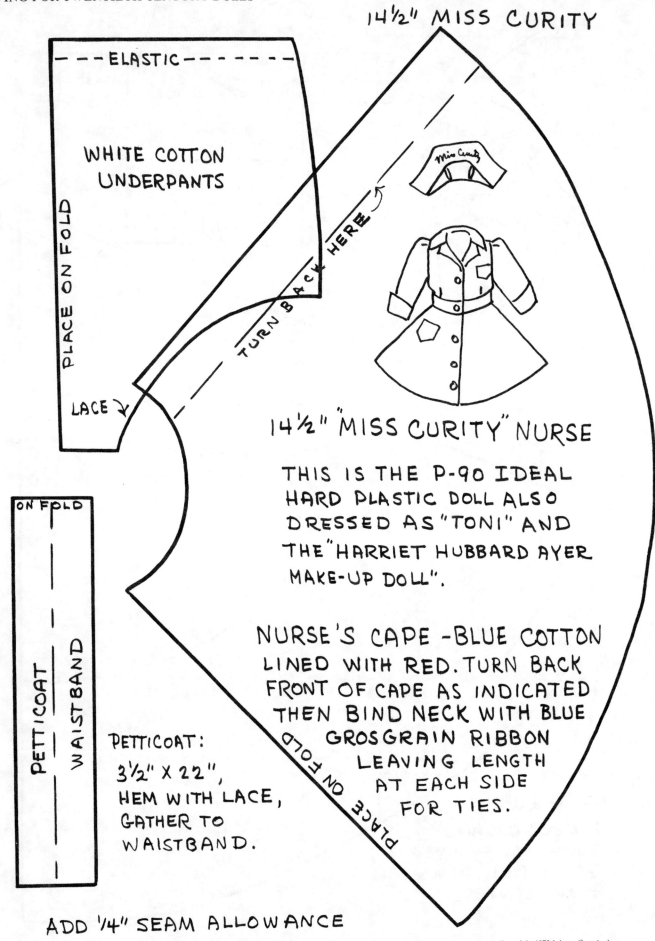

14½" MISS CURITY

ELASTIC

WHITE COTTON UNDERPANTS

PLACE ON FOLD

TURN BACK HERE

LACE

14½" "MISS CURITY" NURSE

THIS IS THE P-90 IDEAL HARD PLASTIC DOLL ALSO DRESSED AS "TONI" AND THE "HARRIET HUBBARD AYER MAKE-UP DOLL".

NURSE'S CAPE - BLUE COTTON LINED WITH RED. TURN BACK FRONT OF CAPE AS INDICATED THEN BIND NECK WITH BLUE GROSGRAIN RIBBON LEAVING LENGTH AT EACH SIDE FOR TIES.

ON FOLD

PETTICOAT WAISTBAND

PETTICOAT:
3½" X 22",
HEM WITH LACE,
GATHER TO
WAISTBAND.

PLACE ON FOLD

ADD ¼" SEAM ALLOWANCE

188

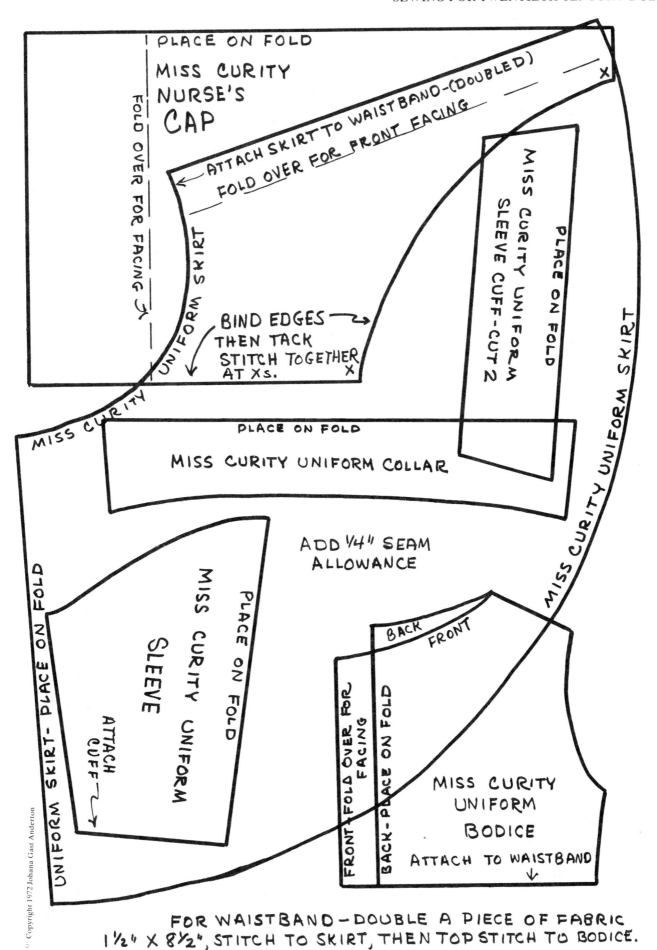

PLACE ON FOLD

MISS CURITY
NURSE'S
CAP

FOLD OVER FOR FACING

ATTACH SKIRT TO WAISTBAND-(DOUBLED)

FOLD OVER FOR FRONT FACING

MISS CURITY UNIFORM SKIRT

BIND EDGES
THEN TACK
STITCH TOGETHER
AT Xs.

X

MISS CURITY UNIFORM
SLEEVE CUFF-CUT 2

PLACE ON FOLD

MISS CURITY UNIFORM SKIRT

MISS CURITY

PLACE ON FOLD

MISS CURITY UNIFORM COLLAR

ADD ¼" SEAM
ALLOWANCE

UNIFORM SKIRT- PLACE ON FOLD

MISS CURITY UNIFORM
SLEEVE

ATTACH
CUFF

PLACE ON FOLD

BACK   FRONT

FRONT-FOLD OVER FOR FACING

BACK- PLACE ON FOLD

MISS CURITY
UNIFORM
BODICE

ATTACH TO WAISTBAND
↓

FOR WAISTBAND-DOUBLE A PIECE OF FABRIC
1½" X 8½", STITCH TO SKIRT, THEN TOP STITCH TO BODICE.

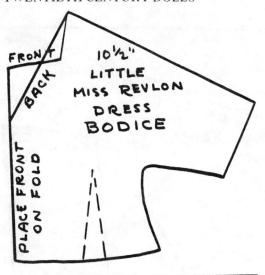

FRONT
BACK

10½"
LITTLE
MISS REVLON
DRESS
BODICE

PLACE FRONT ON FOLD

GATHER TO BODICE ⤴
SKIRT

FOR SKIRT CUT RECTANGLE 4" X 24". ORIGINAL DRESS IS RED WITH WHITE DOTS AND WHITE BIAS BINDING AT NECK AND CUFFS, WHITE FRILL AT THROAT.

5" CIRCLE, DOUBLE AND TOP-STITCHED MAKES "PICTURE HAT".

10½"
LITTLE MISS
REVLON

ALL-PURPOSE
BODICE

←1½→

ALSO FIT 10½" TONI

10½"
LITTLE MISS
REVLON

TOREADOR
PANTS

CUT 4

MAY BE EXTENDED FOR ANKLE PANTS →

COMBINE ALL-PURPOSE BODICE:

1. WITH 10" DIA. CIRCLE SKIRT FOR DAYTIME DRESS.

2. WITH 15" DIA. CIRCLE SKIRT FOR EVENING DRESS.

3. WITH 15" DIA. CIRCLE FOR WEDDING VEIL AND 15" DIA. CIRCLE SKIRT FOR WEDDING DRESS.

ADD ¼" SEAM ALLOWANCE

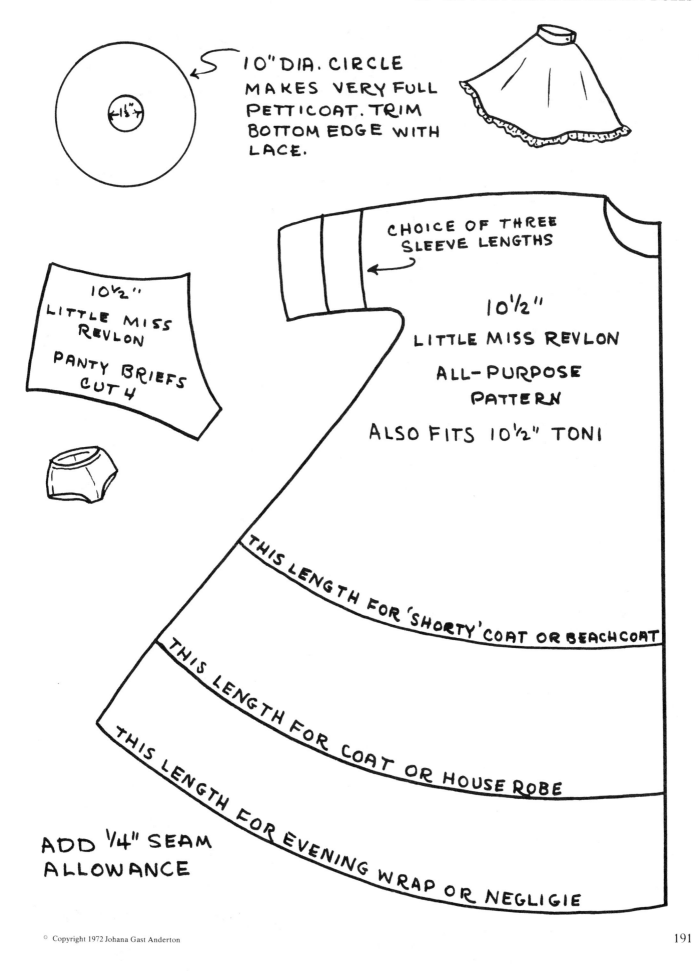

10" DIA. CIRCLE MAKES VERY FULL PETTICOAT. TRIM BOTTOM EDGE WITH LACE.

10½"
LITTLE MISS REVLON
PANTY BRIEFS
CUT 4

CHOICE OF THREE SLEEVE LENGTHS

10½"
LITTLE MISS REVLON
ALL-PURPOSE
PATTERN

ALSO FITS 10½" TONI

THIS LENGTH FOR 'SHORTY' COAT OR BEACHCOAT

THIS LENGTH FOR COAT OR HOUSE ROBE

THIS LENGTH FOR EVENING WRAP OR NEGLIGIE

ADD ¼" SEAM ALLOWANCE

18"
MISS REVLON
"QUEEN of DIAMONDS"

DRESS BODICE

LINE WITH FINE
COTTON

PLACE FRONT ON FOLD

BACK HAS
THREE EVENLY
SPACED SNAPS.

SLEEVE BAND
FOLD OVER
CUT 2
ON FOLD

JEWELRY, NYLON STOCKINGS
WITH SEAMS, AND HIGH
HEELED PLASTIC SANDALS
COMPLETE THE OUTFIT.

"QUEEN of DIAMONDS"

RED VELVETEEN DRESS WITH
PINK RAYON SASH AND 'BOAT'
NECKLINE.

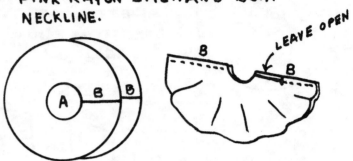

LEAVE OPEN

TO MAKE SKIRT OF DRESS:
CUT 2 CIRCLES 13" DIA.
CUT OUT CIRCLE 1½" DIA. FROM
CENTER OF EACH (A). CUT ALONG
LINE (B). STITCH THE TWO 13"
DIA. CIRCLES TOGETHER ALONG
LINES (B), LEAVING ONE OPEN
1½". ATTACH TO LINED BODICE.

ADD ¼" SEAM ALLOWANCE

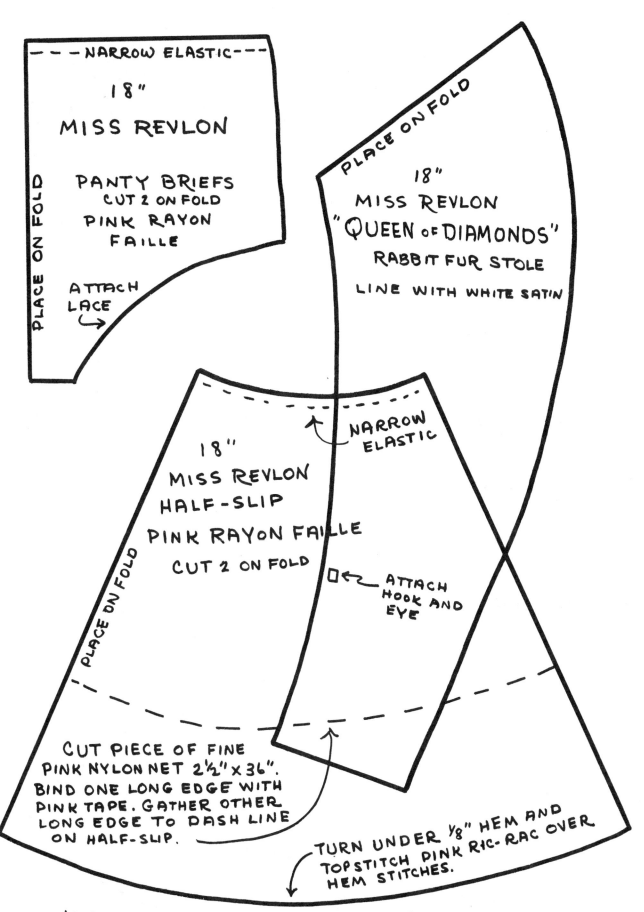

- - - NARROW ELASTIC - - -

18"

MISS REVLON

PANTY BRIEFS
CUT 2 ON FOLD
PINK RAYON
FAILLE

ATTACH
LACE

PLACE ON FOLD

PLACE ON FOLD

18"

MISS REVLON
"QUEEN of DIAMONDS"

RABBIT FUR STOLE

LINE WITH WHITE SATIN

NARROW
ELASTIC

18"

MISS REVLON
HALF-SLIP

PINK RAYON FAILLE

CUT 2 ON FOLD

PLACE ON FOLD

ATTACH
HOOK AND
EYE

CUT PIECE OF FINE
PINK NYLON NET 2½" X 36".
BIND ONE LONG EDGE WITH
PINK TAPE. GATHER OTHER
LONG EDGE TO DASH LINE
ON HALF-SLIP.

TURN UNDER ⅛" HEM AND
TOPSTITCH PINK RIC-RAC OVER
HEM STITCHES.

ADD ¼" SEAM ALLOWANCE

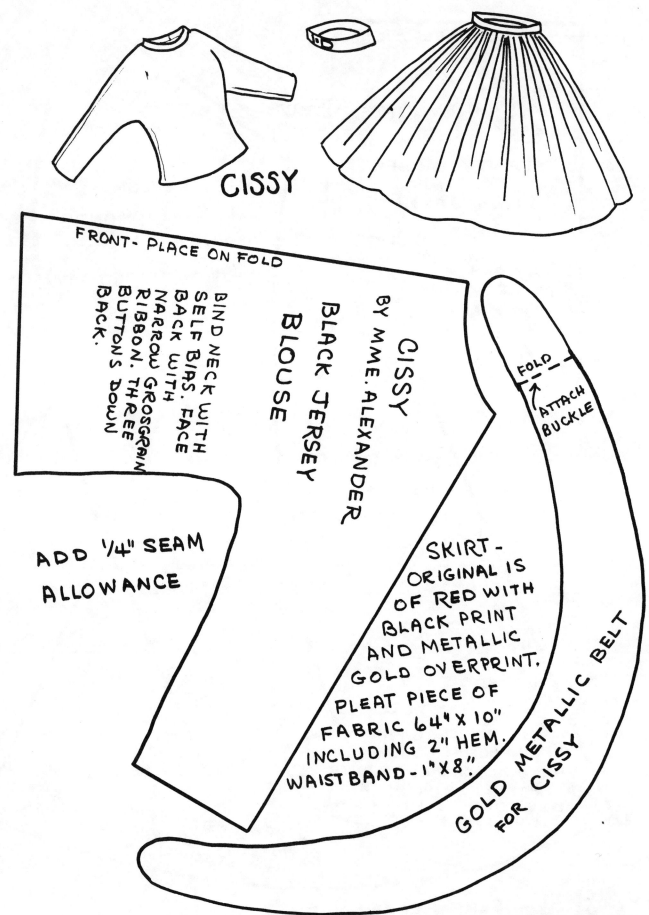

CISSY

FRONT- PLACE ON FOLD

CISSY
BY MME. ALEXANDER

BLACK JERSEY
BLOUSE

BIND NECK WITH
SELF BIAS. FACE
BACK WITH
NARROW GROSGRAIN
RIBBON. THREE
BUTTONS DOWN
BACK.

ADD ¼" SEAM
ALLOWANCE

FOLD
ATTACH
BUCKLE

SKIRT-
ORIGINAL IS
OF RED WITH
BLACK PRINT
AND METALLIC
GOLD OVERPRINT,
PLEAT PIECE OF
FABRIC 64"X 10"
INCLUDING 2" HEM.
WAISTBAND-1"X8."

GOLD METALLIC BELT
FOR CISSY

194

**23" SWEET SUE GIRL
PARTY DRESS**

This dress, found on an old store stock doll, never played with, is of salmon-pink organdy with white flocked dots. Lower sleeves and under-bodice, which makes a dickey effect at front, are of white organdy with salmon-pink flocked dots.

Skirt is 10½ inches by 54 inches long, including a 2½ inch hem. Lace is sewn flat along hem line. Bows are black velvet ribbon, each with a rhinestone set on one tab.

Lower sleeves 3 inches by 12 inches, edged with lace and stitched with elastic thread one-fourth inch from lower edge, and gathered to lower edge of sleeve along other long edge.

Sash is a strip of plain white organdy measuring 3 and three-fourths inches by 45 inches, with the tips angled and a very narrow hem all around.

To complete this outfit a big garden party hat may be made from the same two flock-dotted organdy fabrics, using the white for facing. Cut circles 14 inches in diameter, cut out circles for crown to fit your doll's head, edge with lace, tie with white organdy tie of same measurements as dress tie. This hat is not original to the doll, but would complement the outfit.

195

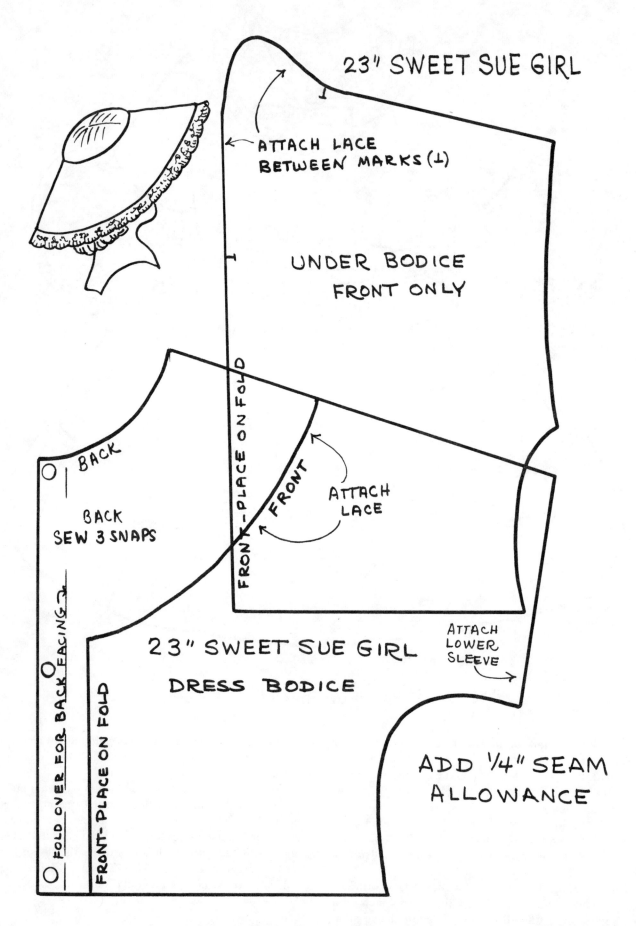

23" SWEET SUE GIRL

ATTACH LACE
BETWEEN MARKS (⊥)

UNDER BODICE
FRONT ONLY

BACK

BACK
SEW 3 SNAPS

FRONT — PLACE ON FOLD

FRONT

ATTACH
LACE

ATTACH
LOWER
SLEEVE

23" SWEET SUE GIRL

DRESS BODICE

FOLD OVER FOR BACK FACING

FRONT — PLACE ON FOLD

ADD ¼" SEAM
ALLOWANCE

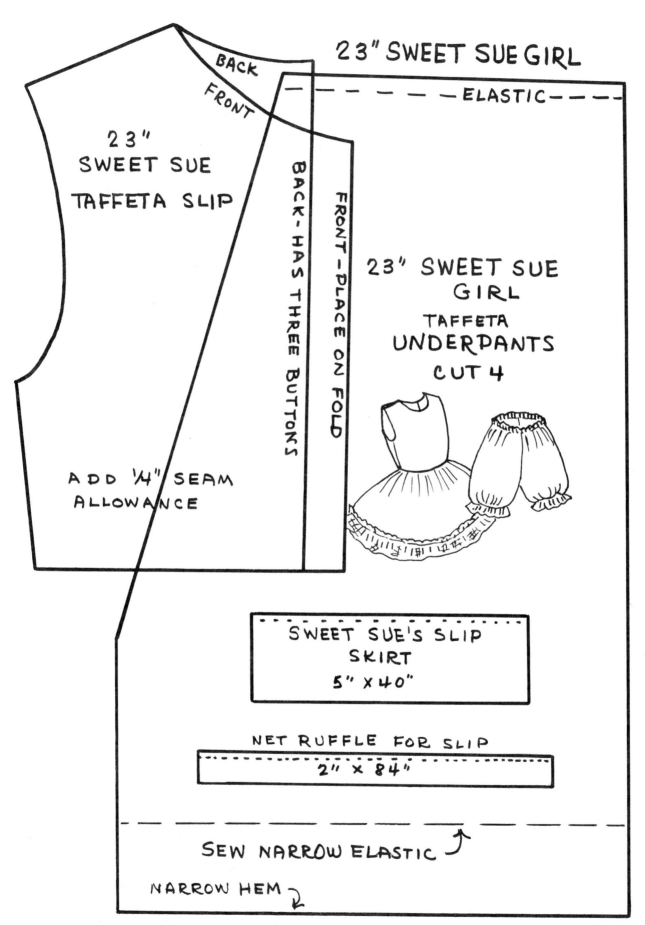

23" SWEET SUE GIRL

BACK

FRONT

--- ELASTIC ---

23"
SWEET SUE
TAFFETA SLIP

BACK—HAS THREE BUTTONS

FRONT—PLACE ON FOLD

23" SWEET SUE
GIRL
TAFFETA
UNDERPANTS
CUT 4

ADD ¼" SEAM
ALLOWANCE

SWEET SUE'S SLIP
SKIRT
5" × 40"

NET RUFFLE FOR SLIP
2" × 84"

SEW NARROW ELASTIC

NARROW HEM

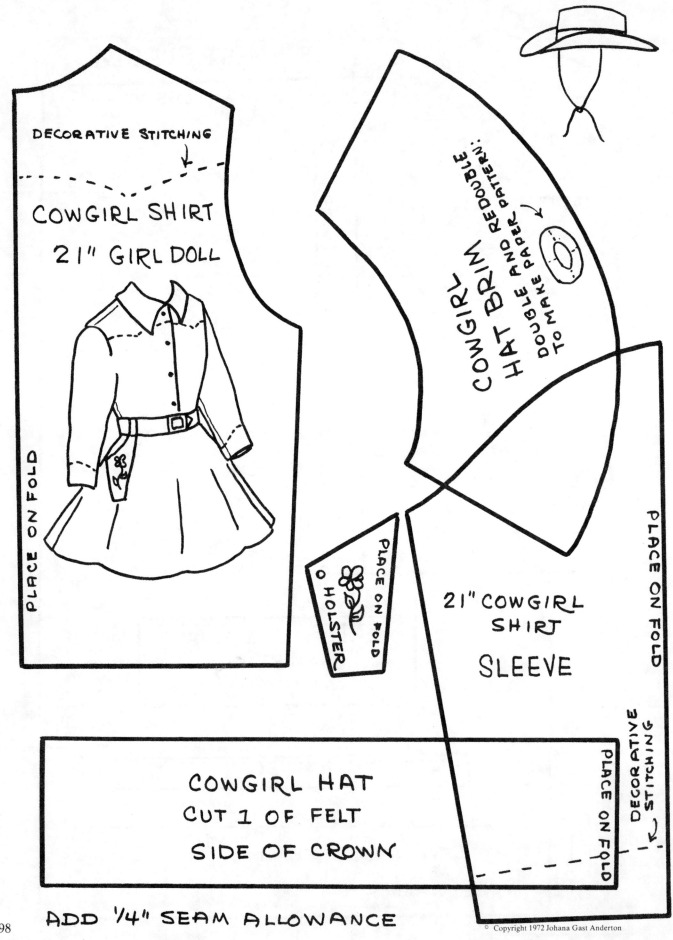

DECORATIVE STITCHING

COWGIRL SHIRT
21" GIRL DOLL

PLACE ON FOLD

COWGIRL HAT BRIM

REDOUBLE: DOUBLE PAPER PATTERN TO MAKE

O HOLSTER

PLACE ON FOLD

21" COWGIRL SHIRT
SLEEVE

PLACE ON FOLD

PLACE ON FOLD

DECORATIVE STITCHING

COWGIRL HAT
CUT 1 OF FELT
SIDE OF CROWN

ADD ¼" SEAM ALLOWANCE

198

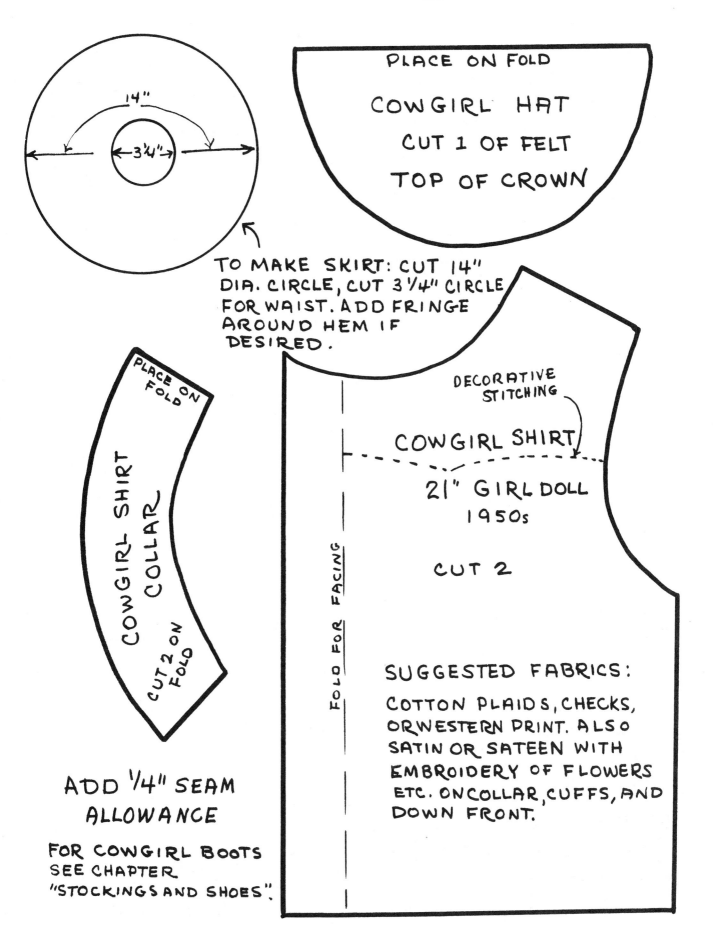

14"

3¼"

TO MAKE SKIRT: CUT 14"
DIA. CIRCLE, CUT 3¼" CIRCLE
FOR WAIST. ADD FRINGE
AROUND HEM IF
DESIRED.

PLACE ON FOLD

COWGIRL HAT
CUT 1 OF FELT
TOP OF CROWN

PLACE ON FOLD

COWGIRL SHIRT COLLAR
CUT 2 ON FOLD

DECORATIVE STITCHING

COWGIRL SHIRT

21" GIRL DOLL
1950s

CUT 2

FOLD FOR FACING

SUGGESTED FABRICS:

COTTON PLAIDS, CHECKS,
OR WESTERN PRINT. ALSO
SATIN OR SATEEN WITH
EMBROIDERY OF FLOWERS
ETC. ON COLLAR, CUFFS, AND
DOWN FRONT.

ADD ¼" SEAM
ALLOWANCE

FOR COWGIRL BOOTS
SEE CHAPTER
"STOCKINGS AND SHOES".

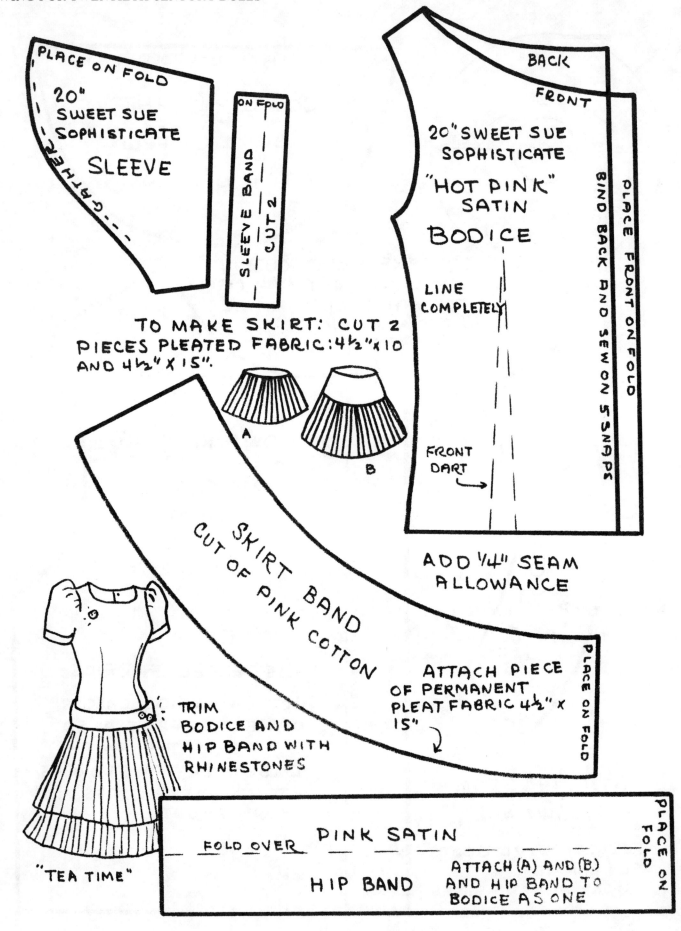

PLACE ON FOLD

20"
SWEET SUE
SOPHISTICATE
SLEEVE

←GATHER→

ON FOLD

SLEEVE BAND
CUT 2

BACK

FRONT

20" SWEET SUE
SOPHISTICATE
"HOT PINK"
SATIN
BODICE

LINE
COMPLETELY

FRONT
DART

BIND BACK AND SEW ON 5 SNAPS

PLACE FRONT ON FOLD

ADD ¼" SEAM
ALLOWANCE

TO MAKE SKIRT: CUT 2
PIECES PLEATED FABRIC: 4½" X 10
AND 4½" X 15".

A

B

SKIRT BAND
CUT OF PINK COTTON

ATTACH PIECE
OF PERMANENT
PLEAT FABRIC 4½" X
15"

PLACE ON FOLD

TRIM
BODICE AND
HIP BAND WITH
RHINESTONES

"TEA TIME"

FOLD OVER   PINK SATIN

HIP BAND

ATTACH (A) AND (B)
AND HIP BAND TO
BODICE AS ONE

PLACE ON FOLD

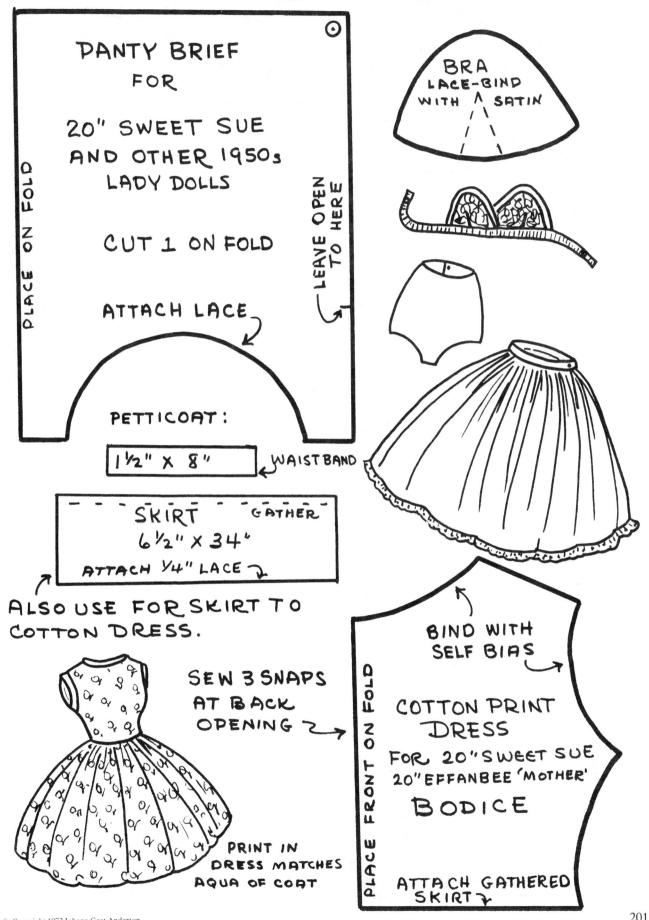

PANTY BRIEF
FOR

20" SWEET SUE
AND OTHER 1950s
LADY DOLLS

CUT 1 ON FOLD

PLACE ON FOLD

LEAVE OPEN TO HERE

ATTACH LACE

PETTICOAT:

1½" X 8"

WAISTBAND

SKIRT
6½" X 34"
GATHER
ATTACH ¼" LACE

ALSO USE FOR SKIRT TO
COTTON DRESS.

SEW 3 SNAPS
AT BACK
OPENING

PRINT IN
DRESS MATCHES
AQUA OF COAT

BRA
LACE-BIND
WITH SATIN

BIND WITH
SELF BIAS

PLACE FRONT ON FOLD

COTTON PRINT
DRESS
FOR 20" SWEET SUE
20" EFFANBEE 'MOTHER'
BODICE

ATTACH GATHERED
SKIRT

201

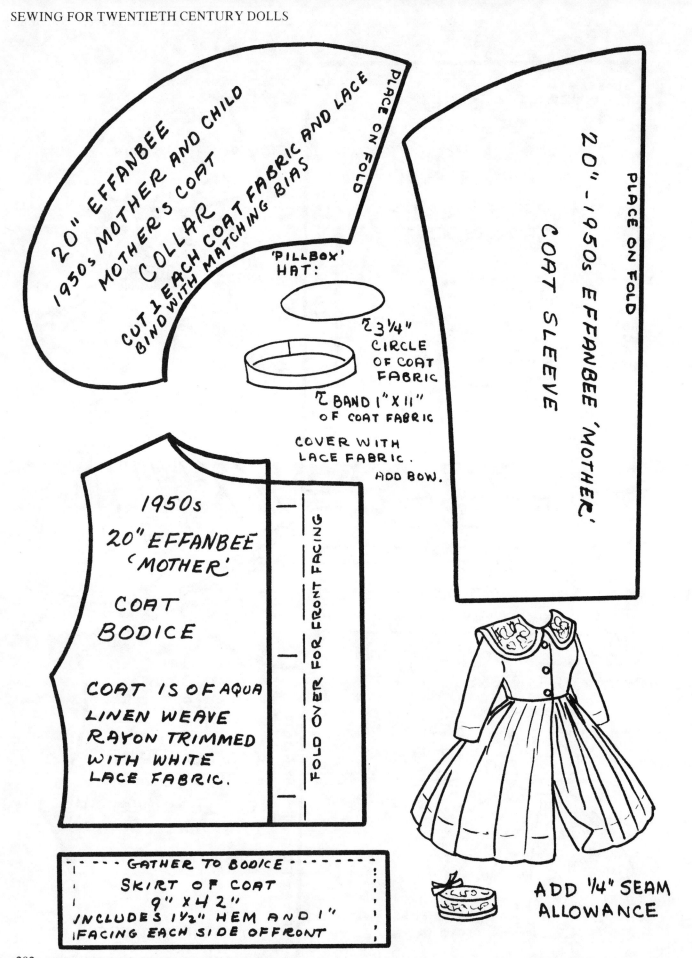

20" EFFANBEE
1950s MOTHER AND CHILD
MOTHER'S COAT
COLLAR
CUT 1 EACH COAT FABRIC AND LACE
BIND WITH MATCHING BIAS

PLACE ON FOLD

20" - 1950s EFFANBEE 'MOTHER'
COAT SLEEVE

PLACE ON FOLD

'PILLBOX' HAT:

3¼" CIRCLE OF COAT FABRIC

BAND 1" X 11" OF COAT FABRIC

COVER WITH LACE FABRIC.
ADD BOW.

1950s
20" EFFANBEE
'MOTHER'
COAT BODICE

COAT IS OF AQUA LINEN WEAVE RAYON TRIMMED WITH WHITE LACE FABRIC.

FOLD OVER FOR FRONT FACING

GATHER TO BODICE
SKIRT OF COAT
9" X 42"
INCLUDES 1½" HEM AND 1"
FACING EACH SIDE OF FRONT

ADD ¼" SEAM ALLOWANCE

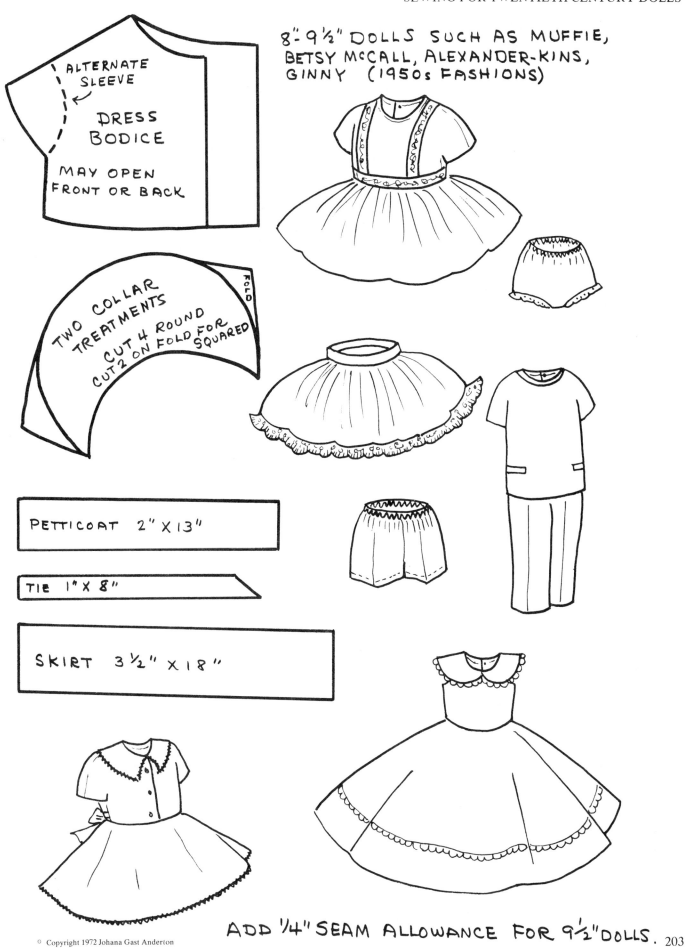

ALTERNATE SLEEVE

DRESS BODICE

MAY OPEN FRONT OR BACK

8"-9½" DOLLS SUCH AS MUFFIE, BETSY McCALL, ALEXANDER-KINS, GINNY (1950s FASHIONS)

TWO COLLAR TREATMENTS

CUT 4 ROUND
CUT 2 ON FOLD FOR SQUARED

FOLD

PETTICOAT 2" X 13"

TIE 1" X 8"

SKIRT 3½" X 18"

ADD ¼" SEAM ALLOWANCE FOR 9½" DOLLS.

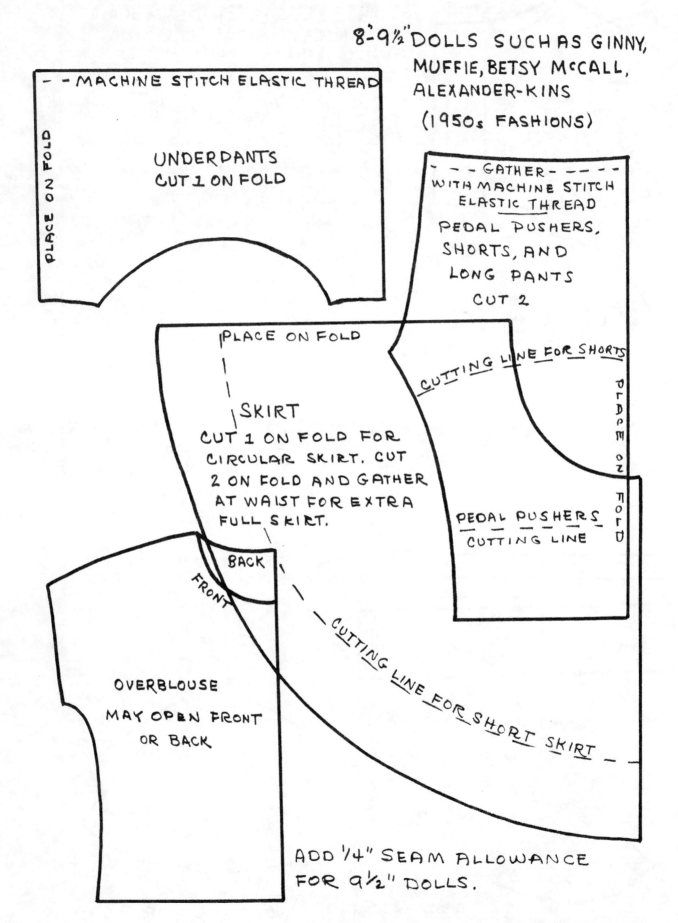

8"-9½" DOLLS SUCH AS GINNY, MUFFIE, BETSY McCALL, ALEXANDER-KINS

(1950s FASHIONS)

- - MACHINE STITCH ELASTIC THREAD

PLACE ON FOLD

UNDERPANTS
CUT 1 ON FOLD

- - - GATHER - - - -
WITH MACHINE STITCH
ELASTIC THREAD
PEDAL PUSHERS,
SHORTS, AND
LONG PANTS
CUT 2

PLACE ON FOLD

SKIRT
CUT 1 ON FOLD FOR
CIRCULAR SKIRT. CUT
2 ON FOLD AND GATHER
AT WAIST FOR EXTRA
FULL SKIRT.

CUTTING LINE FOR SHORTS

PLACE ON FOLD

PEDAL PUSHERS
CUTTING LINE

BACK

FRONT

OVERBLOUSE

MAY OPEN FRONT
OR BACK

CUTTING LINE FOR SHORT SKIRT

ADD ¼" SEAM ALLOWANCE
FOR 9½" DOLLS.

17" RICKEY JR.

FRONT

BACK

RICKEY JR.'s
SHIRT

BLUE AND WHITE
STRIPES

BACK-PLACE ON FOLD

FRONT FACING LINE

RICKEY JR.'s
YELLOW
CORDUROY
CRAWLERS

CUT 2 ON FOLD

SHOULDER STRAPS - CUT 2 ON FOLD

PLACE ON FOLD

PLACE ON FOLD

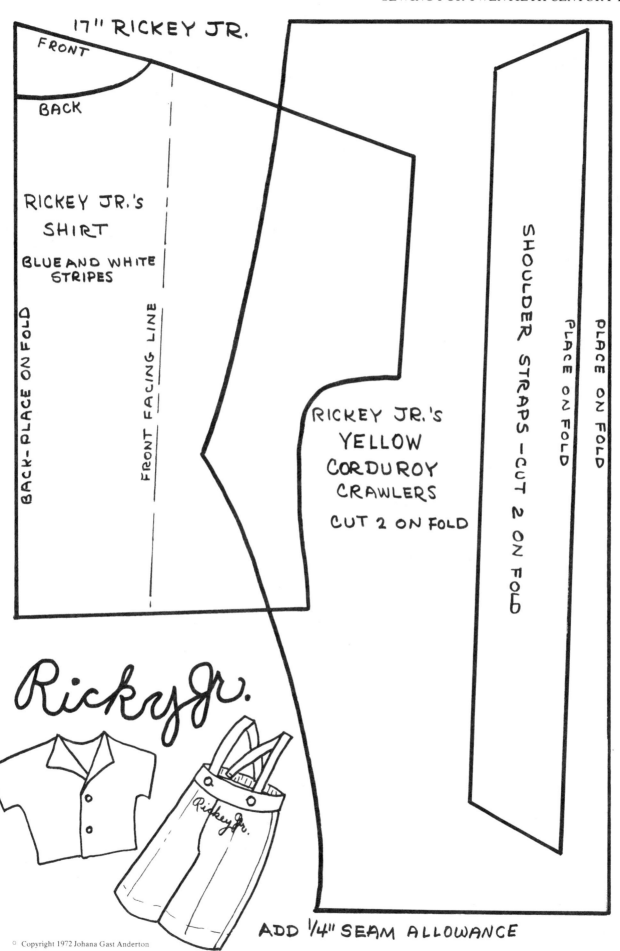

Ricky Jr.

Ricky Jr.

ADD 1/4" SEAM ALLOWANCE

205

THE 1960s

The 1960s saw a swing in fashion from the lady-like styles of the early decade to the kooky, kicky, swingy fads of the later years. Chanel suits with their box jackets and slim skirts, more or less classic sportswear, and slim, basic dinner dresses marked the early years. A return to the styles of other decades created a potpourri of fashion later in the period.

Granny dresses of calico, gingham, and even permanent press fabrics, were a counterpoint to the mini dresses which were no longer than absolutely necessary. Every length in between was considered acceptable and sleeve treatments were just as varied. Juliet sleeves on blouses were popular, as well as leg-o-mutton, and the full bell sleeve, often finished off with a ruffle created by running elastic several inches above the hem. Skirts were short and straight or short and full. Lounge wear became important with the introduction of *at-home* clothes. These ranged from lounging pajamas and hostess pajamas to hostess coats and blouse and skirt separates.

Pantsuits became a symbol of woman's emancipation from the traditional role to a widening circle of interests and activities. Few women failed to include at least one pantsuit or pantdress in their wardrobes. Comfort and utility were two of the factors which contributed to the popularity of this fashion.

Probably one of the most important changes in dress in many years occured in this decade. New fabrics, new fibres, and more importantly, the advent of *permanent press* fabrics offered possibilities heretofore unknown. Many women, freed at last from the tyranny of the ironing board, were able to step into new roles as volunteer workers or even into careers. It is true that permanent press alone did not affect these changes; however, permanent press fabrics coupled with other technological advances in home appliances have wrought great changes in modern life.

The dolls of this decade were fashion's darlings. *Chatty Cathy,* The *Dr. Littlechap Family, Barbie* and her friends, *Penny Brite, Suzy Cute,* and *Coquette* were all products of the early decade. These dolls not only had extensive wardrobes, but also were fully equipped with homes, automobiles, swimming pools, offices, sports equipment and every imaginable accessory.

The dolls of the late years of the 1960s were led by *Beautiful Crissy,* from Ideal. *Crissy* had growing hair, a slender, pre-teen figure, and an up-to-the-minute wardrobe. She was later joined by several other dolls her size (17½") and a smaller version (15"), an equally stylish young lady named *Velvet.*

The reader may note the absence of patterns for *Barbie* and similar dolls. Patterns for this type doll have been marketed commercially almost since the introduction of the doll and it seemed advisable to use the space to better advantage. *Tammy* patterns may be adjusted slightly to fit *Barbie* and other teen-type dolls.

THE LITTLECHAP FAMILY
by Remco (1963)

DR. JOHN'S BUSINESS SUIT

Dark brown suit, three button jacket with narrow lapels, slim tapered slacks, white classic shirt.

Accessories: Striped blue and brown slim tie, black shoes, black socks, pipe and tobacco pouch.

DR. JOHN'S TUXEDO

Black dress suit, satin lapels and dress trousers with satin stripe. White sheer shirt with pleated front and pearl studs.

Accessories: Black bowtie, black satin pleated cummerbund, black socks, black shoes, black wallet, and white carnation.

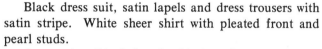

DR. JOHN'S ALL-WEATHER COAT

Natural twill coat for rain or shine lined in red, beige and black cotton plaid.

Accessories: Brown hat, red scarf, doctor's bag containing tongue depressor, fountain pen, stethoscope, hypodermic needle, pill bottles, and doctor's mallet.

DR. JOHN'S WARDROBE

DR. JOHN'S GOLF OUTFIT

White wool cardigan sweater, black jersey polo shirt, red twill golf slacks.

Accessories: Plaid cap, two golf clubs, golf balls, golf trophy, black socks, black shoes.

DR. JOHN'S MEDICAL TUNIC AND SLACKS

White oxford cloth slacks and tunic with stand-up collar and side closing of regulation white metal snaps.

Accessories: White shoes, white socks, stethoscope, tongue depressor, fountain pen, wristwatch and doctor's bag.

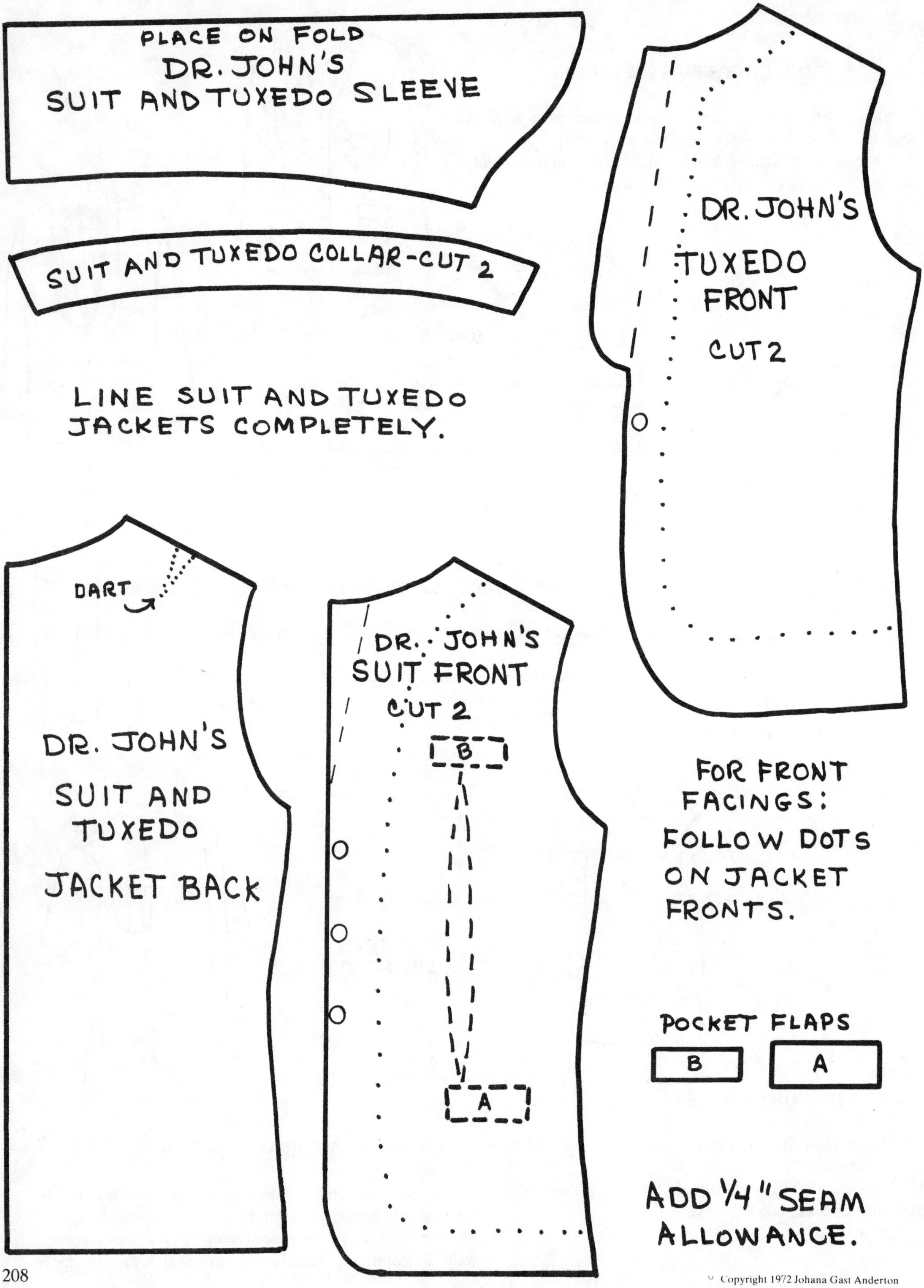

PLACE ON FOLD
DR. JOHN'S
SUIT AND TUXEDO SLEEVE

SUIT AND TUXEDO COLLAR-CUT 2

LINE SUIT AND TUXEDO
JACKETS COMPLETELY.

DR. JOHN'S
TUXEDO
FRONT
CUT 2

DART

DR. JOHN'S
SUIT AND
TUXEDO
JACKET BACK

DR. JOHN'S
SUIT FRONT
CUT 2

B

A

FOR FRONT
FACINGS:
FOLLOW DOTS
ON JACKET
FRONTS.

POCKET FLAPS

B   A

ADD ¼" SEAM
ALLOWANCE.

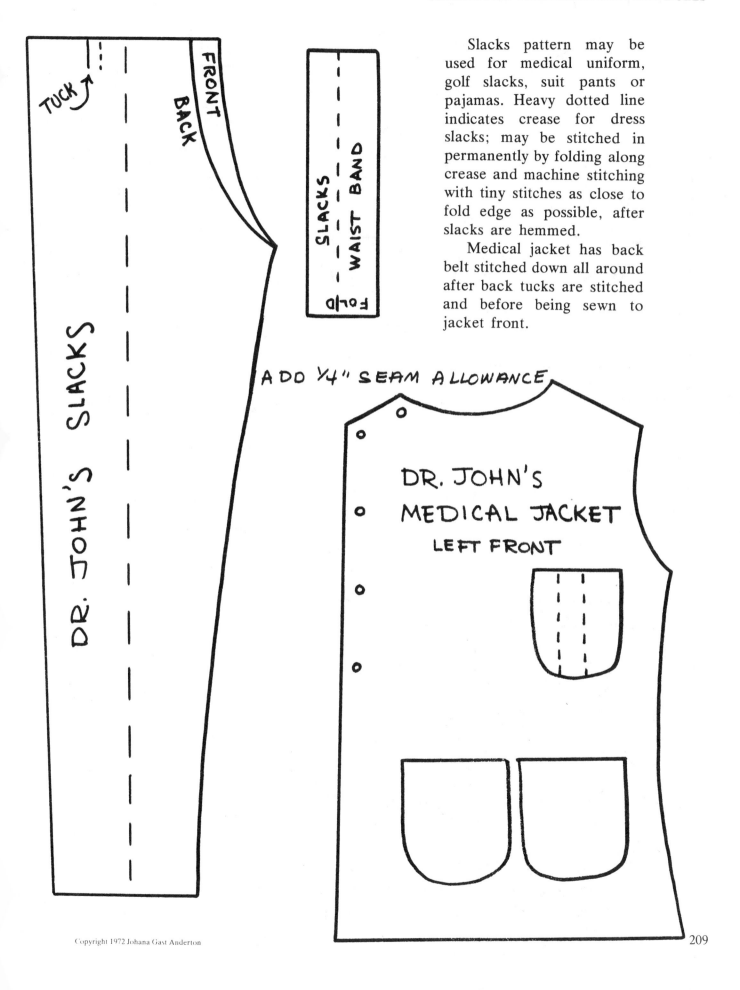

TUCK

FRONT
BACK

DR. JOHN'S SLACKS

SLACKS WAIST BAND

FOLD

Slacks pattern may be used for medical uniform, golf slacks, suit pants or pajamas. Heavy dotted line indicates crease for dress slacks; may be stitched in permanently by folding along crease and machine stitching with tiny stitches as close to fold edge as possible, after slacks are hemmed.

Medical jacket has back belt stitched down all around after back tucks are stitched and before being sewn to jacket front.

ADD ¼" SEAM ALLOWANCE

DR. JOHN'S
MEDICAL JACKET
LEFT FRONT

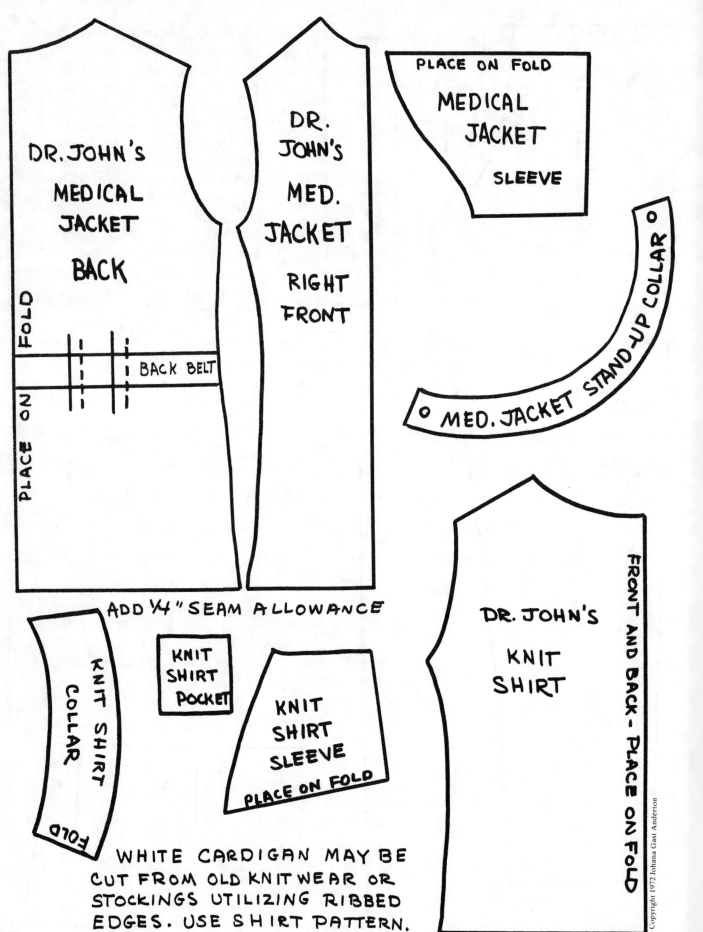

DR. JOHN'S MEDICAL JACKET BACK

PLACE ON FOLD

DR. JOHN'S MED. JACKET RIGHT FRONT

PLACE ON FOLD

MEDICAL JACKET SLEEVE

O MED. JACKET STAND-UP COLLAR O

BACK BELT

ADD ¼" SEAM ALLOWANCE

KNIT SHIRT COLLAR

FOLD

KNIT SHIRT POCKET

KNIT SHIRT SLEEVE

PLACE ON FOLD

DR. JOHN'S KNIT SHIRT

FRONT AND BACK - PLACE ON FOLD

WHITE CARDIGAN MAY BE CUT FROM OLD KNITWEAR OR STOCKINGS UTILIZING RIBBED EDGES. USE SHIRT PATTERN.

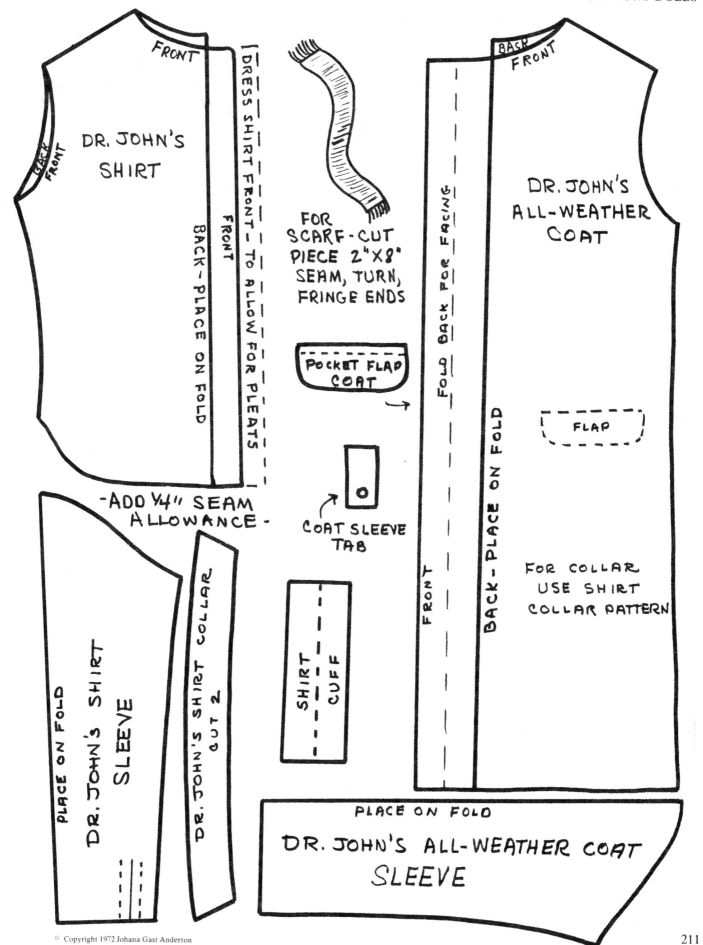

FRONT

DR. JOHN'S
SHIRT

BACK

FRONT

BACK - PLACE ON FOLD

FRONT

DRESS SHIRT FRONT - TO ALLOW FOR PLEATS

FOR
SCARF - CUT
PIECE 2"X8"
SEAM, TURN,
FRINGE ENDS

POCKET FLAP
COAT

COAT SLEEVE
TAB

BACK FRONT

DR. JOHN'S
ALL - WEATHER
COAT

FOLD BACK FOR FACING

FRONT

BACK - PLACE ON FOLD

FLAP

FOR COLLAR
USE SHIRT
COLLAR PATTERN

- ADD ¼" SEAM
ALLOWANCE -

PLACE ON FOLD

DR. JOHN'S SHIRT
SLEEVE

DR. JOHN'S SHIRT COLLAR
CUT 2

SHIRT
CUFF

PLACE ON FOLD
DR. JOHN'S ALL - WEATHER COAT
SLEEVE

LISA'S WHITE TWO-PIECE DRESS

Completely lined two-piece dress with slim skirt and V-necked, long-sleeved overblouse belted in tawny beige suede with gold buckle.

Accessories: Tawny beige printed chiffon scarf, golden tan pumps, golden tan leatherette over-sized tote bag, gold sunburst pin and gold button earrings, beige gloves.

LISA'S FUR-TRIMMED SUEDE COAT

Slim line wrap-around coat in tawny suede cloth, trimmed in creamy beige fake fur with a sheared fur look, matching taffeta lining.

Accessories: Matching fake fur hat, golden tan pumps, large golden tan leatherette tote bag, beige gloves.

LISA'S THREE-PIECE CHANEL SUIT

Straight, slim skirt and box jacket of brown crepe with blue binding, trim, and lining with matching sleeveless blue blouse.

Accessories: Brown fake alligator handbag, gold button earrings, beige gloves, shopping bag, shoes.

LISA'S LINGERIE

Black lace bra, black tricot half-slip with lace trim and matching black lace-trimmed panties, nylon stockings.

LISA'S FORMAL EVENING ENSEMBLE

Sweeping full length coat of blue satin, lined in silver and blue patterned brocade. Standaway portrait neckline, deep cuffs of white ermine-like fur, long slim blue satin evening skirt with fishtail hemline, fitted overblouse with scoop neckline and slim straps of blue and silver brocade.

Accessories: Silver slippers, silver clutch bag, drop earrings, hair ornament, beautiful necklace, opera length white nylon gloves.

LISA'S BASIC BLACK DRESS

Fully-lined black crepe dress, slim skirt, high-waisted effect accented with black velvet bow.

Accessories: Black clutch bag, pearl button earrings, opera length pearl necklace, black pumps, white nylon gloves, black velvet hairbow with net veil.

212

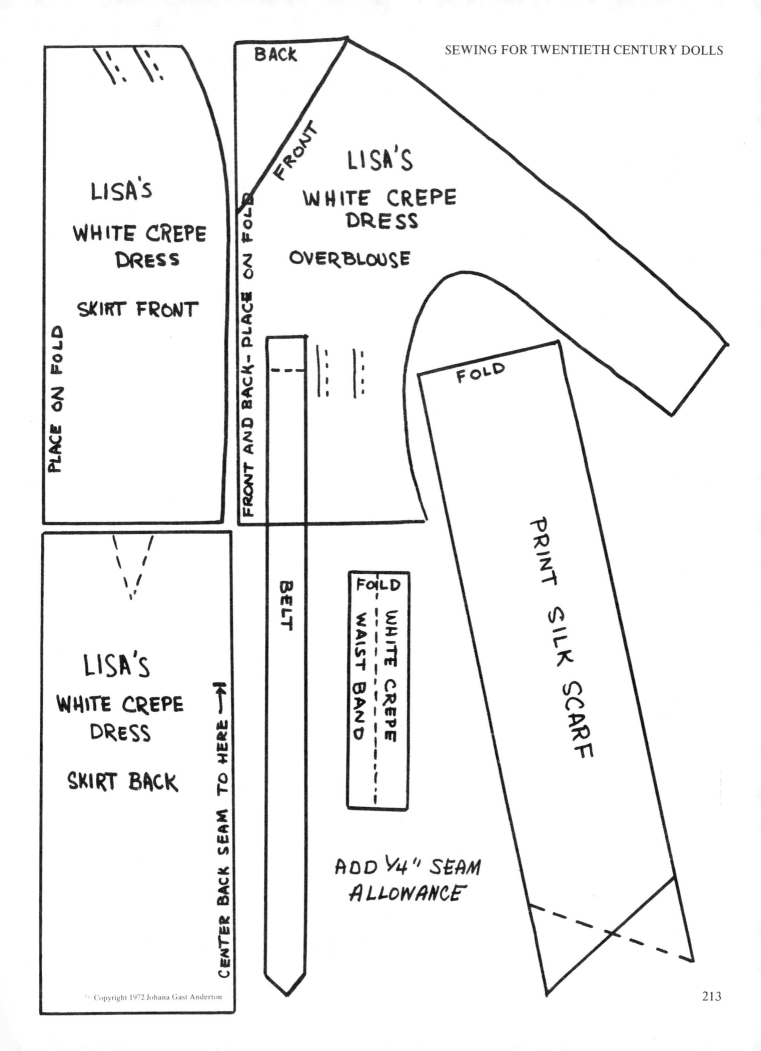

BACK

FRONT

LISA'S
WHITE CREPE
DRESS

SKIRT FRONT

PLACE ON FOLD

FRONT AND BACK—PLACE ON FOLD

LISA'S
WHITE CREPE
DRESS

OVERBLOUSE

FOLD

PRINT SILK SCARF

BELT

LISA'S
WHITE CREPE
DRESS

SKIRT BACK

CENTER BACK SEAM TO HERE →

FOLD

WHITE CREPE
WAIST BAND

ADD ¼" SEAM
ALLOWANCE

BACK

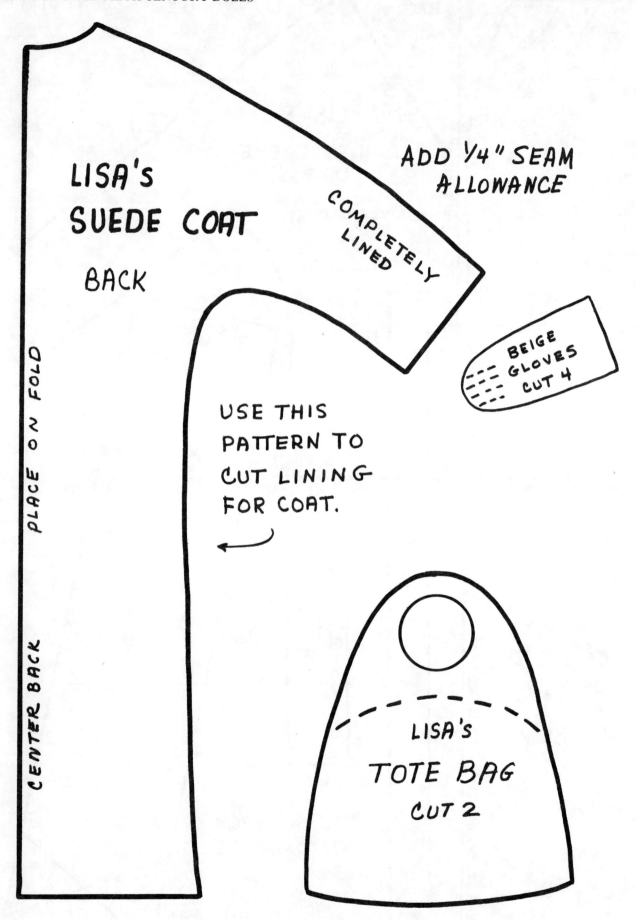

LISA's
SUEDE COAT

BACK

ADD ¼" SEAM
ALLOWANCE

COMPLETELY
LINED

BEIGE
GLOVES
CUT 4

USE THIS
PATTERN TO
CUT LINING
FOR COAT.

PLACE ON FOLD

CENTER BACK

LISA's
TOTE BAG

CUT 2

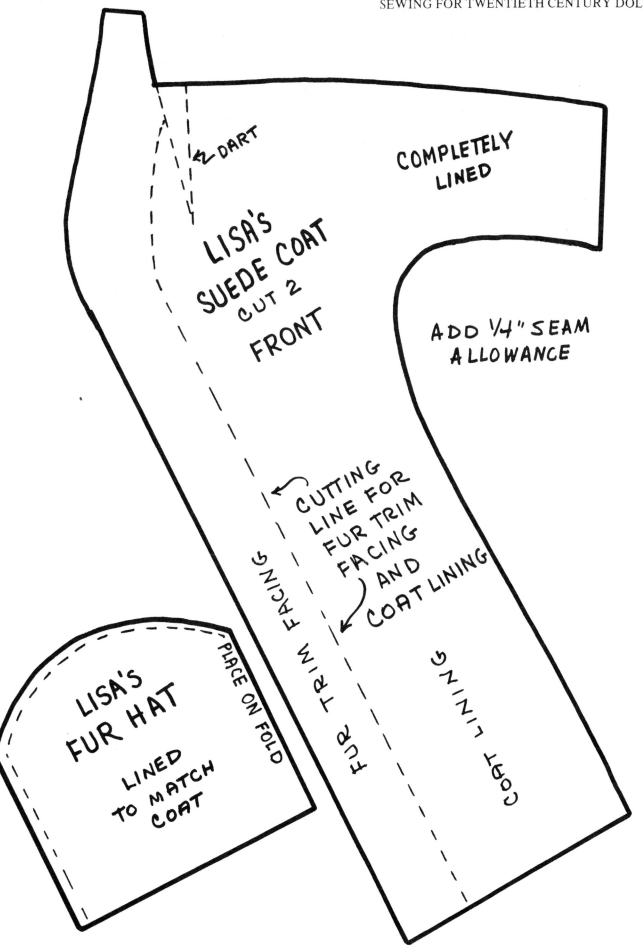

DART

COMPLETELY
LINED

LISA'S
SUEDE COAT
CUT 2
FRONT

ADD 1/4" SEAM
ALLOWANCE

CUTTING
LINE FOR
FUR TRIM
FACING
AND
COAT LINING

FUR TRIM FACING

PLACE ON FOLD

LISA'S
FUR HAT

LINED
TO MATCH
COAT

COAT LINING

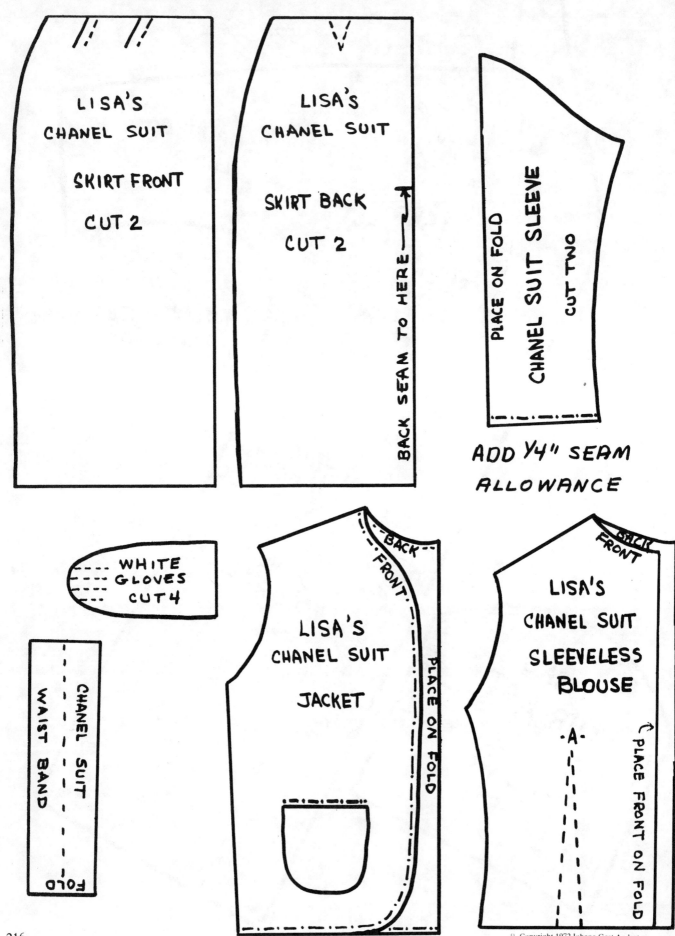

LISA'S
CHANEL SUIT

SKIRT FRONT

CUT 2

LISA'S
CHANEL SUIT

SKIRT BACK

CUT 2

BACK SEAM TO HERE

PLACE ON FOLD

CHANEL SUIT SLEEVE

CUT TWO

ADD ¼" SEAM
ALLOWANCE

WHITE
GLOVES
CUT 4

CHANEL SUIT WAIST BAND

FOLD

LISA'S
CHANEL SUIT

JACKET

BACK

FRONT

PLACE ON FOLD

BACK

FRONT

LISA'S
CHANEL SUIT
SLEEVELESS
BLOUSE

-A-

PLACE FRONT ON FOLD

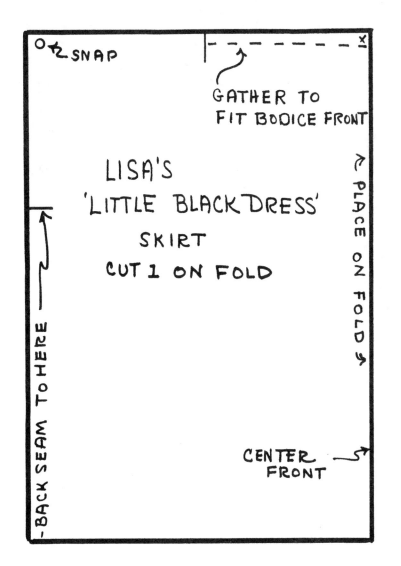

o←₂ SNAP

GATHER TO
FIT BODICE FRONT

LISA'S
'LITTLE BLACK DRESS'
SKIRT
CUT 1 ON FOLD

← PLACE ON FOLD →

- BACK SEAM TO HERE -

CENTER
FRONT

← PLACE ON FOLD →
LISA'S 'LITTLE BLACK
DRESS'
SLEEVE

HAT IS BAND OF
BLACK VELVET
RIBBON TRIMMED
WITH BIT OF
FINE NET.

ADD ¼" SEAM ALLOWANCE

LISA'S
'LITTLE BLACK
DRESS'
BODICE
FRONT

← PLACE ON FOLD →

YY

XX

SNAPS →o

LISA'S
'LITTLE BLACK
DRESS'
BODICE
BACK
CUT 1
ON FOLD

o

o

CENTER
FRONT

PLACE ON
FOLD

YY

UNDERARM

o

MAKE WHITE DRESS GLOVES
BY CUTTING FINGERS
FROM DISCARDED NYLON
GLOVES. HEM TO DESIRED
LENGTH.

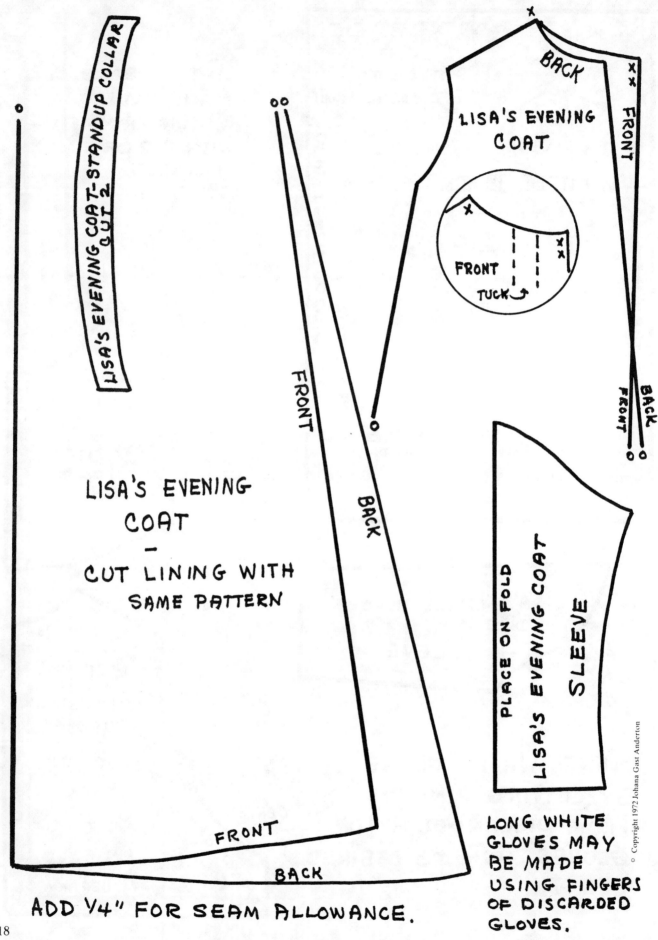

LISA'S EVENING COAT–STANDUP COLLAR CUT 2

LISA'S EVENING COAT

LISA'S EVENING COAT

CUT LINING WITH SAME PATTERN

FRONT

BACK

FRONT

BACK

BACK

FRONT

FRONT

BACK

FRONT TUCK

PLACE ON FOLD

LISA'S EVENING COAT SLEEVE

LONG WHITE GLOVES MAY BE MADE USING FINGERS OF DISCARDED GLOVES.

ADD ¼" FOR SEAM ALLOWANCE.

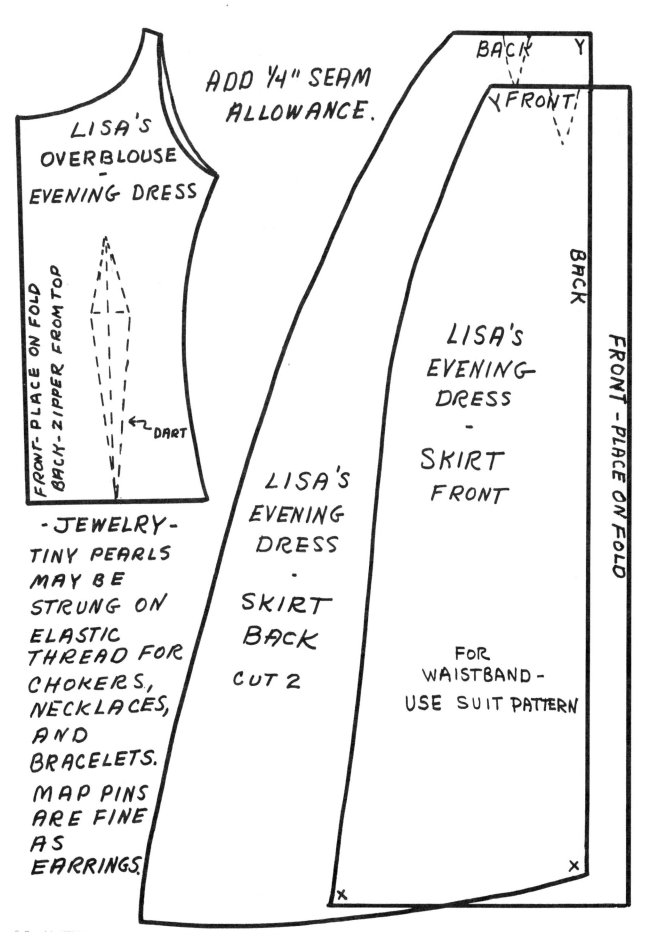

ADD ¼" SEAM ALLOWANCE.

LISA'S OVERBLOUSE - EVENING DRESS

FRONT - PLACE ON FOLD
BACK - ZIPPER FROM TOP

← DART

-JEWELRY-
TINY PEARLS MAY BE STRUNG ON ELASTIC THREAD FOR CHOKERS, NECKLACES, AND BRACELETS. MAP PINS ARE FINE AS EARRINGS.

LISA'S EVENING DRESS - SKIRT BACK CUT 2

LISA'S EVENING DRESS - SKIRT FRONT

BACK Y

Y FRONT

BACK

FRONT - PLACE ON FOLD

FOR WAISTBAND - USE SUIT PATTERN

X

X

JUDY'S PARTY DRESS

Bright pink moire sleeveless dress with low, scooped neckline, bell-shaped skirt and large flat bow.

Accessories: Pink ballet slippers, gold clutch bag, pearl choker, pearl bracelet, pearl button earrings, white nylon shortie gloves.

JUDY'S SPORTSWEAR OUTFIT

Box-pleated, knee tickler skirt (made to be worn above knees) in cream, gray, gold and brown houndstooth check, gold suede jerkin, beige shirt with panel front.

Accessories: Deep red, tie-print triangle headscarf, brown loafers, gold knee socks, gold pin, black framed eyeglasses and play scripe.

JUDY'S RED CHESTERFIELD COAT

Basketweave tweed, pimento red, semi-fitted coat with matching velvet notched collar and lapels, matching red taffeta lining.

Accessories: Leopard print velveteen pillbox hat, ascot, pouch handbag, golden hatpin, beige gloves, black pumps, paper shopping bag containing three colorful packages.

JUDY'S THREE-PIECE SUIT

Red waist-length matador jacket with flap pockets piped in navy, red lining, flared skirt, pencil-striped sleeveless shirt with pert bow.

Accessories: Navy pumps, white shortie nylon gloves, gold button earrings, red tote bag.

JUDY'S DANCE DRESS

Two-piece ensemble with yellow taffeta sleeveless, scooped neckline dance dress, belted in dainty floral embroidered French ribbon, matching yellow velveteen waist-length jacket bound in same French ribbon.

Accessories: Gold ballet slippers, gold clutch bag, pearl choker, white nylon shortie gloves, hair corsage; of red rose on bobby pin in clear plastic flower box, green chiffon triangle headscarf.

JUDY'S LINGERIE

Pink lace bra, pink tricot half-slip with lace trim, and matching pink lace-trimmed panties, nylon stockings.

220

JUDY'S PINK PARTY DRESS

Use patterns for bodice and skirt of yellow DANCE DRESS, cutting only two panels of the skirt. Refer to sketches and description of PARTY DRESS. Add flat bow of dress material. Line dress completely with fine sheath lining.

JUDY'S YELLOW VELVETEEN DANCE DRESS JACKET SLEEVE — LINED — CUT FOUR

- - - GATHER - - - TO FIT BODICE

JUDY'S

YELLOW DANCE DRESS

SKIRT

CUT FOUR

LINED

ADD ¼" SEAM ALLOWANCE

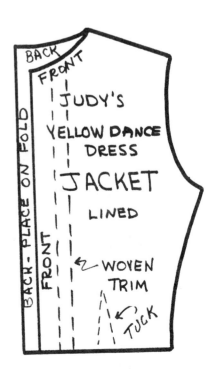

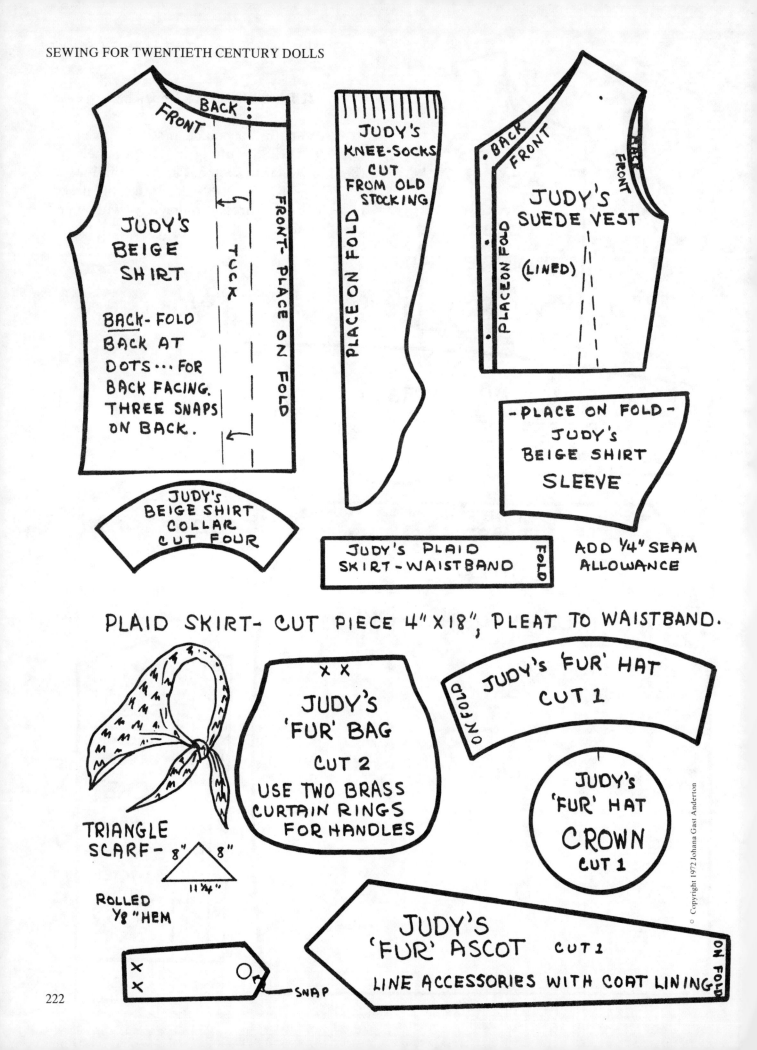

FRONT BACK

JUDY'S BEIGE SHIRT

BACK- FOLD BACK AT DOTS... FOR BACK FACING. THREE SNAPS ON BACK.

TUCK

FRONT- PLACE ON FOLD

JUDY'S BEIGE SHIRT COLLAR CUT FOUR

JUDY'S KNEE-SOCKS CUT FROM OLD STOCKING

PLACE ON FOLD

JUDY'S PLAID SKIRT - WAISTBAND

FOLD

BACK FRONT BACK FRONT

JUDY'S SUEDE VEST

(LINED)

PLACE ON FOLD

-PLACE ON FOLD- JUDY'S BEIGE SHIRT SLEEVE

ADD ¼" SEAM ALLOWANCE

PLAID SKIRT- CUT PIECE 4"X18", PLEAT TO WAISTBAND.

TRIANGLE SCARF- 8" 8" 11¾"

ROLLED ⅛"HEM

XX

JUDY'S 'FUR' BAG

CUT 2

USE TWO BRASS CURTAIN RINGS FOR HANDLES

ON FOLD JUDY'S 'FUR' HAT CUT 1

JUDY'S 'FUR' HAT CROWN CUT 1

XX O SNAP

JUDY'S 'FUR' ASCOT CUT 1

LINE ACCESSORIES WITH COAT LINING

ON FOLD

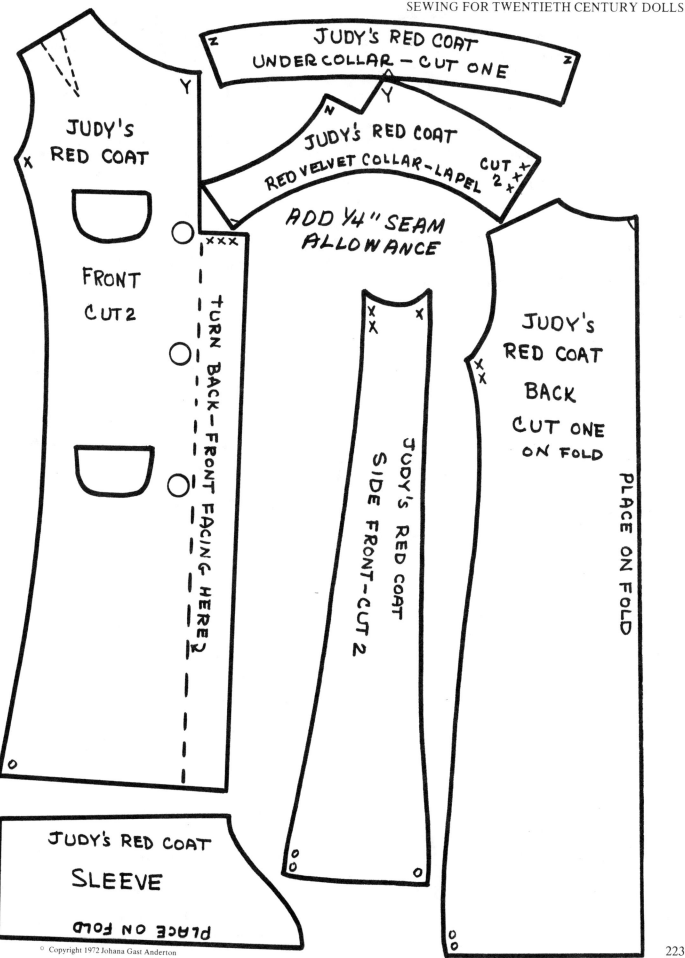

JUDY'S RED COAT
UNDER COLLAR — CUT ONE

JUDY'S RED COAT

RED VELVET COLLAR—LAPEL   CUT 2

ADD ¼" SEAM ALLOWANCE

JUDY'S RED COAT

FRONT CUT 2

TURN BACK—FRONT FACING HERE?

JUDY'S RED COAT
SIDE FRONT—CUT 2

JUDY'S RED COAT
BACK
CUT ONE ON FOLD

PLACE ON FOLD

JUDY'S RED COAT
SLEEVE

PLACE ON FOLD

JUDY'S GORED SKIRT

CUT FOUR

BLOUSE TIE
CUT TWO

BACK

FRONT

JUDY'S STRIPED SLEEVELESS BLOUSE

BACK-PLACE ON FOLD

TUCK FRONT AND BACK

ADD 1/4" SEAM ALLOWANCE

PLACE ON FOLD

JUDY'S RED MATADOR JACKET-SLEEVE

CUT TWO   (LINED)

BACK

FRONT

PLACE ON FOLD

JUDY'S RED MATADOR JACKET

(LINED)

FOLD

SKIRT

WAIST BAND

PURSE HANDLE
CUT TWO

JUDY'S PURSE
CUT TWO

LISA
JUDY
LIBBY

PLACE ON FOLD

BRIEFS

BRA

FOLD

LIBBY'S SLIP BODICE CUT TWO

X   X

XX   XX

HALF-SLIP

FRONT – PLACE ON FOLD

BACK SEAM TO HERE →

JUDY

LISA

ADD ¼" SEAM ALLOWANCE

XX   TUCK TO FIT SLIP BODICE   XX

LIBBY'S SLIP UNDERSKIRT

PLACE ON FOLD

225

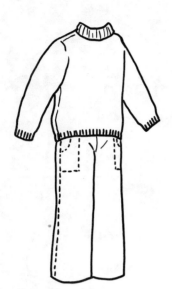

LIBBY'S LEVIS AND SWEATSHIRT

Blue denim levis with fly front and white stitching, classic white sweatshirt.

Accessories: Red and white sneakers, comic book and YoYo, white socks.

LIBBY'S THREE-PIECE BLAZER OUTFIT

Brilliant blue blazer, buttoned in brass with heraldic crest, worn with bright red and blue plaid box-pleated skirt (skirt matches her coat), white tailored shirt blouse.

Accessories: Brown pumps, bright blue knee socks, schoolbook with leatherette strap.

LIBBY'S PLAID REEFER COAT

Bright red and blue plaid, double-breasted coat with patch pockets and self belt.

Accessories: Red, high boots, red knit scarf, red leatherette mittens, red leatherette schoolbag.

LIBBY'S LINGERIE

White tricot lace-trimmed panties, lace-trimmed white cotton slip with petticoat bottom of pleated nylon. A pink puppy came with this set.

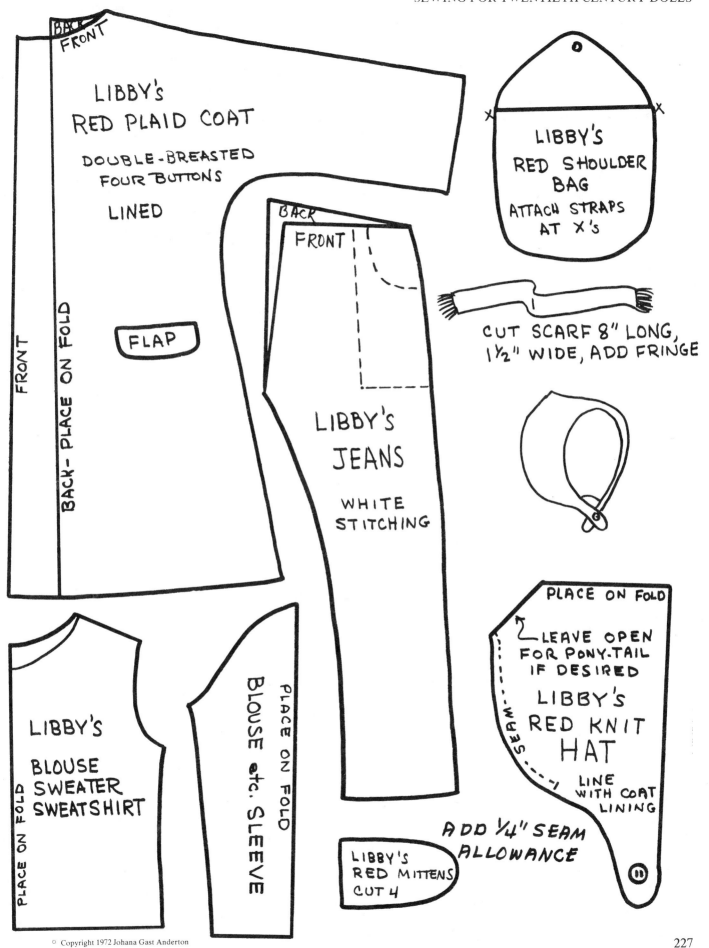

LIBBY'S
RED PLAID COAT

DOUBLE-BREASTED
FOUR BUTTONS

LINED

FRONT

BACK – PLACE ON FOLD

FLAP

BACK
FRONT

LIBBY'S
JEANS

WHITE
STITCHING

LIBBY'S
RED SHOULDER
BAG
ATTACH STRAPS
AT X's

CUT SCARF 8" LONG,
1½" WIDE, ADD FRINGE

PLACE ON FOLD

LEAVE OPEN
FOR PONY-TAIL
IF DESIRED

LIBBY'S
RED KNIT
HAT

SEAM

LINE
WITH COAT
LINING

ADD ¼" SEAM
ALLOWANCE

LIBBY'S
BLOUSE
SWEATER
SWEATSHIRT

PLACE ON FOLD

BLOUSE etc. SLEEVE

PLACE ON FOLD

LIBBY'S
RED MITTENS
CUT 4

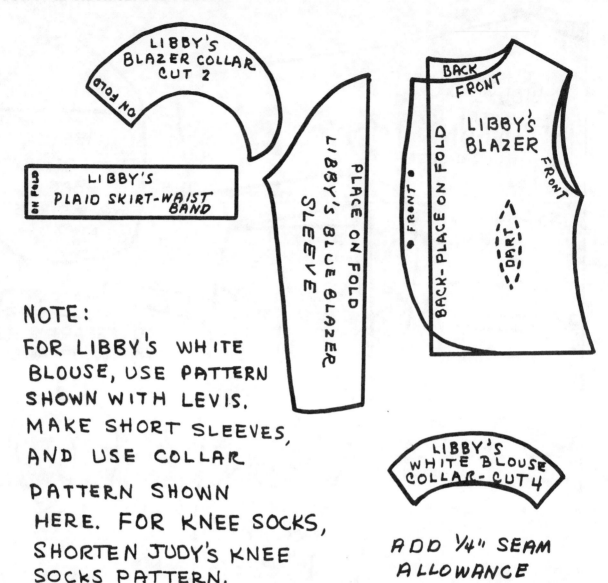

LIBBY'S
BLAZER COLLAR
CUT 2
ON FOLD

LIBBY'S
PLAID SKIRT-WAIST
BAND
ON FOLD

PLACE ON FOLD
LIBBY'S BLUE BLAZER
SLEEVE

BACK
FRONT
LIBBY'S
BLAZER
FRONT
• FRONT •
BACK - PLACE ON FOLD
DART

NOTE:
FOR LIBBY'S WHITE
BLOUSE, USE PATTERN
SHOWN WITH LEVIS.
MAKE SHORT SLEEVES,
AND USE COLLAR
PATTERN SHOWN
HERE. FOR KNEE SOCKS,
SHORTEN JUDY'S KNEE
SOCKS PATTERN.

LIBBY'S
WHITE BLOUSE
COLLAR - CUT 4

ADD ¼" SEAM
ALLOWANCE

— — — LIBBY'S PLAID SKIRT — — — —

PLEAT EVENLY TO
WAIST BAND

THIS PLAID SKIRT MATCHES
LIBBY'S PLAID COAT

PLACE ON FOLD

SUNSUIT for
16" INFANT TOODLES
AND OTHER BABY DOLLS

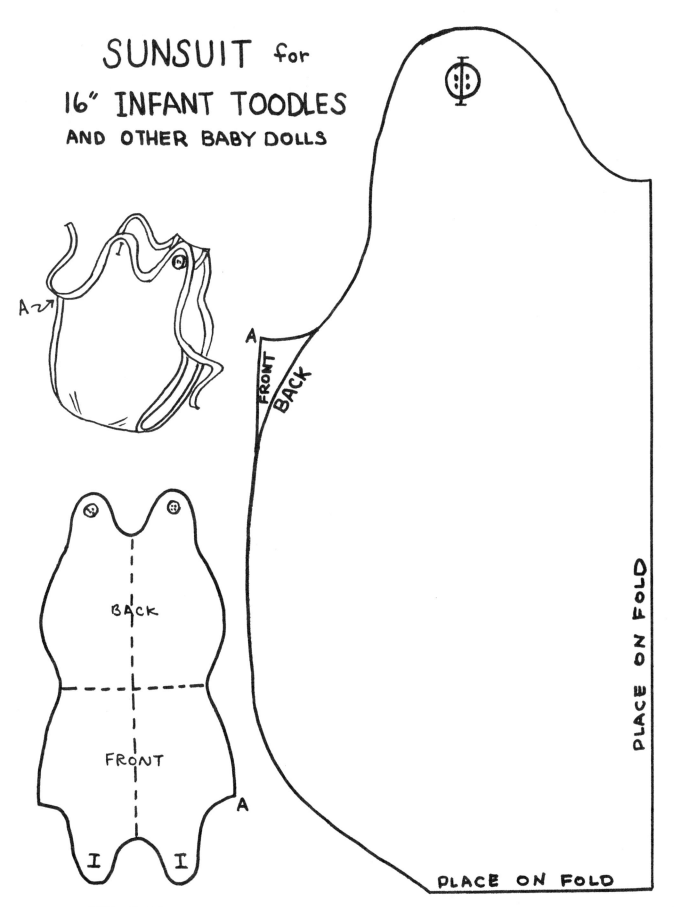

A

FRONT

BACK

PLACE ON FOLD

A

BACK

FRONT

I   I

PLACE ON FOLD

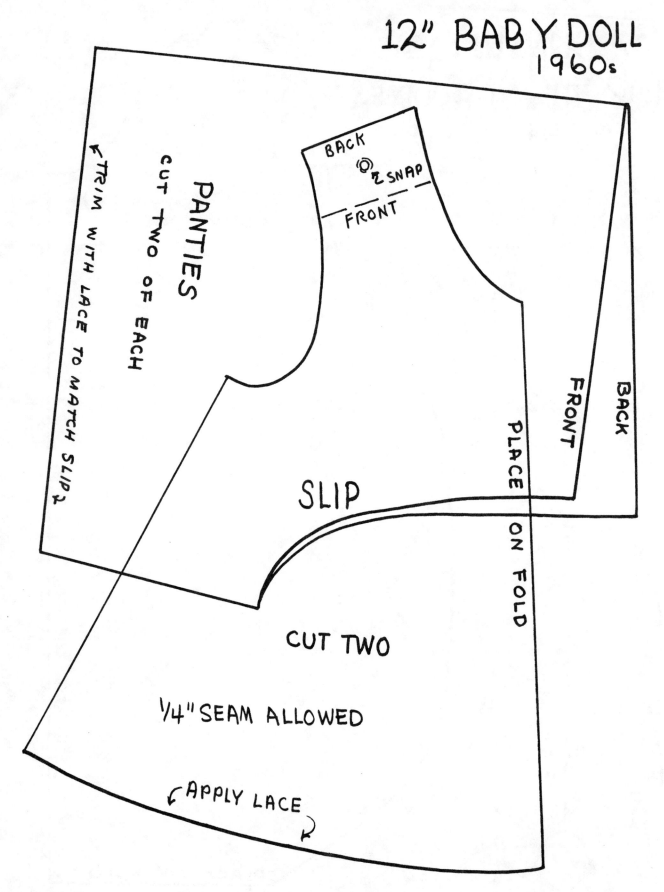

12" BABY DOLL
1960s

PANTIES
CUT TWO OF EACH

TRIM WITH LACE TO MATCH SLIP

BACK
SNAP
FRONT

FRONT
BACK
PLACE ON FOLD

SLIP

CUT TWO

1/4" SEAM ALLOWED

APPLY LACE

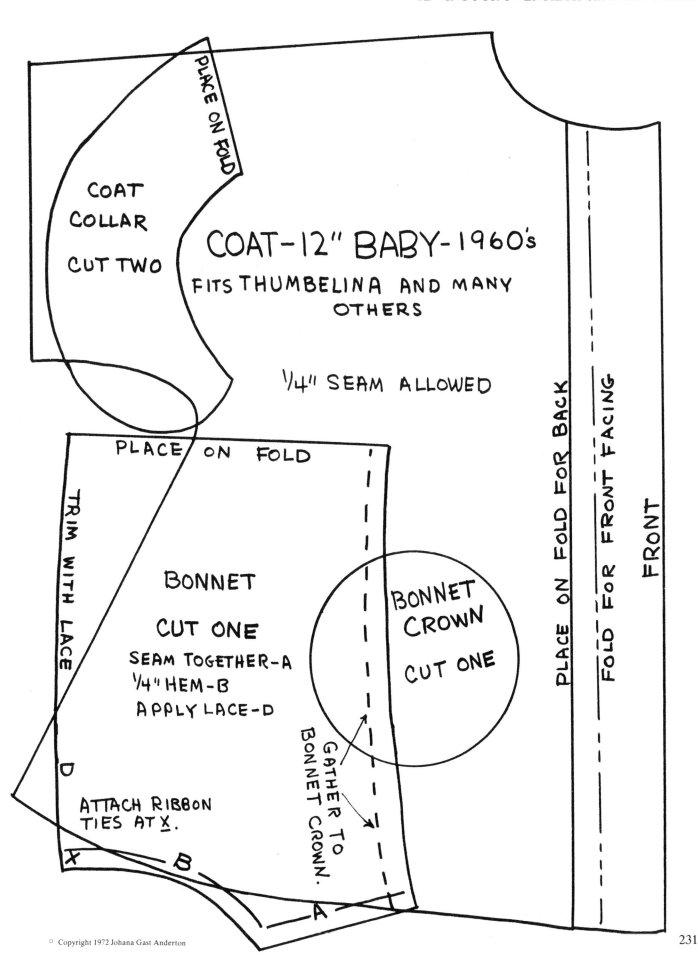

COAT COLLAR
CUT TWO

PLACE ON FOLD

COAT-12" BABY-1960's
FITS THUMBELINA AND MANY
OTHERS

1/4" SEAM ALLOWED

PLACE ON FOLD FOR BACK

FOLD FOR FRONT FACING

FRONT

PLACE ON FOLD

TRIM WITH LACE

BONNET
CUT ONE
SEAM TOGETHER-A
1/4" HEM-B
APPLY LACE-D

BONNET CROWN
CUT ONE

GATHER TO BONNET CROWN.

D

ATTACH RIBBON
TIES AT X.

X

B

A

BABY DRESS FOR 12" DOLL OF THE 1960s.

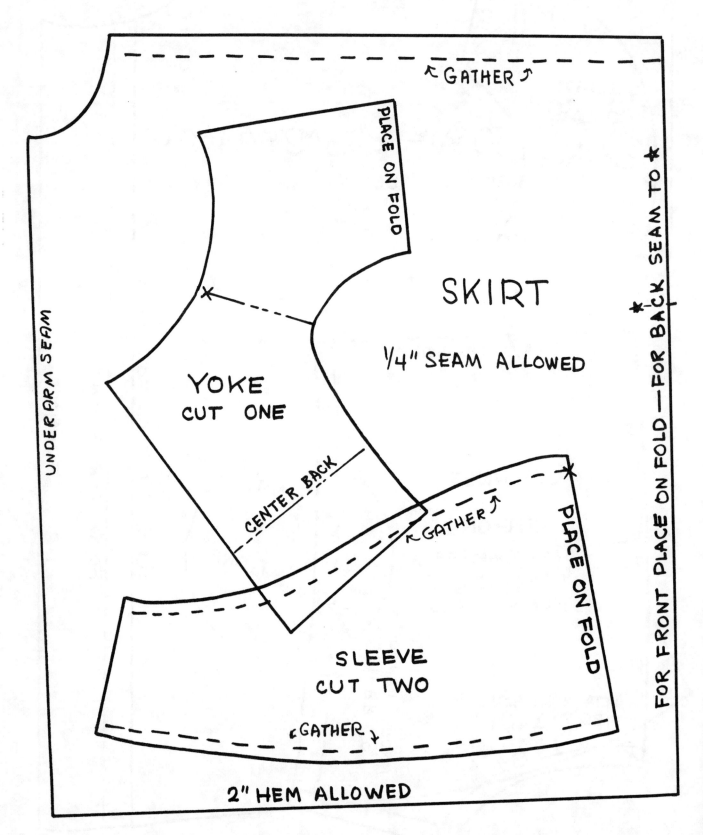

←GATHER→

PLACE ON FOLD

UNDER ARM SEAM

SKIRT

¼" SEAM ALLOWED

YOKE
CUT ONE

CENTER BACK

FOR FRONT PLACE ON FOLD—FOR BACK SEAM TO ✱

←GATHER↑

PLACE ON FOLD

SLEEVE
CUT TWO

←GATHER↓

2" HEM ALLOWED

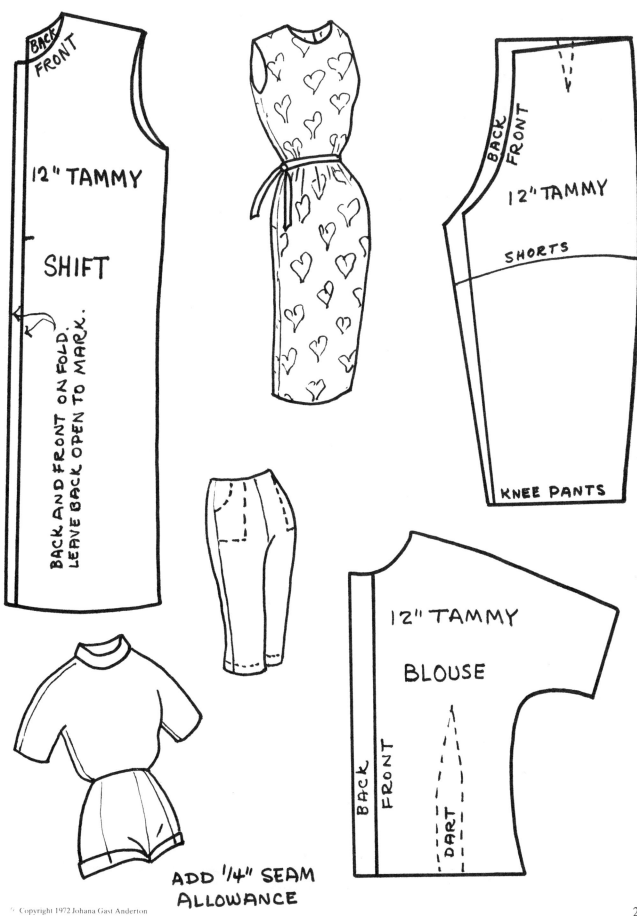

12" TAMMY

SHIFT

BACK AND FRONT ON FOLD.
LEAVE BACK OPEN TO MARK.

12" TAMMY

SHORTS

KNEE PANTS

12" TAMMY

BLOUSE

BACK

FRONT

DART

ADD 1/4" SEAM
ALLOWANCE

ALL-PURPOSE FASHION PATTERN
FOR 20" CHATTY CATHY (BY MATTEL)

These patterns, with only slight adjustment, will fit Charmin' Chatty and Chatty Baby. See chapter "FITTING PATTERNS TO YOUR DOLL".

(A) May be used to design a coat, robe, nightgown, or pajama top. For coat, robe, and pajama top, place back on fold and extend front ¾ inch to allow for overlap. For gown, place both front and back on fold and slit back for opening which is then bound or hemmed.

(B) Rounded collar may be used on dress, pajamas, or robe. Pointed collar is suitable for dress, robe, or coat.

(C) Short sleeve for dress, blouse, or nightgown.

(D) Long sleeve is suitable for coat, robe, dress, pajamas, or blouse.

(E) Bodice pattern gives choice of rounded or squared neckline and arm openings. Use for dress, suntop; lengthen slightly for overblouse. Cut a rectangle of fabric for skirt and gather or pleat to bodice for dress.

(F) Shorts, underpants, or kneepants may be produced with this pattern.

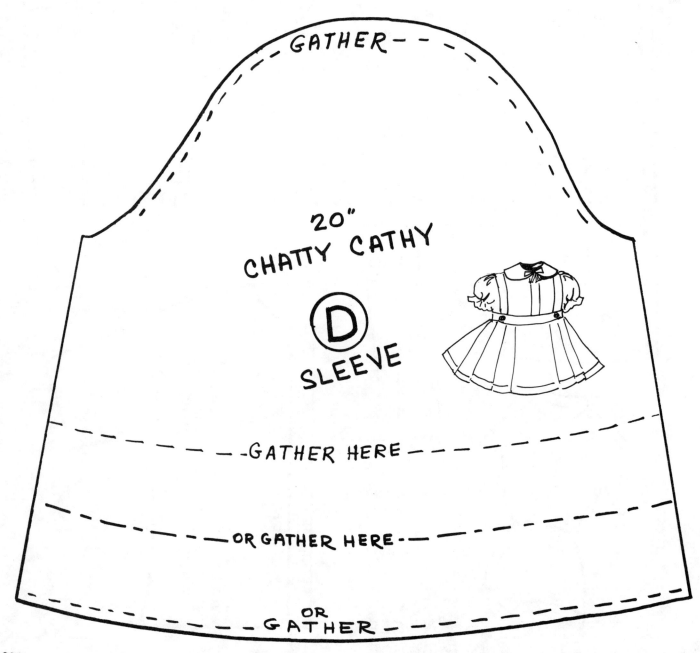

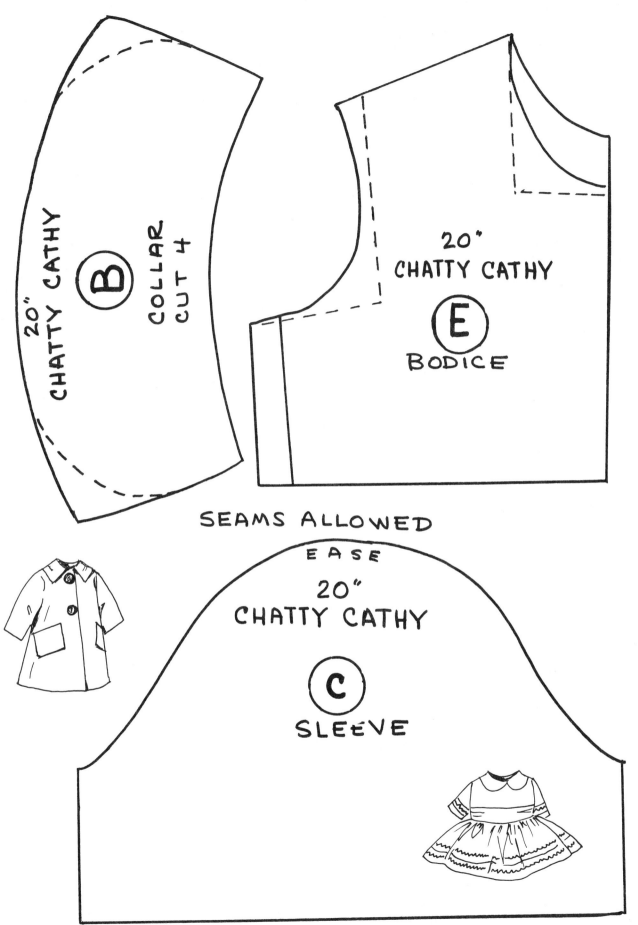

20"
CHATTY CATHY
B
COLLAR
CUT 4

20"
CHATTY CATHY
E
BODICE

SEAMS ALLOWED

EASE

20"
CHATTY CATHY
C
SLEEVE

ROBE
DRESS
COAT
ETC.

BACK
FRONT

20" CHATTY CATHY

(A)

SEAMS ALLOWED

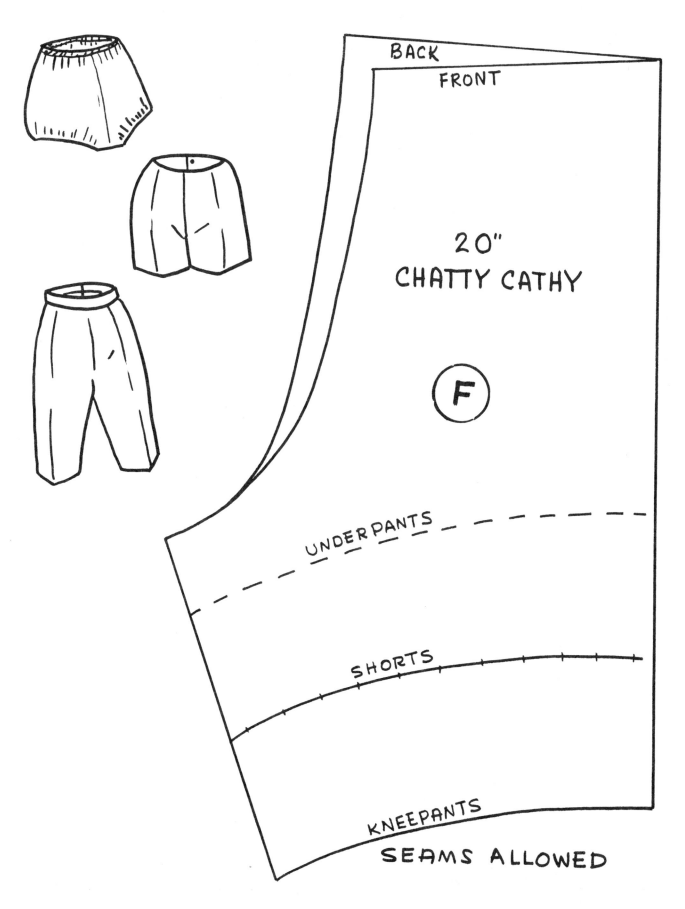

BACK

FRONT

20"
CHATTY CATHY

(F)

UNDERPANTS

SHORTS

KNEEPANTS
SEAMS ALLOWED

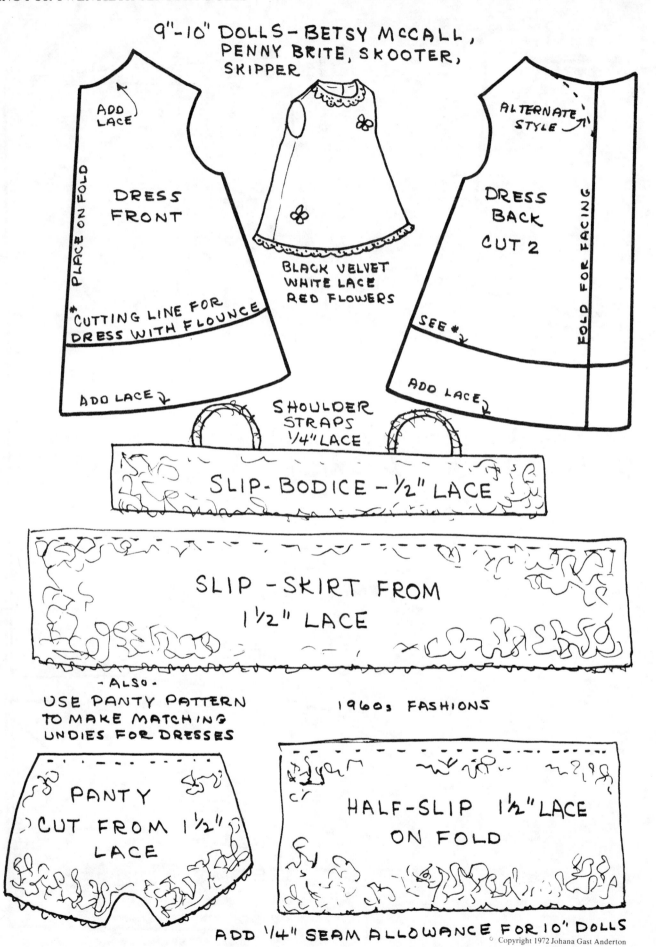

9"-10" DOLLS—BETSY McCALL, PENNY BRITE, SKOOTER, SKIPPER

ADD LACE

PLACE ON FOLD

DRESS FRONT

CUTTING LINE FOR DRESS WITH FLOUNCE

ADD LACE

BLACK VELVET WHITE LACE RED FLOWERS

ALTERNATE STYLE

DRESS BACK CUT 2

FOLD FOR FACING

SEE *

ADD LACE

SHOULDER STRAPS ¼" LACE

SLIP-BODICE — ½" LACE

SLIP-SKIRT FROM 1½" LACE

-ALSO-
USE PANTY PATTERN TO MAKE MATCHING UNDIES FOR DRESSES

1960s FASHIONS

PANTY CUT FROM 1½" LACE

HALF-SLIP 1½" LACE ON FOLD

ADD ¼" SEAM ALLOWANCE FOR 10" DOLLS

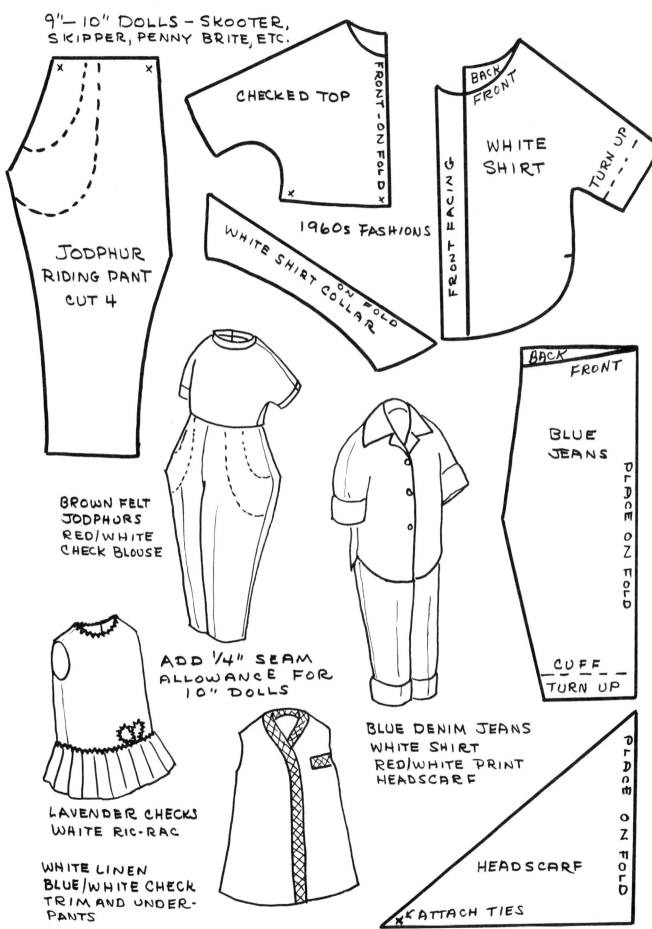

9"—10" DOLLS - SKOOTER, SKIPPER, PENNY BRITE, ETC.

CHECKED TOP

FRONT - ON FOLD

1960s FASHIONS

WHITE SHIRT ON FOLD COLLAR

BACK
FRONT
FRONT FACING
WHITE SHIRT
TURN UP

JODPHUR RIDING PANT CUT 4

BROWN FELT JODPHURS RED/WHITE CHECK BLOUSE

ADD ¼" SEAM ALLOWANCE FOR 10" DOLLS

LAVENDER CHECKS WHITE RIC-RAC

WHITE LINEN BLUE/WHITE CHECK TRIM AND UNDER-PANTS

BLUE JEANS
BACK
FRONT
PLACE ON FOLD
CUFF
TURN UP

BLUE DENIM JEANS WHITE SHIRT RED/WHITE PRINT HEADSCARF

HEADSCARF
PLACE ON FOLD
X X ATTACH TIES

2457   2457   2457   2457   2457

These illustrations show patterns available for *Betsy McCall* and *Tiny Tears*. They are taken from a booklet packed with a *Betsy McCall* doll and are ca. 1960.

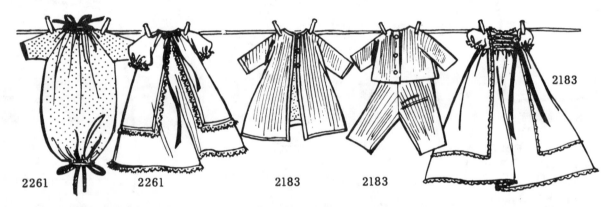

2261   2261   2183   2183   2183

WARDROBES FOR BETSY McCALL DOLLS (sizes 8 1/2" and 30"); McCALL'S 2457.
WARDROBES FOR TINY TEARS DOLLS (sizes 11" to 20"); McCALL'S 2261, 2349, 2183 and 2412.   WARDROBES FOR TOODLES DOLLS (size 25"); McCALL'S 2349 and 2412.   WARDROBES FOR TOODLES DOLLS (size 30"); McCALL'S 2412.

ALL OF THE ABOVE LISTED DOLLS ARE PRODUCTS OF THE ... **AMERICAN DOLL & TOY CORP.**

2349   2349   2349   2412   2412

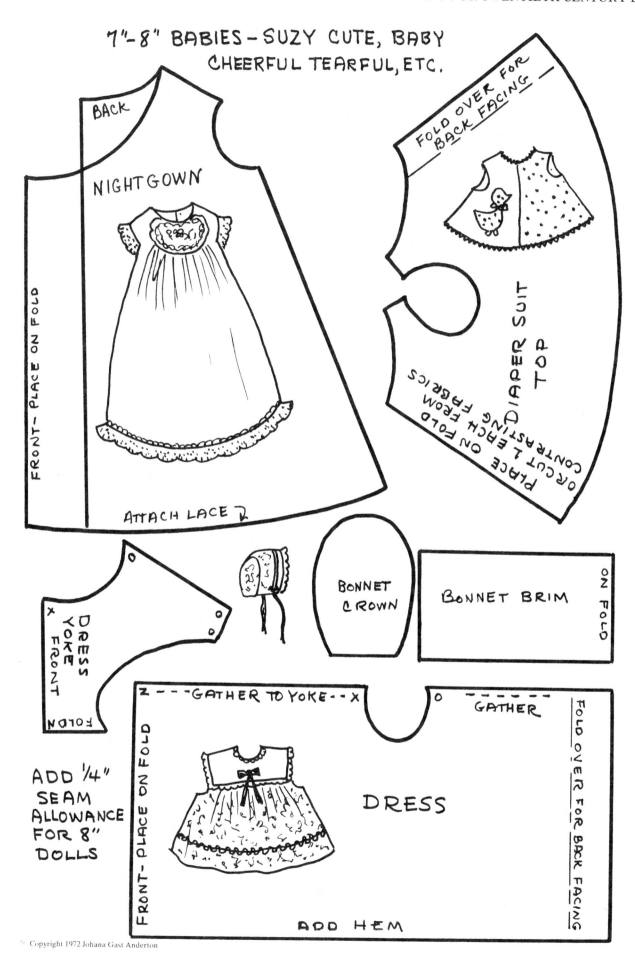

7"-8" BABIES - SUZY CUTE, BABY CHEERFUL TEARFUL, ETC.

BACK

NIGHTGOWN

FRONT - PLACE ON FOLD

ATTACH LACE

FOLD OVER FOR BACK FACING

DIAPER SUIT TOP

PLACE ON FOLD
OR CUT 1 EACH FROM
CONTRASTING FABRICS

DRESS YOKE FRONT

FOLD

BONNET CROWN

BONNET BRIM

ON FOLD

GATHER TO YOKE

GATHER

ADD 1/4" SEAM ALLOWANCE FOR 8" DOLLS

FRONT - PLACE ON FOLD

DRESS

FOLD OVER FOR BACK FACING

ADD HEM

241

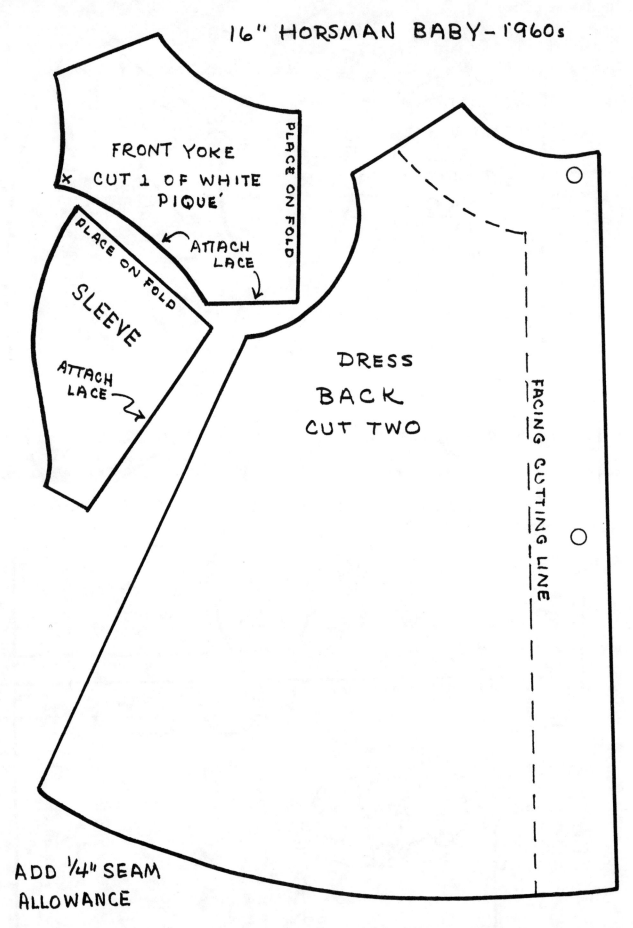

16" HORSMAN BABY-1960s

FRONT YOKE
CUT 1 OF WHITE
PIQUE'

x

PLACE ON FOLD

ATTACH LACE

PLACE ON FOLD

SLEEVE

ATTACH LACE

DRESS
BACK
CUT TWO

FACING CUTTING LINE

ADD ¼" SEAM
ALLOWANCE

242

16" HORSMAN BABY -1960s

ORIGINAL DRESS IS
RED COTTON WITH
WHITE PIQUÉ YOKE
AND WHITE LACE.

FRONT FACING

ON FOLD

PLACE ON FOLD

GATHER
TO FIT LOWER EDGE
OF YOKE

DRESS
FRONT
CUT 1 ON FOLD

ADD 1/4" SEAM
ALLOWANCE

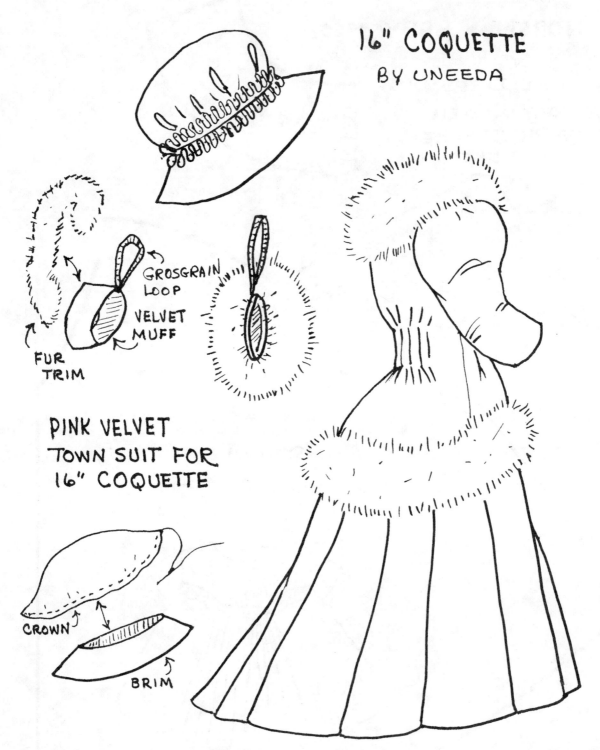

16" COQUETTE
BY UNEEDA

GROSGRAIN LOOP

VELVET MUFF

FUR TRIM

PINK VELVET
TOWN SUIT FOR
16" COQUETTE

CROWN

BRIM

FOR HAT—
    BRIM IS A 6¼" CIRCLE WITH A 3½" CIRCLE CUT OUT
TO FIT CROWN. CROWN IS AN 8" CIRCLE, ONE EACH OF
VELVET AND LINING, GATHERED AS ONE AND SEWN TO BRIM.
BRIM IS VELVET BOTH SIDES, MAY HAVE INTERLINING FOR
ADDITIONAL STIFFNESS. TRIM WITH LACE OR RUTCHING.

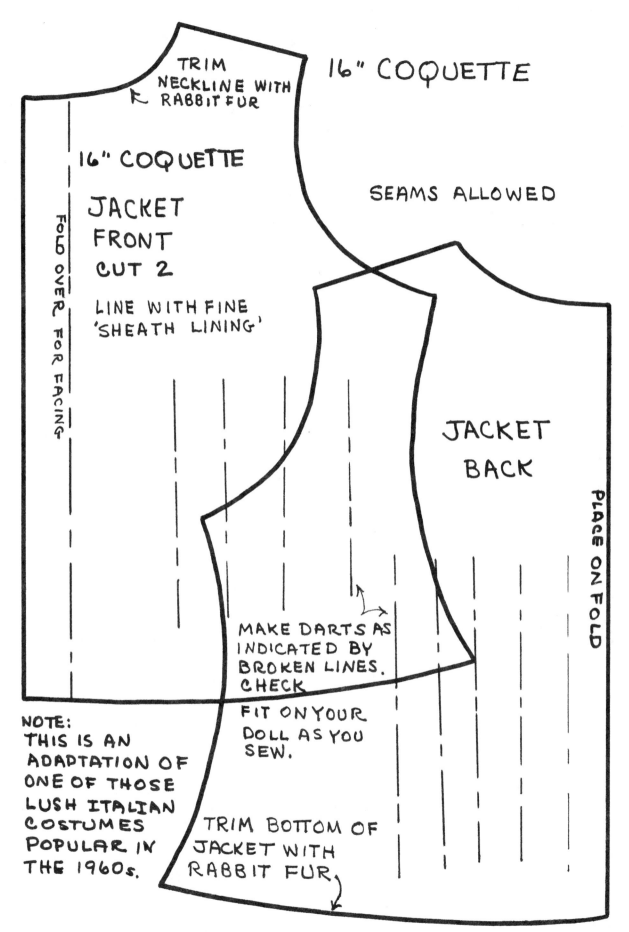

TRIM NECKLINE WITH RABBIT FUR

16" COQUETTE

SEAMS ALLOWED

16" COQUETTE

FOLD OVER FOR FACING

JACKET FRONT CUT 2

LINE WITH FINE 'SHEATH LINING'

JACKET BACK

PLACE ON FOLD

MAKE DARTS AS INDICATED BY BROKEN LINES. CHECK FIT ON YOUR DOLL AS YOU SEW.

NOTE:
THIS IS AN ADAPTATION OF ONE OF THOSE LUSH ITALIAN COSTUMES POPULAR IN THE 1960s.

TRIM BOTTOM OF JACKET WITH RABBIT FUR.

16" COQUETTE

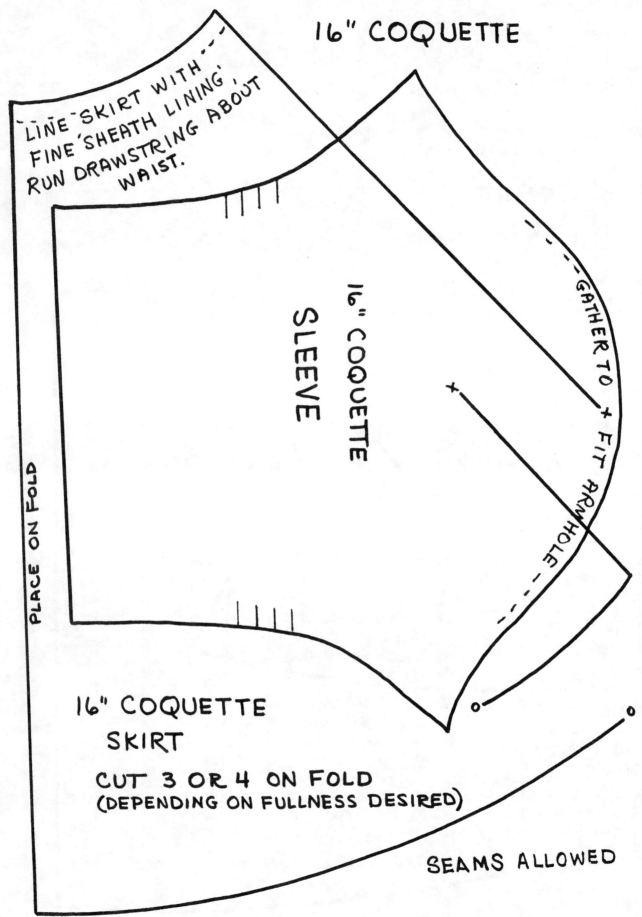

LINE SKIRT WITH FINE SHEATH LINING. RUN DRAWSTRING ABOUT WAIST.

PLACE ON FOLD

16" COQUETTE SLEEVE

GATHER TO FIT ARMHOLE

16" COQUETTE SKIRT

CUT 3 OR 4 ON FOLD
(DEPENDING ON FULLNESS DESIRED)

SEAMS ALLOWED

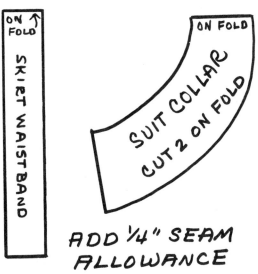

ON FOLD

SKIRT WAIST BAND

SUIT COLLAR
CUT 2 ON FOLD

ADD ¼" SEAM
ALLOWANCE

BACK

⊙ FRONT

10" JACQUELINE
BY MME. ALEXANDER
SUIT JACKET

TUCK

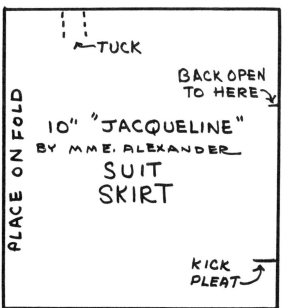

←TUCK

BACK OPEN
TO HERE →

10" "JACQUELINE"
BY MME. ALEXANDER
SUIT
SKIRT

PLACE ON FOLD

KICK
PLEAT →

JACQUELINE'S

HAT CROWN

¼" SEAM ALLOWED

LINE HAT WITH
BUCHRAM OR
PELLON

JACQUELINE'S HAT

ON FOLD

SUIT IS OF VERY
FINE, SOFT BLUE
WOOL. HAT IS OF
SAME MATERIAL.

COMPLETELY LINE SKIRT,
ATTACH WAISTBAND, THEN
OVERLAP BACK TO FORM
TINY KICK PLEAT.
JACKET HAS SNAPS
WITH BUTTONS SEWN
ON FOR EFFECT ONLY.

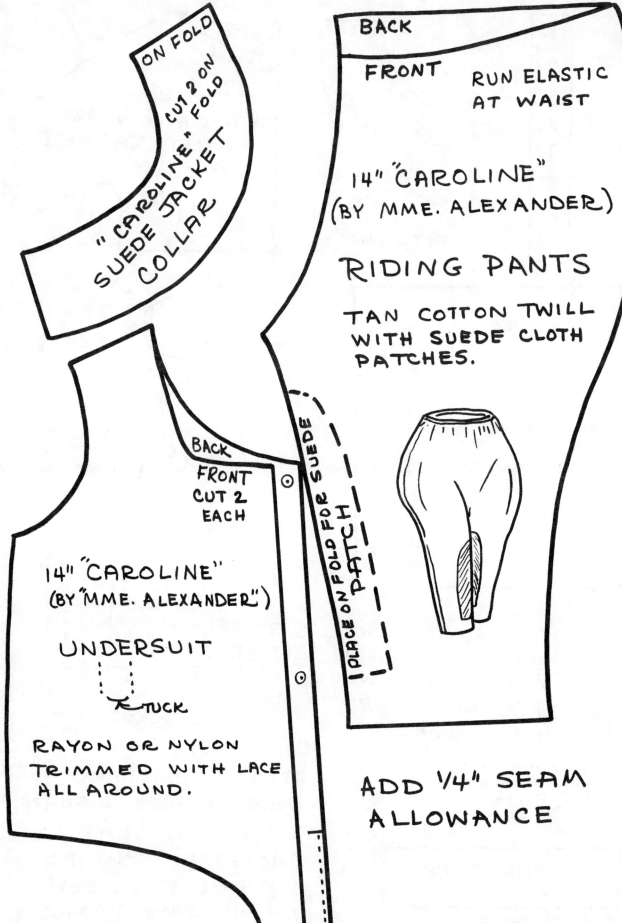

ON FOLD

CUT 2 ON FOLD

"CAROLINE" SUEDE JACKET COLLAR

BACK

FRONT

RUN ELASTIC AT WAIST

14" "CAROLINE" (BY MME. ALEXANDER)

RIDING PANTS

TAN COTTON TWILL WITH SUEDE CLOTH PATCHES.

BACK

FRONT CUT 2 EACH

14" "CAROLINE" (BY "MME. ALEXANDER")

UNDERSUIT

TUCK

RAYON OR NYLON TRIMMED WITH LACE ALL AROUND.

PLACE ON FOLD FOR SUEDE PATCH

ADD 1/4" SEAM ALLOWANCE

248

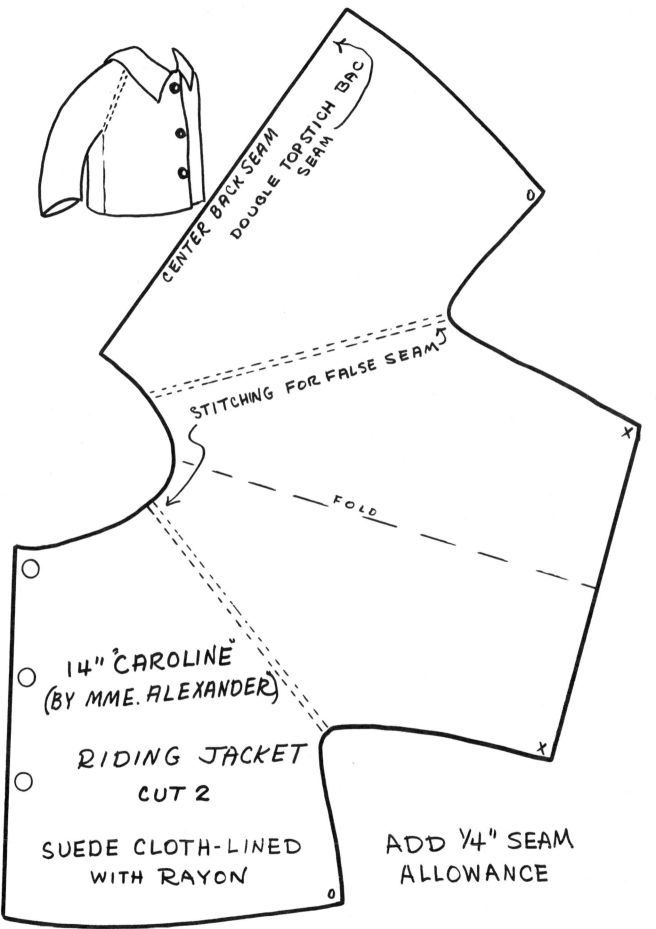

CENTER BACK SEAM

DOUBLE TOPSTICH BAC SEAM

STITCHING FOR FALSE SEAM

FOLD

14" "CAROLINE"
(BY MME. ALEXANDER)

RIDING JACKET

CUT 2

SUEDE CLOTH - LINED
WITH RAYON

ADD ¼" SEAM
ALLOWANCE

17½" BEAUTIFUL CRISSY BY IDEAL

These patterns also fit *Tressy, Dianna Ross,* and *Kerry.* To adjust for *Velvet, Cricket,* and *Mia,* see chapter "FITTING PATTERNS TO YOUR DOLL".

ALL PURPOSE PATTERNS FOR CRISSY

These all-purpose patterns give the versatility needed to represent the potpourri styling of the late 1960s and early 1970s.

PIECE **A** — Follow pattern lines carefully to discover 1) an Empire waistline, 2) a bodice for a natural waistline dress, 3) a bodice for a low or dropped-waist dress, a tuck-in blouse, or long vest, 4) an overblouse, 5) a tunic top or mini-dress, 6) dress, or 7) (now shown) extend pattern to midi (mid-calf) or maxi (ankle length).

A choice of two necklines is given with the alternative of a jumper neckline. Use jumper neckline for a "hippy" vest of simulated leather and add fringe for a swingy look.

Skirts for above dresses are simply rectangles cut to desired length, allowing for amount of fullness desired, and gathered or pleated to bodice of your choice. Thus a skirt for the dropped-waist dress would require a rectangle 3¼ inches by 18 inches, gathered along one long side.

PIECE **B** — This pattern gives a choice of straight or flared (bell) pants. Opening may be placed front, side or back.

PIECE **C** — Three sleeve choices are available: 1) sleeve with some fullness gathered to cuff **E** which may be trimmed with lace or braid; 2) straight sleeve suitable for knit blouse, pantsuit jacket, or coat; and 3) full sleeve in which the fullness is held by a narrow elastic in a casing along lower edge.

PIECES **D** AND **F** — Two choices of collars: **D**) standup collar for dresses, knit blouses, or tunic; and **F**) for coat, jacket, blouse or dress.

PIECE **G** — Briefs or underpants: cut to match dress or cut from tricot, cotton, or other suitable fabric.

In trimming fashions for these up-to-date lasses, use imagination and whatever is at hand. The fashions of the late 1960s and early 1970s featured everything from old-fashioned lace and tatted edgings to permanent press ruffles and orlon yarns. Strings of beads, bangle bracelets, rings on every finger, and headbands were all important additions to the "in" look.

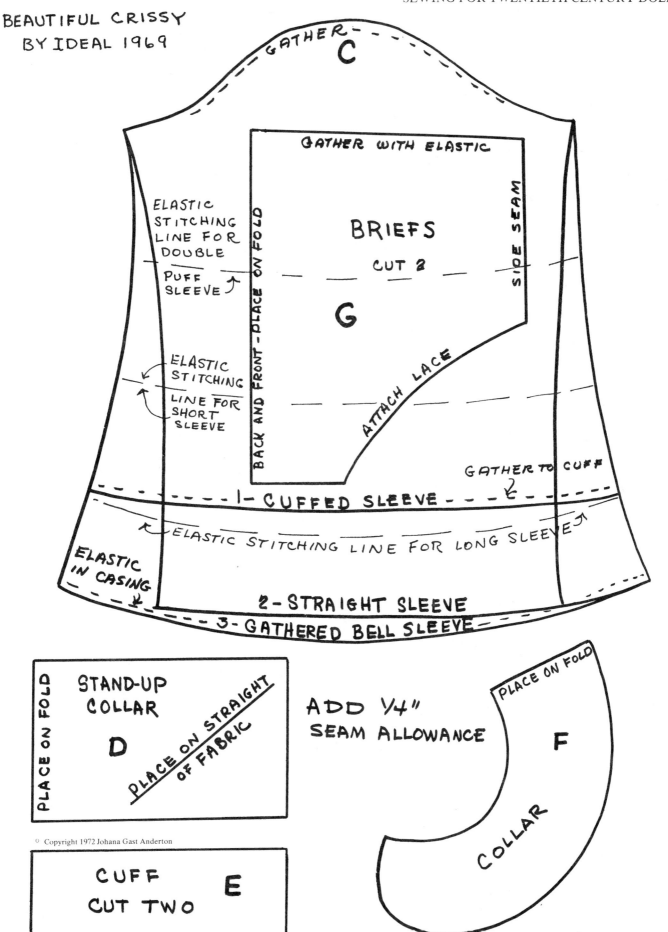

BEAUTIFUL CRISSY
BY IDEAL 1969

GATHER

C

GATHER WITH ELASTIC

ELASTIC
STITCHING
LINE FOR
DOUBLE

PUFF
SLEEVE

BRIEFS

CUT 2

BACK AND FRONT - PLACE ON FOLD

SIDE SEAM

G

ELASTIC
STITCHING

LINE FOR
SHORT
SLEEVE

ATTACH LACE

GATHER TO CUFF

1 - CUFFED SLEEVE

ELASTIC STITCHING LINE FOR LONG SLEEVE

ELASTIC
IN CASING

2 - STRAIGHT SLEEVE

3 - GATHERED BELL SLEEVE

PLACE ON FOLD

STAND-UP
COLLAR

PLACE ON STRAIGHT OF FABRIC

D

PLACE ON FOLD

ADD ¼"
SEAM ALLOWANCE

F

COLLAR

CUFF

CUT TWO

E

251

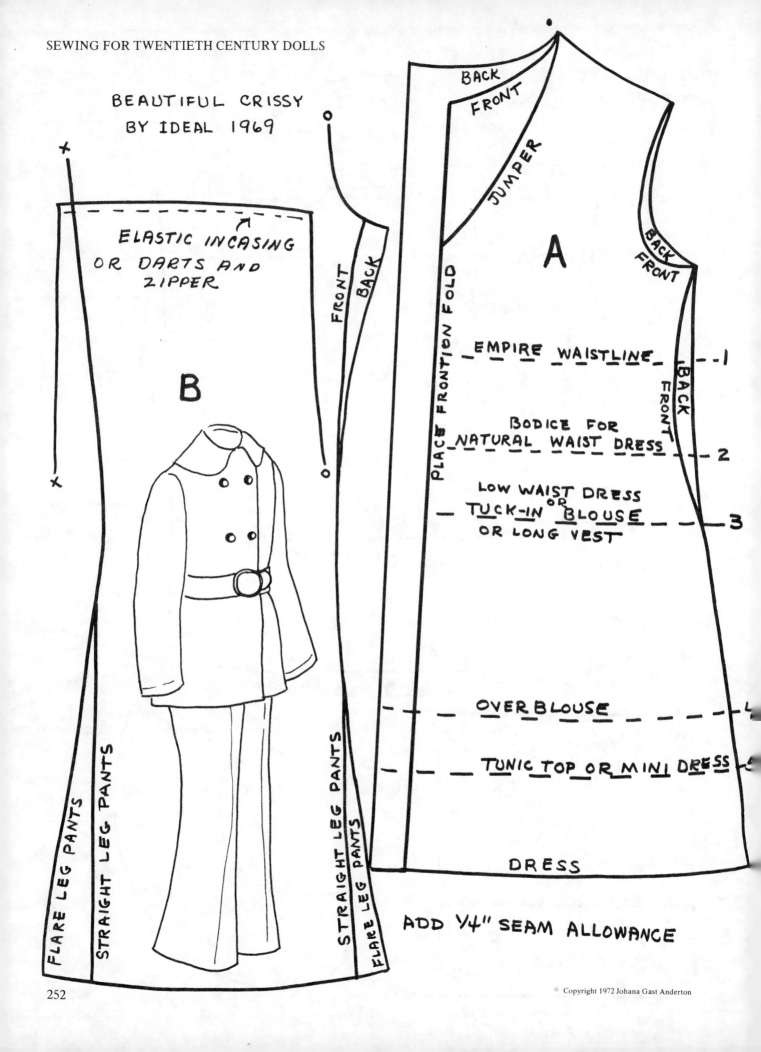

BEAUTIFUL CRISSY
BY IDEAL 1969

B

ELASTIC INCASING
OR DARTS AND
ZIPPER

FLARE LEG PANTS

STRAIGHT LEG PANTS

FRONT

BACK

STRAIGHT LEG PANTS

FLARE LEG PANTS

BACK
FRONT
JUMPER

A

BACK
FRONT

PLACE FRONT ON FOLD

EMPIRE WAISTLINE — — 1

BACK
FRONT

BODICE FOR
NATURAL WAIST DRESS — — 2

LOW WAIST DRESS
OR
TUCK-IN BLOUSE — — — 3
OR LONG VEST

OVER BLOUSE — — — —

TUNIC TOP OR MINI DRESS — —

DRESS

ADD ¼" SEAM ALLOWANCE

252

YOKE LINE
(A)

YOKE LINE
(B)

18"
GIGGLES
by Ideal

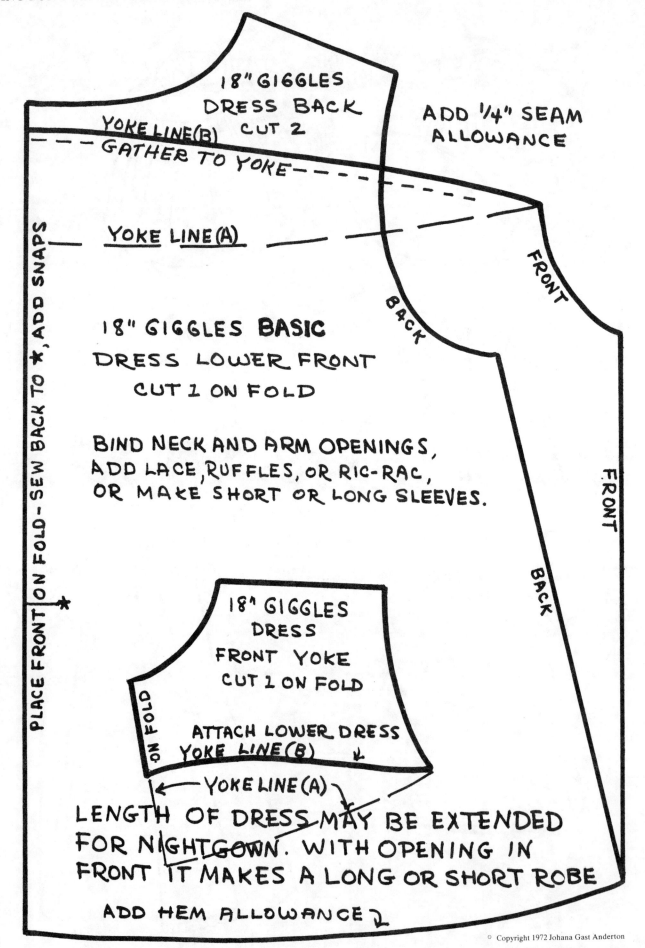

18" GIGGLES
DRESS BACK
CUT 2

ADD 1/4" SEAM
ALLOWANCE

YOKE LINE (B)

GATHER TO YOKE

YOKE LINE (A)

FRONT

BACK

18" GIGGLES BASIC
DRESS LOWER FRONT
CUT 1 ON FOLD

BIND NECK AND ARM OPENINGS,
ADD LACE, RUFFLES, OR RIC-RAC,
OR MAKE SHORT OR LONG SLEEVES.

FRONT

BACK

PLACE FRONT ON FOLD — SEW BACK TO ★, ADD SNAPS

18" GIGGLES
DRESS
FRONT YOKE
CUT 1 ON FOLD

ON FOLD

ATTACH LOWER DRESS
YOKE LINE (B)

YOKE LINE (A)

LENGTH OF DRESS MAY BE EXTENDED
FOR NIGHTGOWN. WITH OPENING IN
FRONT IT MAKES A LONG OR SHORT ROBE

ADD HEM ALLOWANCE

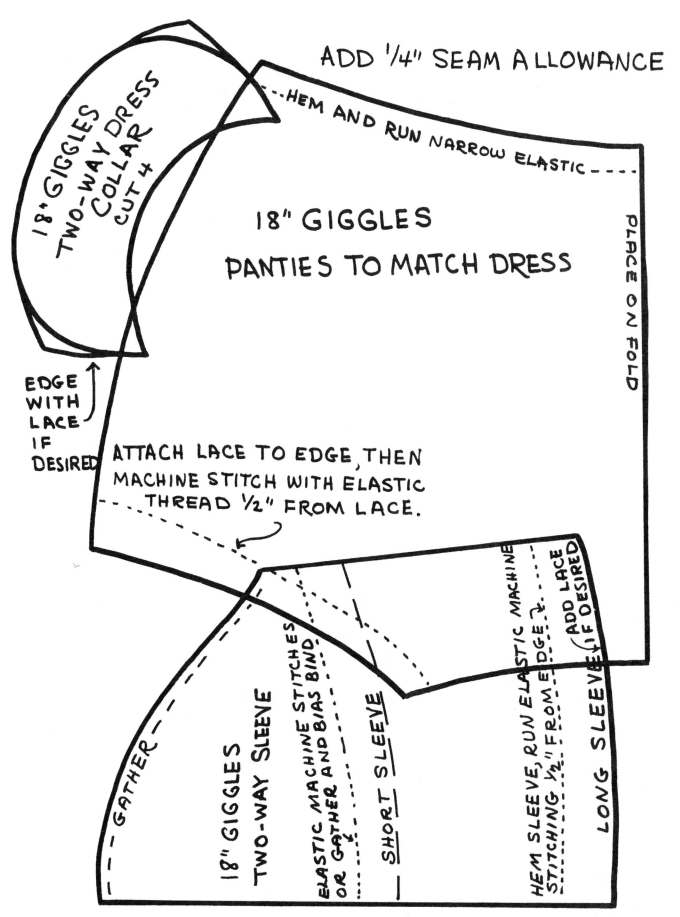

18" GIGGLES
TWO-WAY DRESS
COLLAR
CUT 4

ADD ¼" SEAM ALLOWANCE

HEM AND RUN NARROW ELASTIC

18" GIGGLES
PANTIES TO MATCH DRESS

PLACE ON FOLD

EDGE
WITH
LACE
IF
DESIRED

ATTACH LACE TO EDGE, THEN
MACHINE STITCH WITH ELASTIC
THREAD ½" FROM LACE.

GATHER

18" GIGGLES
TWO-WAY SLEEVE

ELASTIC MACHINE STITCHES
OR GATHER AND BIAS BIND

SHORT SLEEVE

HEM SLEEVE, RUN ELASTIC MACHINE
STITCHING ½" FROM EDGE

ADD LACE
IF DESIRED

LONG SLEEVE

255

18" GIGGLES
BY IDEAL

SHIFT DRESS

ORIGINAL DRESS WAS A "MINI-SHIFT" OF MULTI-COLORED, STRIPED KNIT. GIGGLES WORE SANDALS AND CAME WITH "FUNNY FACE" ACCESSORIES.

DRESS MAY ALSO BE MADE OF GINGHAM OR PRINT AND EDGED WITH LACE, RUFFLES OR BRAID. THIS MODERN MISS SHOULD BE DRESSED IN PERMANENT PRESS AND OTHER 'MOD' FABRICS.

BACK - FOLDOVER FOR BACK FACING

FRONT - PLACE ON FOLD

SEE CHAPTER "STOCKINGS AND SHOES" FOR GIGGLES' SANDALS.

SEW 3 SNAPS ALONG BACK OPENING.

LENGTHEN SHIFT TO MAKE NIGHTGOWN OR ROBE.

1/4" SEAMS ALLOWED

SEW ON NARROW ELASTIC AFTER HEMMING

16" BABY GIGGLES DIAPER SUIT
PANTY

BACK–SEAM TO TOP

16" BABY GIGGLES
DIAPER SUIT TOP
YOKE

PLACE ON FOLD

CUT 1 ON
FOLD OF
DEEP PINK

FRONT – PLACE ON FOLD

NARROW HEM

ADD ¼" SEAM ALLOWANCE

DIAPER SUIT

SLEEVE CUFF

ON FOLD

16" BABY GIGGLES
DIAPER SUIT TOP
SLEEVE

PLACE ON FOLD

ATTACH CUFF
BEFORE SEWING
UNDER ARM SEAM
IF DESIRED

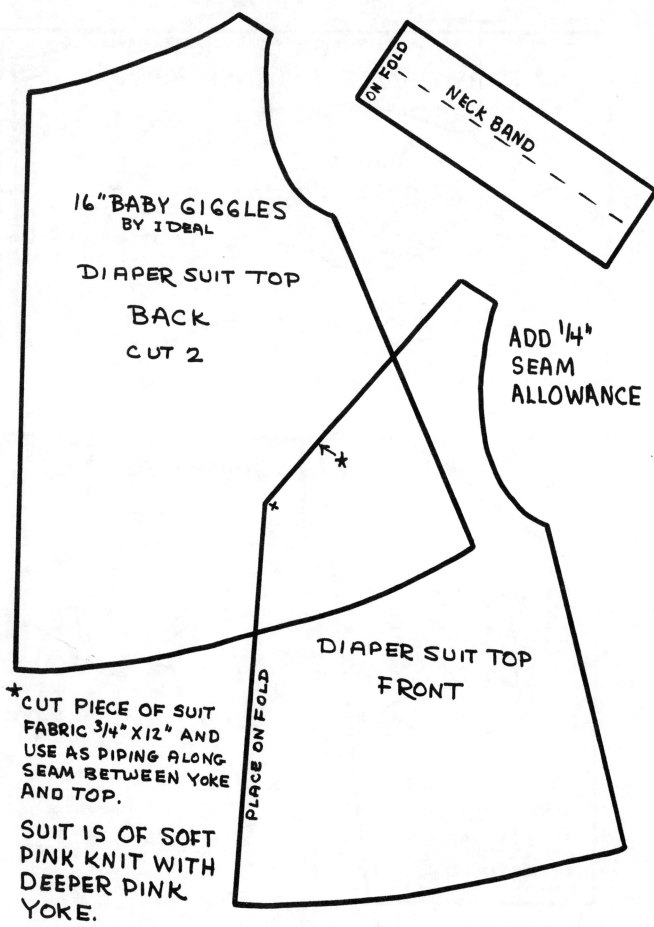

NECK BAND

ON FOLD

16" BABY GIGGLES
BY IDEAL

DIAPER SUIT TOP

BACK

CUT 2

ADD 1/4"
SEAM
ALLOWANCE

DIAPER SUIT TOP

FRONT

PLACE ON FOLD

*CUT PIECE OF SUIT
FABRIC 3/4" X 12" AND
USE AS PIPING ALONG
SEAM BETWEEN YOKE
AND TOP.

SUIT IS OF SOFT
PINK KNIT WITH
DEEPER PINK
YOKE.

258

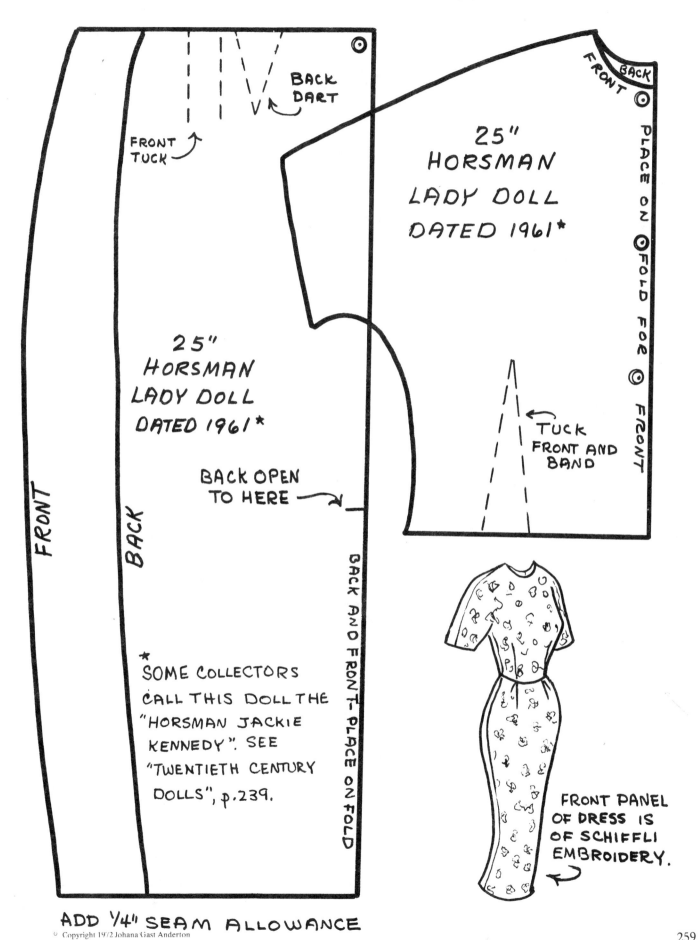

BACK DART

FRONT TUCK

25"
HORSMAN
LADY DOLL
DATED 1961*

FRONT

BACK

25"
HORSMAN
LADY DOLL
DATED 1961*

BACK OPEN TO HERE

TUCK FRONT AND BAND

PLACE ON ⊙ FOLD FOR ⊙ FRONT

FRONT   BACK

* SOME COLLECTORS
CALL THIS DOLL THE
"HORSMAN JACKIE
KENNEDY". SEE
"TWENTIETH CENTURY
DOLLS", p.239.

BACK AND FRONT-PLACE ON FOLD

FRONT PANEL
OF DRESS IS
OF SCHIFFLI
EMBROIDERY.

ADD 1/4" SEAM ALLOWANCE

ENTERING THE 1970s

What can be said of the fashions of the 1970s that hasn't been said about those of other decades? Someone has noted *there is nothing new under the sun* and this is certainly true in the world of fashion where trends come full circle upon themselves. Thus it is we see the 1940s reflected in kick-pleated skirts and long sweaters of the 1970s. The Sloppy Joe sweaters, tennis skirts, and short shorts of the 1940s have become the *knit tops, skooter skirts,* and *hot pants* of the 1970s.

The diversity of early 1970s fashions is striking; bareness and near-nudity co-exist with cover-up, almost Victorian styles. The rule seems to be all or nothing at all. Added to this mainstream of style, or quite aside from it, are the fashions generated by the sub-culture, the world of *hippies* and *drop-outs,* which have profoundly influenced the dress of young people. The floppy hats, fringed leather vests, mocassins, bell-bottom trousers, and put-together styles of this element have influenced even the more sedate styles of the French designers.

Fashion might best be described as a whirling tornado, dancing through the decades, picking up the elements of design here and depositing them there as it continues to whirl along, never at any given moment the same as it was a moment ago.

ILLUSTRATION SOURCES

Butler Bros., New York, catalog, 1933, p. 128

Delineator, The, New York, March, 1918, p. 52; February, 1919, pp. 53, 54.

Designer, The, New York, November, 1915, p.

Home Arts Needlecraft, Augusta, Maine, April, 1936, p. 129; September, 1936, p. 138; September, 1937, pp. 129, 130, 136, 136, 140, 150, 151; September, 1938, p. 131; September, 1939, p. 131; January, 1940, pp. 17, 156, 157.

Ladies Home Journal, The, Philadelphia, December, 1904, pp. 29, 30, 34, 38, 40, 41, 43, 45; March, 1911, p. 48.

McCall's Magazine, New York, September, 1925, pp. 113, 120; September, 1943, pp. 158, 159.

McCall's Needlework and Decorative Arts, New York, Winter, 1930-1931, pp. 16, 17, 102, 103, 127.

Modern Priscilla, Boston, March, 1920, pp. 11, 12; October, 1934, pp. 117, 121.

Needlecraft Magazine, Augusta, Maine, August, 1924, p. 78; February, 1925, p. 126.

Pictorial Review, New York, December, 1910, pp. 26-28, 30-32; October, 1913, pp. 16, 17, 49, 54, 57, 91, 112; October, 1914, p. 17.

Pictorial Review Fashion Book, Spring, 1923, p. 79.

Schoenhut Catalog, 1915, pp. 68-70.

Twentieth Century Dolls, 1971, (frontpiece).

Woman's Home Companion, Springfield, Ohio, October, 1915, pp. 15, 16, 264; January, 1916, pp. 50, 51.

ALPHABETICAL INDEX

A

Accessories 16, 17, 49, 51
Acknowledgments 7
Alexander-kins 203, 204
Alterations 13, 14
Aprons 65, 100, 126, 156
Arranbee 118
Authenticity 9

B

Baby 230-232
Baby Bumps 18, 66
Baby Cheerful Tearful 241
Baby dress 91, 92, 94
Baby Giggles 257, 258
Barbie 206
Beautiful Crissy 206, 250-252
Bed dolls 24, 102-108
Betsy McCall 174, 176, 203, 204, 238-240
Bib 137
Billy Boy 62
Bisque head, body for 19, 22, 23
Bisque head doll 33
Blazer 8, 158
Bloomers 46, 47, 125, 126
Blouses 131
Blue Bird uniform 182
Bodies 8, 18-24
Bonnet 59, 60, 94, 95, 122, 123, 137, 152, 154
Boot 133
Boys 32, 48, 49, 52, 53, 62-64, 70, 128, 159, 168, 205
Bra 201
Braid 157
Bubbles 94, 95
Buddy Lee 2, 13, 80-88
Bye-lo 8, 19, 22, 23, 91-93, 96, 97
Buster Brown suits 70

C

Cape 31, 58
Campbell Kids 168
Cardigan 8
Carmen 2, 160, 161
Caroline 248, 249
Castoffs, using for dolls' clothes 16
Chatty Cathy 234-237
Cinders, Ella 89, 90
Cissy 194
Clown 187
Coat 31, 32, 49, 54, 57, 129, 159, 202
Collars 16, 17, 50, 51
Combinations 93, 101, 117, 125, 148, 152-154
Composition girl 140, 141
Coquette 244-246
Cowgirl 198, 199
Crissy 206, 250-252

D

Deanna Durbin 2, 135, 136
Decreasing patterns 14
Dianna Ross 2, 250-252
Diaper suit 257, 258
Dimples 121-123
Dionne 2, 152-154
Dream Baby 19, 22, 23, 91-93
Dr. John Littlechap 207-211
Dr. Littlechap Family 207-228
Durbin, Deanna 2, 135, 136
Dy-Dee 137

E

Ella Cinders 89, 90
Embroidery 11, 12, 127, 130, 137
Emelie Dionne 2, 152-154
Enlarging patterns 14
Evening dress 131

F

Fabrics 9, 10
Face of Fashion 9
Fashion Mannequin 169-172
Flapper 24, 102-108
French bed doll 102-108
Frog leg body 19
Furs 10

G

Garland, Judy 2, 138, 139
Giggles 253-256
Giggles, Baby 257-258
Ginny 203, 204
Girdles 17
Girl doll 140, 141
Girl Scout 183-185

H

Hairbows 30
Hair styles 10
Handwerck 38-41
Harriet Hubbard Ayer make-up doll 188
Hat 15-17, 31, 32, 49, 52-54, 59, 60, 63, 111, 116, 131, 132, 149, 166, 198, 199, 202, 244
Hem allowance 13
Henie, Sonja 162-165
Horsman baby doll 242, 243
Horsman child 121-125
Horsman Jackie Kennedy 259
Housecoats 157

I

Ideal P-90, 188
Increasing patterns 14
Introduction 8

J

Jackie 247, 259
Jacqueline 247, 259
Jerri Lee 178-181
Jewelry 17
Judy Garland 2, 138, 139
Judy Littlechap 220-225

K

K (STAR) R 8, 33-37, 42-47
Kathe Kruse 100, 101
Kennedy, Jackie 247, 259
Kennedy, Caroline 248, 249
Kid body 20, 21

L

Lady doll 192, 193, 200-202, 212-219, 225
Lee, Buddy 2, 13, 80-88
Lee, Jerri 178-181
Lee, Terri 177-186
Leggings 61
Libby Littlechap 225-228
Lisa Littlechap 212-219, 225
Littlechap Family 207-228
Little Miss Revlon 190, 191
Little Rickey, see Rickey, Jr.
Lounging pajamas 99

M
McCall, Betsy 203-204
Majorette 132-134
Mannequin 169-172
Martin, Mary 166, 167
Mary Martin 166, 167
Men's clothing 32, 207-211
Mickey Mouse 128
Middy dresses 158
Miranda, Carmen 160, 161
Miss Curity 188, 189
Miss Revlon 192, 193
Mother-daughter fashions 156, 157
Muffie 203, 204

N
Nautical 8
Nurse 188, 189

O
Old doll clothes patterns 51-54
Original clothes 9
Overalls 137, 155

P
P-90 188
Pajamas 99, 114, 115, 147
Paris says 50, 51
Party dress 195-199
Pattern
        alterations 14
        decreasing 14
        enlarging 14
        file 13
        layouts of 1920s 78
Patsy 2, 109-120
Patsy Ann 109-117
Patsy-ette 119-120
Patsy type 118
Penny Brite 238-240
Pinafores 157
Princess frocks 157
Proportion 9

Q
Queen of Diamonds

R
Raggedy Ann and Andy 63-65
Raincape 58
Revlon, Little Miss 190, 191
Revlon, Miss 192, 193
Rickey, Jr. 205
Riding Habit 248, 249
Robes 30
Rompers 66, 78, 98
Ross, Dianna 2, 250-252
Russian suits 70

S
Sailor dress 69, 158
Sailor suit 128, 166, 167
Schoenhut dolls, 67-76
Seam allowance 13
Sheath dress 259
Shirley Temple 2, 142-151
Shirtwaist 8
Shoes 8, 25-28, 39, 40
Shoulders 14, 129
Skating costume 164, 165

Ski costume 162, 163
Skipper 238-240
Skooter 238-240
Sleeves 9, 127, 129
Slip 33
Smocks 156
Sonja Henie 162-165
Soldier uniform 52, 53
Spare heads 8
Stockings 8, 25-28, 38, 39, 128
Suits, boys 52, 53
Suits, girls 158
Sunsuit 147, 229
Suzy Cute 241
Sweet Sue 195-202
Sweet Sue girl 195-199
Sweet Sue Sophisticate 200-202

T
Tammy 233, 234
Teen doll 220-225, 233
Temple, Shirley 2, 142-151
Terri Lee 177-186
Tiny Tears 240
Tiny Terri Lee 182
Tippet 61
Toni 175, 176, 188
Toodles 229, 240
Tracing patterns 13
Trim 127, 129, 130, 157
Trousers 9

U
Underclothes 38, 41
Underwear 16, 33, 36, 37, 42-47
Uneeda Coquette 244-246

W
Wigs 10

Size Index
7" — 241
8" — 203, 204, 241
8½" — 174
9" — 119, 120, 238-240
9½" — 203, 204
10" — 96, 97, 182, 238-240, 247
10½" — 19, 91, 92, 175, 190, 191, 225-228
11" — 62
11½" — 22, 23
12" — 66, 230-234
13" — 66, 137, 169-172
13½" — 18, 220-225
14" — 67-76, 94, 95, 162-164, 176, 212-219, 225, 248, 249
14½" — 166, 167, 188
15" — 207-211
16" — 147, 177-181, 229, 242, 243, 244-246, 257, 258
17" — 67-76, 205
17½" — 250-252
18" — 100, 101, 132-134, 138, 139, 143-146, 192, 193, 253-256
19" — 109-117
20" — 118, 121, 124, 125, 176, 200-202
21" — 38-41, 135, 136, 160, 161, 198, 199
22" — 121-123
23" — 195-197
24" — 140, 141
25" — 33-37, 259
28" — 24, 42-47, 102-108
30" — 102-108